The Most Fun I Never Want To Have Again

A Midlife Crisis in Community Banking

Robert D. Koncerak

Library of Congress Control Number: 2013900175
CreateSpace Independent Publishing Platform
North Charleston, South Carolina

Cover illustration by *Laurkon Designs* and The Cheeb

To Bill

For the most fun neither one of us *ever* wants to have again

The author and Bill Short at the opening of Touchmark National Bank's Alpharetta, Georgia headquarters in October 2009. In color, our ties match the palate of the Touchmark company logo.

Contents

Index of Charts, Graphs and Data

Introduction

What Was That All About?

Those of us who've spent the past several years managing financial institutions remember with fondness the good ol' days of 2006. Christmas that year was exciting: we all had good jobs, and many of us were eyeing better ones. Deal making of one kind or another was the subject of most lunch conversations, golf outings, and quail hunts—frequent golf outings and quail hunts. The financial services industry, from simple hometown community banks to arcane and nebulous private equity funds, was on a historic roll— and its trajectory had been stunning. As industry consolidation reduced the number of FDIC insured institutions by 27 percent between 1995 and 2006 (from 11,971 to 8,680), industry profits soared by $89 billion—more than 2.5 times over the period. Cash dividends from banks, thrifts, and credit unions increased by 266 percent between 1995 and 2006. Employment across the financial services industry amounted to 1,735,000 at the end of 1995. By fourth quarter 2006, employment had reached 2,207,000. Those years draw a wistful sigh from many who now refer to that time as the "Golden Age of Banking." For the vast majority of us, though, it wasn't anything like the "irrational exuberance" described by former Federal Reserve chairman Alan Greenspan. It was hard work, hand-shake integrity, and a whole lot of fair-trade prosperity.

In contrast, the years since then have felt like a hard fall down a flight of concrete stairs. On October 9, 2007, the Dow Jones Industrial Average closed at an all-time high of 14,164.53. Since then, the stock market has halved and then doubled, bonds soared, the real estate markets crashed and then stabilized, energy prices spiked, tanked, and recovered. As this book went to print in May 2013, the Dow Jones was again reaching record highs. All the while, the US government has been racking up massive new debts with no clear path to recovery—or a strategy as to how this debt will ultimately be repaid.

While the number of chartered institutions continues to decline, it is institutional *closures* rather than acquisitions that have driven consolidation across the industry over of the past five years. There were 7,083 banking companies in the US on December 31, 2012— 1,577 fewer than existed at the end of 2006. Eight were closed by the FDIC during 4Q12. More than 20 others were being merged or consolidated as 2012 came to a close. Industry employment has declined by over 100,000 *people* since the downturn began. And profits, well...let's just say that many of us are still filling in the hole.

In many ways, banks are the *least* of what has disappeared. The market confidence, the enthusiasm, the prosperity of so many businesses and households has dimmed since the industry's hey-day. Both hard-earned fortunes and easy-money affluence were smashed to pieces in a slow-motion train wreck that has continued unabated for nearly six years. Is it a cycle? Most likely. Will things get better? In many sectors, times are certainly better than they were during the abyss of 2008–2009. But the memories are painful, and some of the wounds are still raw. The scars we carry mean that the gaping holes in our careers, our egos, and our finances have managed somewhat to heal. In that sense, others of us are still looking forward to scars.

Gad!—what a downer of an opening page, huh? Well, the story gets better—because the story goes on. Volumes will be written about banker-entrepreneurs who dusted themselves off during these challenging times and came back to revolutionize the industry. Some of those success stories no doubt are being lived out even today.

But *this* story is about real people in real times, pursuing opportunity as they saw it *at* the time. I am confident that recollecting such an adventure has lessons to offer for us all.

This writing project has been as much a therapeutic memoir for me as it is a work of commercialism. This book is part documentary, part biography, part life lesson, and part cautionary tale. The past several years have given most everyone in the banking industry a story worth telling...and this one is mine. I've spent the past fifteen years of my working career in some aspect of banking and investment management as of this writing. Finance has come to be my hobby as much as it is my career, and I've pursued it with ambition and curiosity.

When she tires of my ramblings, my wife occasionally reminds me that not everyone reads the *Financial Times* with their coffee at 6:00 a.m. Her loving (if pointed) reminder is a reality check on my quirkiness, and I'm pleased to know that she means well (at least I think so!). There aren't many people who do what I do...even fewer who *like* to do what I do. That's OK by me, as so far this preoccupation has afforded me a pretty good living. My good friend Bill Short (now a self-styled "recovering banker") is fond of saying that, to the average American, the importance of his banking relationship lies somewhere between the loyalty he feels toward his dry cleaner and the soft spot in his heart for the local beer distributor. Bill is right, of course. The general population expects banking to be convenient, dependable, affordably priced–if not free, ubiquitously available, and secure. They don't want to *care* how it works. They *want* it to be a friendly customer service rep and an app on their iPhone at the same time. Those are high and carefree expectations indeed! For those of us in the industry, though, this business is our livelihood, and the past several years have been anything *but* dependable or carefree. Instead, these years have been consuming, exhausting— and morbidly, utterly fascinating. Many of us in banking have been caught up in quite the roiling drama. From bank directors to small business lenders, fortunes large and small have vaporized, careers have been set adrift, and a flamethrower has been taken to our stock options and pension plans. We in the industry know that stock and options were not only awarded to high-rolling executives, but to deserving secretaries and loan assistants as well. The Golden Age of Banking made it common-place to reward all levels of employment with a share in the company's success (you might want to skip back and re-read those employment statistics). The crater left by the impact of this downturn is deeper and wider than most outside of banking can possibly comprehend.

So I promise to do my best to keep this story interesting. Since business is ultimately about people and personalities, I am confident that some of the characters and characterizations in this book will keep it entertaining and worthwhile. If you like charts and graphs, there's some of that, too. Chapter Four – *Running Up The Bank*, includes a few passages and explanations that some may find technical. I included them because I felt they were important to the story.

This work is predominantly a documentary. The names and the places are all real. This is a story about launching an Atlanta-based bank as a new business venture late in a spectacular economic cycle; growing the business and gaining altitude just as the economy was lurching into crisis, ejecting as the project careened from its initial course...and then strapping in to try and save a second institution that was doomed to failure for no worse an offense than impeccably bad timing in the marketplace. We level the wings of that flailing vessel and bring her in for a landing as failure #70 of the eighty five banks that were closed across Georgia between September 2007 and December 2012. A total of 467 banks "failed" and were closed across the U.S. during this period.

In case you're wondering, this is not another tale about some Wall Street wunderfolk who struck out to set the banking world on fire. I can assure you that it's *truly* not that. This is a nuts-and-bolts tale of what happens when the expectations of accomplished and self-styled entrepreneurs collide with the cold, hard circumstances of reality. Like most business starts, the story begins with a perception of opportunity and profit, moves forward with enthusiasm, and ultimately goes to market through a combination of persistence, resolve...and chutzpah. Jangled nerves and seeds of conflict are the stuff of life that get mixed in along the way.

What purpose does this book serve beyond documentary? Well, it's an insider's view as to how a financial start-up gets organized and launched—or at least used to! It's a case study for the importance of forming a well-vetted board of directors and leadership team. It's a testimony as to how visioning and strategic planning can get crossways with human nature and how the best-intentioned people can find themselves with conflicting agendas when outcomes bear no resemblance to the forecasts. I've done my level best to not be critical of anyone in the process. Instead, I try to tell an objective story with documentary evidence and the recollections that I've gathered from the experience of my past several years in community banking.

I ask your indulgence for my colloquial writing style. The AP business writing standard this is not! This book is essentially expository—a story about events I have researched and experienced—and as such it's peppered only with the most pertinent of references and footnotes. While at heart I'm an optimistic finance guy with an academic bent, I am satisfied that I'll prove myself to be more of a storyteller in these pages than a dyed-in-the-wool business writer. I aim to tell a story that can be both understood and enjoyed—and I hope that you'll think so, too.

The book is organized in chapters that contrast the 2007 launch of a Georgia community bank with the national financial nightmare that had its roots in the fall of 2006. The first chapter is about career choices and the circumstances that lead to selection. It's my personal-professional story and it serves as a foundation for pulling this volume together as a writing project. Then we review Georgia's most recent community banking boom and bust with both local and national references. A "community bank" is defined here as an FDIC-chartered institution with less than $1 billion in total assets—which constitutes the vast majority of US banks in existence. The "big-picture" chapter is the work of John Mauldin, an accomplished hedge fund advisor and financial writer. John has graciously allowed me to reprint one of his weekly missives that provides both a history lesson and perspective between the local and the national scene. John's references help us see the community bank downturn as a small part of a great global unwinding that is still a debacle in progress. Similarly, articles reprinted with permission from the *Atlanta Business Chronicle* offer plenty of local and historic context. The *ABC* has done a great job of chronicling the growth of community banking in Georgia, and I am grateful to include some of their best work as color commentary that is inset throughout these pages. You'll find this symbol at the end of each external article:

As a final chapter, I am delighted to include several important thoughts from Karl Nelson on what's ahead for the community banking industry. Karl is president and CEO of KPN Consulting and is a well-known and highly regarded professional. He is also a good friend. Lastly—and perhaps most important, I am grateful for support from ex-Touchmark directors who have provided me with a wealth of input and reference material. Because I left Touchmark National Bank with specific expectations for non-disclosure, I have been careful to only publish information that was available from public sources or provided to me by individuals not subject to non-disclosure arrangements. In every case, information published is respectful, relevant and non-privileged. The collective project offers perspective on how the best-laid plans of accomplished and ambitious people can be thrown off course by a once-in-a-generation firestorm.

One unique aspect of this story will be helpful to bear in mind as you turn the pages: half way through the capital raise, our use of the trademarked name "Touchstone" was challenged by another company and we changed our name to Touchmark National Bank. The entities are one and the same—though occasionally both names appear in the same paragraph.

April 22, 2002

Community banks at risk, FDIC reports

Atlanta Business Chronicle - by Jim Lovel, Staff Writer

Community banks in Atlanta and throughout the Southeast could falter if the housing industry slows.

The Federal Deposit Insurance Corp. noted the risk in its latest quarterly report on the nation's banking industry. Community banks issue more, and often riskier, home mortgages and construction loans as a percentage of their total business than other banks and would be vulnerable if home sales dropped or borrowers couldn't pay their mortgages, according to the **FDIC**.

In metro Atlanta, about 40 community banks, or one-half of the area's community banks, are at risk, said Jack Phelps, regional manager of the division of insurance and research for the Atlanta office of the FDIC.

Those banks have more than 15 percent of their assets invested in mortgages for new construction, which have a higher rate of default than mortgages for existing homes.

Of those 40, about 18 have more than 25 percent of their assets in construction loans. The average for community banks in the metro area is 15.6 percent of their assets in construction loans.

Those are risky numbers. During the last recession in the early 1990s, banks with that many construction loans were twice as likely to have financial problems than other banks, the report states. The national average is for community banks to have about 9.5 percent of their assets invested in construction loans. The FDIC wants to see the level remain below 15 percent.

The report cites Atlanta specifically as an example of a city at risk because "residential construction activity was accelerating as local economic conditions were deteriorating" last year.

The FDIC also is concerned that many of the community banks were chartered during the unprecedented economic growth of the past decade and are operating with business plans that depend on that rapid growth.

"Banks with concentrations in traditionally higher-risk assets or that have adopted a business model that relies on rapid economic growth should evaluate their ability to operate during a period of slow economic growth," the report states.

I've come to describe my experience with launching Touchmark National Bank as *the most fun I never want to have again.*" That phrase on its own would have made for an interesting book title, but I felt the need to combine it with the urgency of a midlife crisis—because on several levels, that's really what it turned into for me.

In the early days of our start-up, Bill kept a quotation on his desk that read, *"In Confusion There Is Profit."* That would have made a good title, too. As you'll read, it certainly drove some of our early success!

The experience of my past few years has taught me that wealth and wisdom are not loyal traveling companions. We were all wealthier—and felt smarter when we started our business—and grew less so as the experience wore on for reasons outside of our control. I feel safe in writing that all of us bankers have learned lessons in the past few years in areas where we'd rather have remained ignorant. If the moral of this story helps a similarly minded individual to travel a better-informed path, then this tale will also have a legacy—

which is all that a mortal can hope for. In hindsight, my adventure is one that I neither regret nor would recommend to others.

Two quotations before we begin, both courtesy of Dick Jackson, who in 2005 published an entertaining volume of his own about a career in community banking. It's titled *Too Stupid To Quit*, and I heartily recommend it to those interested in a wider reading on this subject.

"A good banker should be bald, overweight and have hemorrhoids. Baldness conveys maturity. A paunch reflects wealth. And hemorrhoids give a look of concern to one's eyes."

Advice given to a bank trainee, author unknown

And for Bill Short, the "recovering banker":

"Banking is a career from which no man really recovers."

John Kenneth Galbraith

Touchstone Bancshares, Inc.
(A Proposed One Bank Holding Company)
3434 Howell Street N.W. Suite B
Duluth, Georgia 30096

February 28, 2007
Karen Bryant
Licensing Manager
Comptroller of the Currency
Administrator of National Banks
Southern District Office
xxxxxxxxxxxxxxx
Dallas, Texas xxxxx

Re: Proposed formation of "Touchstone National Bank",
and Parent One-Bank Holding Company "Touchstone
Bancshares, Inc." in Duluth, Georgia

Dear Ms. Bryant:

Thank you for your telephone call yesterday regarding the scheduling of a pre-filing meeting for our organizing group. Should there not be adequate space for all of us at the OCC Field Office, we will be happy to reserve a meeting room in Duluth at the 1818 Club. We understand that the FDIC representative will also be in attendance, and also provide this material for their use.

The formation of the organizing group was initiated by Bobby Williams in the summer of 2005. The market was researched and studied in light of competitive and economic conditions and was found to have attractive and sustainable components for economic growth. In particular, the Duluth-Suwanee area and the Chamblee area are the northern and southern points along a natural corridor within a supporting and growing infrastructure. This corridor from inside Interstate 285, the "Perimeter Highway", up to the southern end of Lake Lanier is the most diverse and contiguous representation of future economic growth in Metropolitan Atlanta.

In January of 2006, Bobby Williams met Vivian Wong who shared his beliefs about the market potential given the continuing cycle of mergers. They strongly believe this has an effect of under serving the small to medium size business customer, particularly the large and growing Indian and Asian community within this international corridor.

Together, they developed a profile for their potential organizers and directors. Each organizer should have a successful and diversified business and personal history and be a person of unquestionable character and integrity. In addition, the group should represent diverse business backgrounds to represent the market to be served. Additionally, the group will have a representative amount of banking experience.

Over the next six months our organizing group was formed and represents a broad range of business, banking and professional experience. Their Biographical sketches are attached to this document.

The organizers propose William R. Short to be the President and Chief Executive Officer of the bank. Bill has been in the Atlanta banking market for over thirty years with Wachovia Bank and its predecessor First National Bank of Atlanta. We believe his executive administration; lending and operating experience in this market demonstrates the organization skills that are uniquely suited to our goals. His attached biographical information indicates this. He was hired this past December.

We have hired Robert D. Koncerak as our Chief Financial Officer. Bob's resume is also attached.

Nineteen of the 23 organizers will be directors of the bank.

Those who are organizers only do not have the ability to attend regular board meetings.

We believe that the collective banking experience of our group is in accordance with OCC guidelines.

The following table outlines our group, the proposed directorate, and the bank board experience within:

			Bank Board	Local	Bank Board exp.
1		John W. Burnett	x		x
2		J. Egerton Burroughs	x		x
3		J. William Butler	x	x	
4		Daniel B. Cowart	x	x	x
5		Barry A. Culbertson	x	x	
6		Emily M. Fu	x	x	
7		Howard R. Greenfield	x	x	
8		Yuling R. Hayter	x	x	
9		John L. Johnson	x	x	greater than 5 years ago
10		Daniel J. Kaufman	x	x	
11		Moon K. Kim	x	x	
12		C. Hiluard Kitchens, Jr.	x	x	
13		Paul P. Lam			

14		Sudhirkumar C. Patel	x		
15		Thomas E. Persons, Sr.	x		greater than 5 years ago
16		J.J. Shah	x	x	
17		Meena J. Shah	x	x	
18		William R. Short, CEO/Spokesperson	x	x	
19		Larry D. Silver			
20		Haskumkh P. Rama	x		
21		Debra D. Wilkins			
22		Bobby G. Williams	x	x	
23		Vivian A. Wong	x		
24		Robert D. Koncerak, CFO			

Each organizer has executed a joint venture and contribution agreement and contributed $20,000 for the initial phase of organizational costs.

The bank will be wholly owned by a holding company to be formed that will raise between $25 and $40 million in a public offering, at least $20 million of which will be for the initial capitalization of the bank. We are currently constructing our business plan to determine the level of the offering.

We envision that the bank can achieve a deposit growth as high as $250-$300 million within five to seven years, with three to four offices; one of which is contemplated to open approximate six months after the bank opens. The enclosed Market Feasibility Study demonstrates a reasonable likelihood of success within our intended market. Initial deposit projections within a preliminary ten year forecast have been performed at multiple capital scenarios and are included therein.

We are currently constructing pro forma projections for our five year business plan which tracks our initial market assessment of potential growth. This plan will be presented to our organizing board at its meeting on March 21st. With the recent addition of Bob Koncerak as CFO, we are refining our projections as we move through a list of interviews with a multitude of vendors that will give us the best possible estimate of overhead expense.

We are careful to forecast our loan and deposit composition and are influenced by numerous peer bank comparisons in the local market. We seek to depict accurately what we expect to achieve. The committees of the organizers are heavily tasked in the development of our business plan.

Collectively, we are committed to investing from a minimum of six million to as much as ten million of the total offering. Each organizer will subscribe to a minimum of $200,000 in the offering, and receive one warrant for each share purchased.

The warrants will vest over three years and be exercised within ten years at the original purchase price. The structure conforms to OCC guidelines for Tier 1 and 2 plans. The executive committee of the organizers is formulating an incentive stock option plan for management.

The organizing group is negotiating an offer under a letter of intent for the bank's initial location to be leased subject to our obtaining preliminary approval. The proposed site is strategically located and highly accessible in Duluth at the Northeast side of the intersection of Hwy 120 and Peachtree Industrial Boulevard, Duluth, 30096. The premises are approximately 2,700 square feet with a drive thru facility.

Additional space of approximately 2,500 square feet will soon be located near to this location and will not only serve as offices for our organizational phase, but will continue as banking offices upon opening.

We plan to open our second location within the first year of operations in Chamblee and have executed a letter of intent to lease space from a business interest of one of our organizers. This transaction is subject to the organizing board receiving an MAI appraisal and conforming to OCC guidelines for insider transactions.

The organizing group has held regular board meetings since the spring of last year. Each organizer has been provided with a copy of the OCC Licensing Manual, the E-Banking Guide, as well as the OCC Licensing Manual. We have scheduled a director's college for our group to attend on April 27 & 28.

The Organizers feel that the Bank's focus and its physical location will provide the opportunity for individuals and businesses to obtain traditional banking services from a financial institution with local ownership and with management and staff that is experienced in the market.

We have engaged consultants and attorneys, and are interviewing accounting firms. The organizing group has planned to file the application within sixty days of the pre filing meeting. We believe we have made significant progress toward accomplishing this timeframe. As soon as we complete our business plan and file the application, we will continue our policy development in conjunction with the selection of a Chief Credit Officer and the remaining bank staff.

Should you need any further information or clarification, please do not hesitate to call me at (770) 363-xxxx. We look forward to our meeting with you and the FDIC representative.

Very truly yours,

William R. Short
CEO/Spokesperson

cc: Board of Directors

   F.D.I.C.

Chapter 1

It's All About Getting Chosen

Midlife crisis *is a term coined in 1965 by Elliott Jaques and used in Western societies to describe a period of dramatic self-doubt that is felt by some individuals in the "middle years" or middle age of life, as a result of sensing the passing of their own youth and the imminence of their old age. Sometimes, a crisis can be triggered by transitions experienced in these years, such as extramarital affairs, andropause or menopause, the death of parents or other causes of grief, unemployment or underemployment, realizing that a job or career is hated but not knowing how else to earn an equivalent living, or children leaving home. The result may be a desire to make significant changes in core aspects of day-to-day life or situation, such as in career, work-life balance, marriage, romantic relationships, large expenditures, or physical appearance.*

Wikipedia

Only those who will risk going too far can possibly find out how far one can go.

- T. S. Eliot

It's All About Getting Chosen

I went to primary school in the late 1960s at Circleville Elementary in Irwin, Pennsylvania. I remember kickball games on the playground like they happened yesterday. Our teacher would write the names of the week's two captains on the blackboard. The captains would meet before Monday recess to choose up teams for that week's games. For most of the class, it was a celebrated process of selection. For a few of us, though, it was a weekly humiliation. Our class would stand in an arc around the two captains. The first picks were rapid-fire: both captains knew the kids that they most wanted on their teams. The middle pick was more deliberate and contemplative: the B-team, after all, required consideration and strategy. "If I pick Randy, then he's going to take Dale...and that means I'll get either Roy or John." The last of the bunch, the "dregs," as we called ourselves, stood glumly with our hands in our pockets, waiting for the embarrassment to be over. I remember my "place," late in the process, standing between four-foot five-inch Pam Shirley and a somewhat taller—but just as petite—Marcia Hunniford. I liked standing next to Marcia Hunniford, because she was really cute. Marcia would get picked, the other side would take me, and then Pam would go over to the side that took Marcia. When the captains were boys, they would always pick Marcia next to last...because at least she was cute.

There's nothing in life that compares with the privilege of being chosen. "I pick *you*" is one of the most valued phrases in all of the English language. Those words are earned, they are gratifying, and they are almost always memorable.

Pam and Marcia: wherever you are, I pray that you have chosen, and that you have *been* chosen well.

The Season of Epiphany

To begin with, I'm a man of modest intelligence and perhaps some above-average writing skills. I view preschoolers as my intellectual peers because they are fascinated by the world and everything in it. It's probably that wide-eyed naiveté that first got me interested in such common and yet complicated things like money and financial services.

I have realized through most of my working career that the most valuable business attribute I possess is that I often *look* like I know what I'm talking about. I have an outgoing nature, I present myself with a general confidence, and I'm a passable public speaker when I need to be. Lucky for me, that combination can get one a very long way in the banking business.

By the summer of 2006, I was forty-five years old and had been employed by Wachovia Bank in Atlanta for several years. My first job was that of chief financial officer for the company's Capital Markets division. After the bank's 2001 merger with First Union, I landed a similar role in the "new" Wachovia's Wealth Management group. I was good at my job, and as time passed I developed a reputation for being a clever technician. Among other tricks of the trade, I had a knack for mastering the annual budgeting process and for helping division executives to exceed their corporate goals. This was no small feat in a large bank, because exceeding the annual budget meant a whole lot of money from the incentive comp pool—and an outsized share of stock options to boot. Because Wealth Management was the most expensive distribution channel in the bank, we were always on the lookout for ways to fatten our revenue line while at the same time dodging overhead allocations. Lucky for me, I was also pretty good at ferreting out the most profitable banking products to promote across my client teams—which in turn expanded revenues and made for happy executives. It was this favorable combination of networking and right-brain skills that enabled me to work in such comfortable environs as Palm Beach, Naples, and Fort Lauderdale (for you youngsters, this was long before the real estate crash of 2008. Palm Beach *boat slips* were selling for $200,000+ in those days). The division's managing directors liked me, my bosses gave me good reviews, and I always managed to stay one step ahead of the central treasury trolls. Life was good so far as performance was concerned. Problem was, my technical success never translated much into significant "wealth management" for me. The better I did *what I thought my job was*, the more I helped my executive teams to succeed...and the more frustrated I became in the process.

You see, large banks (and all companies in general, for that matter) tend to lay out significant compensation packages for the "client-facing" staff. As a practical matter, this tends toward *in*significant compensation packages for those responsible to *equip* the client-facing staff.

Epiphany #1: Sales rarely influences the staff incentive pool. Helping sales folks to succeed, while greatly appreciated by Sales, doesn't typically get Staff rewarded come profit sharing time.

Though it took a couple of years, I eventually figured out that the *reason* I knew how to work the system so well was because I actually *understood* the rules of transfer pricing and management finance better than most of my Wachovia peers—especially those central treasury trolls that were responsible for the annual budgets.

This realization that I *knew* what I was doing came as a bit of a surprise to me. I remember that moment...because my *next* thought was that I'd never really felt that way before. I had a high level of confidence in what I was doing...and I was fairly *good* at it. Was that because of my on-the-job training...or my age...or what?

My elemental worldview led me then to a profound and personally dramatic conclusion: I was reaching Middle Age. And based on my understanding of what happens when a person reaches that place in life, I was either destined to become reconciled to my lot in life…or time was fast approaching for a head-on confrontation with the milestone of a Midlife Crisis.

Epiphany #2: I approached my job differently than other folks in my position. While everybody else in Finance was focused on accuracy and equity, I also wanted my teams to *win*. But as a finance employee, I wasn't being paid to win. Once I knew that I *wanted* to be paid to win, I decided that it was time to put my native skills to better use.

A related learning that didn't become clear until I was responsible for building a business and leading people: **One of the fastest ways to disenchant your top performers is to tolerate mediocre performance on the team. When your best employees come to understand that average performance will be tolerated—or that exceptional performance will not be appropriately compensated—the best will either move on to better opportunities or cease to strive for exceptional results. Neither outcome is healthy for the organization.**

Follow The Herd

While the number of FDIC-insured institutions in the United States has been in decline for years (Chart 1), start-up banks across Georgia were something of robust cottage industry in the early 2000s (Chart 2).

Chart 1

All FDIC-Insured Institutions		
Number of Institutions Yearly at June 30		
Year	**Georgia**	**US**
1995	420	**12,289**
1996	439	**11,694**
1997	391	**11,189**
1998	389	**10,738**
1999	379	**10,346**
2000	382	**10,119**
2001	369	**9,757**
2002	364	**9,474**
2003	359	**9,256**
2004	368	**9,065**
2005	367	**8,855**
2006	375	**8,767**
2007	380	**8,605**
2008	383	**8,441**
2009	359	**8,185**
2010	321	**7,821**
2011	292	**7,523**
2012	236	**7,255**

Source: FDIC

Strong demographics and a willing investor base fed start-ups and M&A activity through much of the 1990s and early 2000s. Success stories like Darrell Pittard's Premier Bank, which acquired 12 charters between 1993 and 1998 (at 2-2.5x book) and then sold to BB&T in 1999 for nearly 3x book, made investors a *lot* of money. Premier Bank—and other Georgia aggregators like Mainstreet and Flag that followed it, caused many a commercial real estate developer to look up from his site-grading project and take notice. After a brief dip at the beginning of the decade, the market strengthened considerably. In August 2005, Synovus Financial Corp. paid 3.6 times book value for Riverside Bancshares Inc. Transactions like that one kept relative valuations at high levels—and did the same for seller expectations. Behind them, new bank starts quickly filled in the gaps. Georgia spawned no fewer than 149 banking start-ups or "de novo" community charters between 1997 and 2007*.

Chart 2

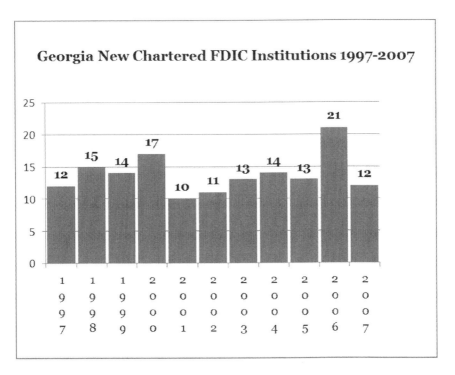

Source: FDIC

Consider the implications: the state of Georgia on its own stamped out 149 newly minted banking enterprises over a span of ten years. In the face of a declining national trend, the number of new Georgia charters was a standout. Only Florida and California christened more charters over this period—and those states claim more than two times and four times the respective populations!

Westside Bank was one of the best 'home-run' success stories during this period. Ed Milligan and his team sold stock at $10 per share and opened Westside Bank in Kennesaw, Georgia in May 1990. The bank loaned heavily on Cobb county real estate development, which was booming. In 1993, their holding company changed its name to First Sterling Banks and began posturing for growth. After a 2 for 1 stock split and several handsome dividends, shareholder basis amounted to $3.16. Sterling merged into Mainstreet Bank in 2006, continued its trajectory, and ultimately sold to BB&T in June 2006 for $28.50 per share. For those without a calculator handy, total return for a shareholder who hung on for the whole ride approaches *1,000 percent* (excerpts from the press release announcing the Mainstreet sale appear later in this chapter). US housing prices peaked during the second quarter of 2006. The timing of Milligan's sale was impeccable.

The timing of Darrell Pittard's sale of Premier to BB&T was also exquisite. Unfortunately, Mr. Pittard went on to build Magnet Bank, which came to a very different end.

When I began following this trend with interest from the fifth floor of 191 Peachtree Tower, no one I recall speaking with at the time (or have been able to identify since) felt that there were too many new banks in the Atlanta market. The Georgia Department of Banking and Finance used to maintain a wall in their offices that touted the growing crop of state chartered institutions (it's gone now). The only practical concern of bank boards and regulators at the time was the challenge of finding qualified executives to *run* them. And recruiting was a valid concern. After all, at what point between the launch of de novo bank #1 and de novo #149 did the qualified talent pool of capable and experienced bank CEOs begin to thin out? Who was available to run bank #78? How about bank #115? What CFO candidates within reasonable transfer distance were willing to help with start-up #34...who did they find for #135? In reality, a number of bank presidents over this period were called up from the ranks of the state's commercial lending force. Others were recycled in the process of charter acquisitions and sequential new start-ups. De novo CFOs were often former auditors, controllers, big bank finance guys, or they came into community banking from outside the industry altogether.

John Kline, president of John B. Kline & Associates, began assisting de novo banks in 1997—the first year of the cycle covered in this book. John, who earlier in his career served as deputy commissioner for the Georgia Department of Banking, says that the ranks of de novo executives were routinely replenished by "recycling" the exiting presidents and CEOs of acquired institutions. "Between Regions, BB&T, SouthTrust, and Wachovia", he says, "bank presidents were freed up by the dozens through the late 1990s and early 2000's. On the heels of Georgia roll-up bankers like Darrell Pittard and Joe Evans— Evans first with BCG and then Flag, the regionals came in behind them, bought out their roll-ups and put all those executives back on the market. Many contacted me on the very same day that their banks were signed over to the new owners." John says that in the 90's few buy-outs included non-compete agreements, and so out-placed executives were immediately available in the market. It was only in the early 2000's he says, that the regionals got smarter and started getting non-competes to avoid business run-off. "Even then", John adds, "those agreements never lasted longer than twelve months, which is about the time it takes to start a new bank". In all, Kline & Associates assisted with 60 bank starts across the southeast through 2007—with 26 of those opening for business between 2005 and 2008.

The outsized growth of commerce and construction in Georgia over this period stands as firm evidence that the preponderance of executive lending experience was relegated to real estate—or what we bankers call "dirt lending" ("Get the dirt and you'll never get hurt!").

As I read through *Atlanta Business Chronicle* coverage from this period, I noticed that there seemed to be a lot of good *lenders* in the community banking market, but by comparison there were fewer well-rounded *bankers* taking on boom-time executive roles.

The *Atlanta Business Chronicle* has featured a litany of stories over the years about former lending officers donning appointments as bank CEOs, opening storefront temporary offices, hiring commercial lenders, constructing impressive headquarters buildings, and then gushing to the press about the business opportunities afforded by so and so and the tremendous opportunities of such and such. Those archives sure look different on this side of the bubble.

Indeed it seemed like an attractive proposition...and I began thinking that I would like to try it for myself. To my way of thinking, I was reaching The Age where either I had to start digging a protective moat around my existing job...or start a search for my own construction project on the erstwhile foundations of Middle Age.

*Note: The total number of new bank charters between 1997 and 2007 was actually 152. Three, however, were for large bank expansions into the state as opposed to charters capitalized predominantly by in-state individual investors.

Friday, December 7, 2007
Bank picks interim exec after CEO search fails
Atlanta Business Chronicle - by Joe Rauch Staff Writer

A Norcross-based bank is the latest to struggle in filling its top management spot. First Covenant Bank appointed Vice Chairman Bill Blanton as interim CEO on Nov. 30, replacing founding CEO Henry Vick, whose contract was due to expire in February.

The move is the latest by several de novo and community banks that have struggled to fill key executive roles, like CEO, because of the explosion of new Atlanta banks in recent years.

First Covenant's fill-in comes after a six-month search for a permanent CEO came up empty, and the bank's board concluded it was unlikely a permanent replacement could be found in two months. Vick will be a First Covenant consultant until March 1.

The job is Blanton's third current position in Atlanta banking. The former CEO of First Capital Bancorp is also the chairman of NBOG Bancorporation, which owns Gainesville's First Century Bank.

So how does Blanton, as bank director, describe the CEO and senior executive talent left?

"Abysmal," he said.

The state has ranked at, or near, the top of national new bank growth during the last few years, primarily driven by Atlanta bank expansion.

Atlanta boasts 162 banks, according to Federal Deposit Insurance Corp. figures. That means the need for 162 CEOs and an exponentially larger staff of senior executives has tapped the market of not only talented executives, but also those who would be approved by bank regulators to run these institutions.

"We've got a lot of stuff to get accomplished," Blanton said. "But there's just nobody out there."

First Covenant opened in September 2006 and according to FDIC data, has $180 million in assets, two branches and 62 employees a year later.

The bank expects to name a permanent CEO in the spring.

A note of personal admission ahead of this next section:

Self-deprecation aside, I have two other faculties that led me to believe I could help launch a banking enterprise from investor funds, ambition and a business plan; I'd had good experience throughout my career in *selecting capable people* and in *building organizations through teamwork*. Most of my experience in these areas didn't come easy, and the "prequel" that follows is key to understanding how the theme of this book holds together.

Humbled Beginnings: My Prequel

I grew up in a traditional neighborhood along the far eastern suburbs of Pittsburgh, Pennsylvania. From the perspective of my generation (I was born in 1961), if you were *from* Pittsburgh at that time, then at some point you were *expected* to have worked in the steel business for part of your career. Call it a rite of passage...or just wanting to say that you fit the profile of the city. No matter that my career had a financial bent: by the mid-1990s, I was a treasury officer for a stainless steel manufacturer, following a white-collar path on a parallel plain to my lunch pail-toting, mill-working grandparents in previous generations of the Koncerak clan.

I made a hard-right career turn into the banking business only after a happenstance conversation in 1997 with a next-door neighbor in my driveway. Isn't it a hoot that stuff happens that way? Don Miller and I had been talking about our careers and the stuff that we liked to do when he broadsided me with a Bessemer furnace full of common sense:

Epiphany #3: "If you're going to be a finance guy, then you *ought* to be working for a financial services company." "If you stay in the steel business, the best that you're ever going to be is *overhead*—because that company produces steel...and you don't. If you like finance, move over into financial services," he told me, "and find a job that's responsible for *revenue* rather than expense. It's only then, my boy, that you'll be recognized for adding value to your firm. *The closer you are to the customer, the better off you're going to be.*"

Humph.

My first day of financial services employment in the great state of Georgia was with Wachovia Bank on January 30, 2000. My family's relocation from Pennsylvania took place after I had worked for a time in Mellon Bank's capital markets division in Pittsburgh.

I took the job—and the transfer to Atlanta only after several conversations with some of Mellon's corporate officers, key among them Paul Dimmick—who at the time headed up the bank's capital markets and the mid-corporate banking divisions. During the time that I worked for Paul, Mellon was undergoing a strategic assessment that ultimately led to its exit from retail and corporate banking. "If Mellon doesn't want to be a corporate bank," Paul counseled me at one point, "then what on *earth* do you think it's going to do with a capital markets group?"

At the time, my wife and I had been married for sixteen years. Our three girls were eleven, nine, and four years of age. So the move away from "home" carried with it the mix of heartache and adventure that I imagine is always associated with such relocations. The independence and initiative that enables such a move—as all know who have done it—is significant. We endured the requisite bumps and misfortunes; we strengthened as a family and ultimately settled into a comfortable life in the northwest reaches of Cobb County.

Then, on the morning of April 16, 2001, news broke all over the media that Wachovia was merging with the First Union banking empire. Less than a year and a half into my "career change of a lifetime," the position for which I had relocated my family presented me with an uncertain future.

You could have believed that a bomb had exploded inside the offices of 191 Peachtree on the day that the merger was announced. The genteel, Southern, storied institution—the bank that had never had a layoff in 140 years, the bank that had stepped in for the state of North Carolina to make payroll and keep its finances solvent during Reconstruction, the bank that had financed tobacco and textile empires across several Southern states, and the bank that my boss occasionally referred to as "Mother Wachovia"—announced that it was merging with the "evil empire" of American financial commerce. Wachovia was legendary for inspiring a loyalty and a culture that set the standard for Southern professionalism. By comparison, "Wachovians" perceived First Union as a swashbuckling, abrasive conglomeration of miscreant acquisitions. The market perception of First Union was almost as stark: in a PR disaster still fresh in Atlanta at the time, First Union had tried unsuccessfully to institute a five-dollar fee for customers who preferred to transact at a teller window in lieu of using its new-fangled online banking terminals. The move sparked a howl of customer protest in a town accustomed to high-touch, relationship-centered banking—and the effort was ultimately abandoned. First Union management had a reputation for being hard-charging, transaction-oriented street fighters. And we were supposed to merge? With *them*?

At 5:05 p.m. on the afternoon of the announcement, my phone rang. It was Paul. "*So...*" he inquired with an amusing (read: satirical) lilt in his voice, "What do you think of Wachovia *now*?"

A sheepish "*Help!*" was all I could muster by way of a response.

What followed that taunting salutation was—and remains, the most helpful career advice that I have ever received: "If you're looking for a way back to Pittsburgh, Bob, then of course I'll be glad to help. But I have a recommendation for you in the meantime (picture a finger waving at the other end of the phone). *No matter what else happens*, find a way to come out with a job on the other side of this merger. While there's no doubt you'll learn a lot about banking along the way— you'll learn even more about *people* and the way they behave in tough situations. You'll learn what people do when they feel threatened, and you'll become a better manager of people in the process. *Pay attention and keep good notes. Help good people when you can. And above all else, conduct yourself so that you'll be proud of your work and your reputation regardless of whether you stay or you leave.*"

Paul's admonition proved to be spot-on through the months of transition that followed. I saw highly regarded Wachovia managers—folks I felt certain would land significant positions in the new company—who proved to be painfully inept at navigating redrawn channels and were quickly cut loose. I saw others who got buried deep in the strata of a corporate layer cake, left to asphyxiate in the frosting. And I saw people I knew to be little more than conniving, brown-nosed sycophants (opportunists...I just really wanted to use the word "sycophant") who managed to maneuver themselves into surprising positions of authority, responsibility, and compensation.

Across all divisions of the merger, Wachovia's "legacy" capital markets group would serve as the sacrificial lamb on our side of the deal; every significant leadership position was awarded in succession to the First Union side of the lineup. Wachovia capital markets folks felt understandably threatened...and some handled the pressure better than others. On more than one occasion, employees from related areas of Wachovia's finance division came to my office and asked if they could informally report up through my group for a while, because their managers refused to even acknowledge them in the politics of posturing for a new job. The six accomplished analysts who worked for me during this time all wanted *out* of the new Wachovia environment. While I insisted that every member of my team interview for at least one position in the new company (for the experience of sitting in front of an interviewer if nothing else), all of them eventually left to take jobs outside of the company. I couldn't blame them. Many (though not all) First Union managers and their analysts treated our employees like ugly stepchildren. On more occasions than I'd like to remember, our advice and reporting was solicited by e-mail, only to have all reference to our input cut off before communications were finalized and passed up the management chain. Adding insult to injury, we were often cc'ed on the final plagiarized work product that was attributed to some snot-nosed First Union rookie! While I'm sure that most of these were capable, ambitious people, their management culture tolerated—even *encouraged*—a ruthless approach to self-promotion (and self-preservation) as the First Union juggernaut had piled on serial acquisitions over the years. It could not have been a very fun place to work for those who didn't thrive on blood sport. Wachovia's native culture fostered external competition. First Union's fostered internal competition. There were many career Wachovians who were simply not equipped for such a battle.

In retrospect, I'd wager that the Wachovia/First Union hookup was one of the more extreme examples of culture clash in the annals of corporate merger-dom. While the combined entity lumbered along for eight years, few areas of the business ever seemed to settle into a rhythm of accomplished performance. By my recollection, those who had not stretched themselves to take advantage of education and advancement opportunities in the "old" Wachovia found muted opportunity in the merged company—because the competition for available job slots was fierce. That part, however, is surely *not* unusual in the annals of corporate merger-dom.

When he read through the draft of this section of the book, Bill Short told me about a defining moment that he experienced shortly after the WaFU announcement. Bill was invited to a senior management meeting one afternoon that included representatives from both sides of the merger. Several of the First Union managers sported comfortable and confirming smiles as their leadership crowed on about the image and respect that the combined companies would command in the marketplace. They were open about sharing why: "We're no longer going to be known as the "FU" bank!"

Epiphany #4: Take care of your people and position them for *their* next move. The best performers will always have career opportunities both inside and outside of the company hierarchy—and it's better if they consider their next move along *with* you rather than behind you or without you. While it's fair to expect loyalty over a reasonable term (you hired them to do a job, not just to train them for the next one), one of the biggest privileges in life is to have *choices*. When you're good at what you do, opportunities will arise that suit your interests and long-term goals. The important decision, then, is *which* choices to make. Those less capable in the ranks are left to carry on under the thumbs of those who prefer to control rather than champion the existence of underlings.

I decided that I *liked* having choices, and I liked feeling capable. I chose to adopt the outlook that I was responsible for navigating my own course...and that I did not want to find myself hostage to a position or a culture for the sake of a steady paycheck.

A great analogy that I remember reading at the time was that, like people, you can't evaluate what's inside of a tea bag until it gets dropped into hot water. Regardless of how much vetting and research is done on the front end, situations change, people disappoint, and trust is warranted for a very, very few.

Epiphany #5: Choose both your managers and your underlings carefully—and don't be afraid to walk away from either when the longer term goals of your career— or the shorter term interests of your integrity—stand at risk of compromise.

Here are three worthwhile sidebars on the subject of *choice*:

1: When you hit your thumb with a hammer, you can't help but be in pain—because the fact is that it *hurts* to smash your thumb with a hammer. Being *miserable* in one's circumstances, however, is a *choice*. While we cannot choose whether or not to feel pain, we do *choose* whether or not to be miserable. Being miserable is a *choice*—and it comes from assuming a negative attitude in the face of adverse circumstances.

2: My grandfather once told me "every day that you wake up and get out of bed, you trade your life for something. Every once in a while you need to step back from the mattress and think about whether or not you're happy with the trade. If you don't like what you're doing, nobody can fix it but you."

3: The ability to choose wisely is a gift. *Having* choices—alternatives to choose *from*—is a blessing. The ability to choose means you get to pick the best among available options. It is when you have no choice in a matter that you become most vulnerable in your circumstances.

I spent the rest of 2001 helping to disassemble Wachovia's capital markets division and ship off the pieces to Charlotte, North Carolina. While I was eventually offered an attractive job in the same line of work, I chose instead a division role in what was the "sacrificial lamb" of the First Union side—Wealth Management. The choice enabled me to spend the next five years building out a significant industry platform—and to work with accomplished people, many of whom I still count as friends.

The lessons I learned from the organizational management blender of that merger have served me well—and I thank Paul Dimmick for the majority of my hard-won perspective.

A Higher Class of Overhead

I remember joking with my wife, Carol, around 2005 that if I was destined to have a midlife crisis, then I was going to make mine as *big* and as *organized* as it possibly could be. "After all, I *am* a creature of organization—and I like to take on big things. So if I'm going to have a crisis *anyway*, then it may as well be *big* enough to make it worthwhile…and *organized* enough to make sense of it once it's over!" I remember Carol getting that worried look…it's an expression I've since come to recognize.

I first considered that it was time to become a *revenue generator* like my neighbor Don had recommended…but by then it seemed that I might have missed my chance. I interviewed for several sales jobs within the new Wachovia organization, but I was type-cast as a finance guy. At my age and with my resume, it was going to be tough to move into the client-facing position that Don had recommended. There were simply too many good candidates who were younger than me—and most had more relevant experience than I did.

It was then, for the very first time, that I thought about becoming a higher class of overhead.

Epiphany #5: If you're destined to be overhead, then be *executive overhead*. It's better to be an expense at the *top* of the corporate ladder rather than anywhere closer to the bottom.

And that's where the idea came from that I wanted to be the CFO of a bank. To my way of thinking, it seemed like a both a good challenge *and* an impressive career goal. In hindsight, I have no bloody idea why I thought I could manage a full-scale banking enterprise—but I was confident that if I could talk someone into letting me try, I could figure it out just fast enough to avoid getting fired. In early 2005, I started following the banking industry and started reaching out to recruiters for interviews.

One of my first efforts was a meeting with Sam Hay, then president of Mainstreet Bank in Covington, Georgia, around April of 2005. Mainstreet, as noted earlier, was an early Atlanta success story. Founded in 1972, Mainstreet raised $6 million of capital in 1994 and used it to acquire local competitors Northside Bank and Eastside Bank in 2003. By 2006, Mainstreet had grown to $758 million and was posturing to either continue an acquisition strategy, or sell and provide its shareholders with a "liquidity event." I spent most of an afternoon with Sam, an upbeat guy who seemed to be shopping for an interim manager more than someone who could help advance his business model. The current CFO was leaving to pursue "other business opportunities." Hmmm.

Covington was too far of a drive from my Cobb County home, and I apparently didn't come across as much of a caretaker. Mainsteet ultimately hired another Wachovia veteran for the role. On May 6, 2005, Mainstreet announced the appointment of David Brooks as CFO...and sold to BB&T less than a year later. The significant premium in the deal really caught my attention. Value was being created through the development of a franchise, and the sale of that franchise was adding both wealth and future opportunities to its shareholders. I wanted some of that. I hope that David fared well, too.

News Release
BB&T to acquire Main Street Banks Inc. of metro Atlanta

PRNewswire-FirstCall
WINSTON-SALEM,N.C.
(NYSE:BBT)
Dec 15, 2005

WINSTON-SALEM, N.C., Dec. 15 /PRNewswire-FirstCall/ – BB&T Corporation (NYSE: BBT) today said it plans to buy Main Street Banks Inc. (NASDAQ: MSBK) of Atlanta in a $622.7 million stock swap that would strengthen its presence in some of the most economically vibrant communities in the country.

The merger would bump BB&T from sixth to fifth in deposit market share in both metropolitan Atlanta and Georgia. It would mark the first bank acquisition for BB&T since it acquired St. Petersburg, Fla.-based Republic Bancshares in April 2004.

With $2.5 billion in assets, Main Street Banks is the largest community bank in metro Atlanta. It operates 24 full-service banking centers and five insurance offices in the Atlanta and Athens, Ga., metropolitan statistical areas.

The transaction, approved by the directors of both companies, is valued at $28.50 per Main Street share based on BB&T's closing price Wednesday of $43.17. The exchange ratio will be fixed at 0.6602 of a share of BB&T stock for each share of Main Street stock. The merger, which is subject to regulatory and shareholder approval, is expected to be completed in the second quarter of 2006. Main Street shareholders will receive a 64.5 percent increase in dividend income, once the transaction is complete.

"Our acquisition strategy remains the same – to pursue very high quality banks and thrifts that improve our financial performance and franchise value," said BB&T Chairman and Chief Executive Officer John Allison. "So we could not be more pleased with the prospects of a merger with Main Street Banks, one of the best community banking franchises in the Southeast.

"This merger will enhance our ongoing commitment to organic growth by adding state-of-the art, strategically located branches in some of the fastest growing and economically attractive communities you'll find anywhere."

Main Street operates four branches in Fulton County, three in Cobb County, three in Newton County, three in Rockdale County, two in Forsyth County, two in Dekalb County, two in Gwinnett County, two in Walton County, one in Barrow County and two in metro Athens, Ga., located east of greater Atlanta.

***

Main Street was founded as The Bank of Covington in 1901. It changed its name to Main Street Banks in 1996. In May 2000, it entered into a merger of equals with Kennesaw, Ga.-based First Sterling Banks Inc., creating a $900 million bank with 21 branches. First Sterling was the surviving entity in the merger of equals and adopted Main Street's name. Since then, Main Street has acquired three Atlanta-based banks (the last in May 2003) and three independent insurance agencies.

***

The merger would increase BB&T's deposits in Georgia to nearly $6.5 billion. BB&T expects a 35 percent cost savings in the first year after systems conversion.

BB&T bought 17 banks and thrifts from 2000 to 2004 before announcing a moratorium on bank acquisitions to refocus on organic revenue growth and expense control.

In May 2006, I interviewed with Charlie Crawford, who at the time was organizing The Private Bank of Buckhead, which opened in December of that year. After about fifteen minutes of interrogatories, Charlie informed me that I was too much of a "big bank" manager and that I was unlikely to be suited for the wide-ranging responsibilities of a community bank CFO. "You seem compartmentalized, and you're probably accustomed to having plenty of resources around," I remember him telling me.

It never feels good to be told you're not a good fit. The fact that he was probably right was totally beside the point. I responded respectfully, but assertively, that I didn't agree with his assessment and that I felt certain I could handle the responsibilities of the job. We never spoke again. As of this date, his bank still seems to be doing fine without me. Imagine that.

By mid-2006, Wachovia was beginning to flounder under the grandiose expectations of its executive team. The bank's last major acquisition was Golden West Financial, the California subprime lender that pioneered the concept of "pick-a-pay" mortgage banking. Yeah, I know: it sounds like a stupid idea. A lot of us thought it was stupid back in 2006, but we weren't executive overhead at the time. In 2009, Wells Fargo would ultimately pay less for the entire empire of Wachovia than Wachovia itself had paid for Golden West. Unfortunately, Wachovia's new mortgage customers had interpreted Golden West's payment plans as "pick-whether-or-not-to-pay"...and lots of them apparently decided not to.

I was getting increasingly restless in my job, and I felt like I'd pulled all of the rabbits out of my hat. It was time for a new hat. For a few months, I toyed with the idea of starting my own bank around a concept for condominium lending. I couldn't get traction with investors. Finding no other bank CFO jobs in the market, I was bored one afternoon and threw my hat into the ring for a relationship manager (client-facing!) position that had opened up on a wealth management team supervised by one William R. Short.

Bill Short looks like a bank executive that a movie producer might have called up from central casting: he's tall, thin, impeccably mannered, always well dressed (I kid him that he probably wears a matching terrycloth tie with his bathrobe), and he had great business contacts around the city. While my interview request may have come as a bit of a surprise to Bill, it turned out that I was actually a viable candidate for the opening. Bill and I had worked together in Wealth Management for about five years. While we weren't personal friends, our paths had crossed many times over client strategies and the politics of financial reporting.

Several weeks into the process, I had survived all the interviews and was starting to believe that my "driveway dream job" might finally come true. As a practical matter, it was fairly rare for a staffer to navigate his way into a client-facing role, and I was on the verge of getting considerable satisfaction in having done so.

Epiphany #6: Some folks believe that where you start has a lot to do with where you'll end up. Sure, if you let it. Your life's adventure can't be measured from where you start...but only by looking back from the place where you end up.

Friday, June 10, 2005
Sprouting Banks
Atlanta Business Chronicle - by Lori Johnston Contributing Writer

Georgia trails only Florida and California in the number of new banks opening each year. Community bankers say the trend will continue as customers get used to personalized service.

Forget the Peach State. Georgia's nickname might as well be The New Bank State. Georgia is a hotbed for new banks due to consolidation, a high demand for financial services, residential construction and population growth. In the past five years, de novo banks, which are banks that are less than 5 years old, have reported impressive deposit and asset figures that show customers are willing to put their trust in a new, locally grown operation.

"Bigger doesn't necessarily mean better. That's a big aspect to why a lot of de novo banks have been popping up," said Mark Tipton, chairman and CEO of Atlanta-based **Georgia Commerce Bank**, which was founded in July 2003. "Their friendly banker they used to deal with is no longer there."

Although he admits regional and national players have done well, too, the turnover created by mergers and acquisitions results in customers looking for better service and to deal directly with the decision-makers.

"The bigger a bank gets, the more they build a box, and if you fit into that box, everything works great. When you don't, things begin to short-circuit and you're not getting your needs met," he said. "We try to build the box around our customers' needs. That's why community banks continue to pop up and grow in this market, is to fill that need."

Georgia ranks third-highest in the number of new banks, closely behind Florida and California. In the past five years, 67 banks have opened in Georgia, compared with 69 in Florida and 71 in California, according to data from the **Federal Deposit Insurance Corp.** From 1992 until April 2005, 131 banks opened in Georgia, compared with 171 in Florida and 133 in California.

Metro Atlanta is the primary location for de novo banks, with 252 new branch openings from 1995 to April 2005, according to the FDIC. About 56 percent of the state's new banks since 1995 have been in the metro area.

Jack Phelps, regional manager of the FDIC Division of Insurance and Research, said displaced bank managers running community banks have improved the quality of management in today's new banks, many of which are founded by veteran bankers.

He also noted a strong correlation with the economic boom in the late 1990s. De novo activity in Atlanta peaked from 1998 to 2000, with 21 banks in '98, 25 in '99 and 37 in 2000. That slowed down with the recession, but is starting to pick up, he said.

"With the regionals moving in, people, for the most part, when they are banking with a community bank and it sells to a regional, there's something lost there," said Mark Stevens, president and CEO of **New Southern Bank** in Macon, which has grown to $325 million in deposits in less than three years.

After buying community banks, regional banks don't protect management, which causes longtime bankers to start up new operations, he said.

"That's really happened in Macon," he said. "It was attractive for people to move from the regionals and to where the management is local."

***

Rodney Hall, president of Georgia Commerce Bank, said the trend in de novo banks has diversified the opportunities for commercial customers by giving small businesses more choices and more access to capital.

"There is a huge opportunity to deliver a high level of service to those companies and do very well," he said. "The community banking market has thrived over the last five or 10 years."

Georgia Commerce focuses on privately held, owner-operated small businesses and the professional and executive market, such as doctors and lawyers. In less than two years, the bank has grown to $92 million in assets and $75 million in deposits.

It was November 2006, and I was vacationing with my family at Disney World in Orlando when Bill phoned me with news that would prove to have nothing to do with my next job: he called to offer me a relationship manager position in Wealth Management. *"You got the job!"* he was happy to relay—and congratulations to me for it! However, he continued, I wouldn't be working for *him* in my new position. Bill hadn't shared it during the interview process, but now he told me that he'd decided to retire from Wachovia and take on a new job as start-up CEO for a community bank that was organizing in northeast Atlanta. While he wasn't sure who would be taking his place in Wealth Management (and he had no earthly reason to care), Bill felt certain that I would hit it off swimmingly with whoever would be managing the team... (Blah, blah...).

I thanked Bill profusely for the call and for the good news, I offered him my congratulations and best wishes for *his* new venture, and then I mouthed something appropriate about looking forward to the announcement of a new managing director.

Then I hung up the phone, allowed my mind to turn a few revolutions, collected my thoughts, took a deep breath...and called him back.

I can't say I remember much about how that conversation went, but it must have included something about my interest in community bank start-ups, my considerable experience in building organizations (cough!), and my sincere enthusiasm for taking on a new and exhilarating challenge. I told him that I'd been in contact with a few community bankers myself over the past few months and that I would sincerely appreciate an opportunity to meet with him sometime and compare notes on common contacts in the community banking business...

Whatever it was I said, it was enough to get Bill to invite me to lunch when I got back to Atlanta and to talk with him further about his new venture. I snapped shut my clamshell phone, cast a glance toward heaven, and exhaled with the realization of what had just happened: I had a *meeting* with a soon-to-be de novo CEO who would need a de novo CFO for a start-up bank in Atlanta. Bill was familiar enough with my reputation...and he was going to need a CFO. Heck, he'd just offered me a job. He knew that I was a finance guy with enough chutzpah to try to move into sales...and he was going to need a CFO.

On January 6, 2007, Bill and I met for lunch at Houston's restaurant on Lenox Road in Buckhead. The group he had joined up with, Bill explained, was coming at a de novo bank start in an opposite fashion from the way most groups come together. Most new banks get started with a prospective CEO selecting and vetting organizers who ultimately work together and sit on a board of directors. In contrast, this organizing group had been forming for some time and then undertook a search for the CEO. Bill had been recruited and offered the job after several interviews with a selection committee. Some important cards had already been dealt by the organizing group: the bank was going to have an OCC charter (issued by the Office of the Comptroller of the Currency), and the capital raise would be conducted by way of a public stock offering through registration with the Securities and Exchange Commission. An OCC or "national" charter meant that the bank would be able to branch anywhere in the country as opposed to a state-level charter, which limits branching to pretty much within the state's borders. The "public" or SEC registration was intended to support a capital raise across a wide base of shareholders and across a range of states. The group had aspirations for a $40 to $50 million capital raise, followed by an additional raise to be accomplished after the bank had outgrown its capital in the first few years of operation (those were glorious days indeed!). After an extensive conversation about expectations and backgrounds, Bill told me straight out that he was in favor of my pursuing the CFO role for his new company. While he acknowledged that neither of us had ever managed a start-up before, Bill said that he knew many of the guys who had started banks across the state and had become successful...and we were at *least* as smart as they were! There's some real irony in there somewhere if you think about it...

We compared calendars and scheduled dates for our next meetings. Within days, I was interviewing with organizing board members for a midlife crisis that was cleverly disguised as an adventure. It was destined to be a fine crisis—a fantastic crisis, larger and more exhilarating than any I could have imagined on my own. Be careful what you ask for: God does indeed have a remarkable sense of humor.

My first organizer interview was with Dr. Dan Kaufman, a retired brigadier general, a Harvard/MIT grad, and a former academic dean at West Point. He said that he just wanted to meet me and see if I could walk and chew gum at the same time. I made it a point to not bring gum to the interview, and I was careful not to trip on the carpet in his office. We had a good conversation. Dan acknowledged that he didn't have a banking background and that he had no idea what sort of questions to ask me. Even I wasn't fooled by that approach: his capacity for assessment was obvious. In his final analysis, "I seemed competent," and he expressed confidence that "I could probably manage to find my way out the door even if I *had* brought chewing gum" into the interview. It was a compliment that stayed with me. I'm even more confident now that Dan is an excellent judge of character—as well as a remarkably accomplished individual. Dan would eventually serve as the first chair of the bank's Audit Committee.

This was a job beyond my ultimate "driveway opportunity." Indeed, this seemed to me to be the ultimate in a "higher class of overhead"...and it was beginning to find some traction. I asked around for introductions to executives at several community banks in order to compare notes and gather advice in pursuing the role. Those meetings proved helpful and yielded excellent insights and guidance. Some of it turned out to be darn near providential. The most important thing those meetings accomplished was to help me prioritize the job responsibilities and to speak with more authority as I went through the interview process.

I interviewed next with John Johnson, a former bank CFO himself who subsequently ran a de novo advisory firm that assisted with launching successful banks all across the country. John had been lobbying for an experienced community bank CFO for this group since the CEO hadn't been down this road before. After our meeting, he endorsed me anyway. Thanks, John.

I remember kidding with Carol about the potential change coming my way: "Forget about the blonde," I told her. "Don't worry about a convertible, and don't even *think* that I'd consider a middle-age comb-over...I might just go off and help start a *bank* for my midlife crisis!" Carol asked about the prospect for paychecks, and she asked about health care insurance. We were raising three girls, after all. We would have both, I assured her (both a paycheck and the insurance). In fact, I would likely be the one to recommend the benefits package to our board of directors (only *executive overhead* can do that)! I had answers, and Carol trusted me, though with that same expression I'd come to know from our previous conversations...

As a practical matter, there was sufficient funding to get the project underway. Each of the twenty-two organizers (John Burnett withdrew early in the process) had chipped in $20,000 to fund initial expenses. That placeholder was their "ante in" that entitled them later on to equity warrants. What made the project viable was not that we had $440K in our start-up fund—but that we also had a $2.5 million organizing line of credit from a local correspondent bank. More on that later.

My third interview took place in late January. Several of the out-of-state organizers met with me in Greenville, South Carolina. As Bill and I were driving back to Atlanta after the meeting, the group called Bill's cell phone and offered me the job.

And thus the privilege of choice: On February 5, 2007, I turned down what I thought I had always wanted: a revenue-generating, client-facing role at a legendary financial institution...in order to serve as executive overhead for a bank that didn't even exist yet. Go figure.

Newly Minted Bankers In The Merry Land Of Oz

Monday, February 12, 2007, was my first day on the job as CFO for our bank "in organization" (I.O.). It had been ten years since my driveway conversation with Don Miller, and my opportunity was finally shifting into gear.

The adventure began at a posh and peculiar conference at the legendary Ritz Carlton in Atlanta's toney Buckhead district. In retrospect, the Banker's Bank De Novo Banking Conference of February 2007 was a high-water mark for the irrational exuberance (there's that phrase again) that propelled the final stage of Georgia's bank-ing start-up boom between 2005 and 2007. The Banker's Bank was a correspondent lender—a bank for bankers, that made a busi-ness of providing start-up services, lines of credit, and transaction management to its base of community bank clients (within a year, The Banker's Bank would change its name to Silverton Bank). Our generous sponsor spared no expense in hosting the event for us giddy prospects. It was exciting and insightful...but for reasons entirely different than I could ever have anticipated.

As a rookie, I'd fully expected that the breakout conversations surrounding the conference would continue the same line of discussion: *Picking the Right Partners; Meeting Regulatory Expectations; Identifying the Needs of Your Community,* etc. (yes, I still have the binder). The reality, however, was decidedly more capitalistic. Over drinks and hors d'oeuvres on the sump-tuously thick carpeting, the buzz was all about which banks had just got bought, what were the payouts, who would be running the next deal, and whether or not non-compete agreements might open the door for a new group to enter the zip code. There was a whole lot more preening and deal talk going on than anything akin to note-taking by studious conferencees.

For me, the evening was a rolling series of epiphanies. At first I felt naïve, then unprepared—and finally more than a little incredulous. I was alert enough to keep my mouth shut, make introductions, and take notes in my pocket-sized Moleskine. I recall Bill and I glancing at each other at moments throughout the conference and us shaking our heads with a silent chuckle. While Bill was track-ing more with the agendas of those in attendance, we both were getting our first introduction to the feeding frenzy that was puls-ing through the entrepreneur bankers in this business. I'd spent the past several years working among platoons of bankers who were incented to do exactly that: *banking*. They made loans, they took deposits, and they offered fee-based advisory work. Now, crowded all around me and overflowing into the halls were bank-ers who seemed to be more about *dealing in banking companies*.

And if "dealmaker" seems a discourteous adjective, then perhaps "businessman" would better suffice. Regardless, this multitude of community financiers was a breed apart from the corporate Mellon folks and the polished Wachovians that *I* was accustomed to navigating. After thirty minutes of banter at the evening reception, I was alarmed that I really didn't understand this business. This wasn't Kansas...and that wasn't Auntie Em up there on the podium. To me this was banking bewilderment.

By the time dinner was over, though, I realized that there was more of a variety of folks in attendance than had I first thought. I remember labeling some of the attendees as "traders;" their mission was to establish, grow, and sell. Others seemed more the "buy and hold" variety, keeping abreast of trends but not overtly on the prowl for a deal. Lastly, there were the bankers that bore expressions like I imagined I was wearing: fascinated by the success of the business, pleased to be in attendance, but incredulous as to the paths of some of their brethren. I left the Banker's Bank de novo conference having established some friendships that I keep to this day...and with the realization that this business model had far more testosterone associated with it than I had anticipated. Just the ticket for a guy having a midlife crisis!

I bought laptops for Bill and myself, and we started hammering out a business plan that very week. We established a quintessential office in Bill's basement (on the "terrace level" as he likes to call it). He kept it stocked with Budweiser and Coronas, and we bolstered our efforts with an occasional "medicinal beverage" while we worked. As we finished portions of the OCC application and gathered background paperwork from the organizers, we took advantage of Bill's spacious pool table for sorting and assemblage. Ultimately, we mailed 105 pounds of paper to the OCC just ahead of Memorial Day weekend in May 2007, constituting our full application and the required copies for regulatory consideration. Yes, I said *one hundred and five* pounds of paper. A note to future generations: de novo bank chartering was a driver of deforestation in the early years of the twenty-first century.

There Will Be Regulators

On April 22, 2007, the organizers of what would become Touch-mark National Bank were all present in the same room—the first and only time that this would happen in the history of our banking endeavor. The occasion was a required "pre-filing" meeting with representatives of the FDIC and OCC, where regulators would meet eye to eye with an organizing group in order to reinforce the regulated nature of the enterprise that was getting underway. Our group sat at adjoining tables that formed a big square such that we could all look across at each other. The OCC and FDIC participants had taken up positions across one side of the room. We had been prepped earlier by conference call to be mindful of our hosts; the regulators, we were told, staged such meetings in an effort to gauge the maturity, integrity, and agendas of the group assembled. My only specific recollection of this meeting was FDIC Licensing Agent Karen Bryant asking chairman-elect Tom Persons—and then each organizer in succession—a single, pointed question: "*So why do you want to start a bank?*" She made it sound like an odd question, as though we were attempting to undertake something a little peculiar.

As each organizer in turn answered her question, the responses were methodical and scripted: "Supporting our community," "Building a business," "Promoting commerce while earning a reasonable return," etc. When the full group finally finished, Ms. Bryant turned the tables: "Why, then, do you imagine that *we* are here?" she asked, motioning across the regulatory panel that was amassed along her side of the table. Our organizers chuckled respectfully, and then cast glances at each other to see who would answer her question.

All eyes fell on Tom, and he took the queue. "Well...we *assume* that you're here to assess our qualifications and to make sure that we understand the nature of regulatory oversight," he responded. Tom looked confident that he had nailed their primary objective.

Karen looked out across the organizers, raised her eyebrows with purpose and then fixed her gaze directly on Tom. After allowing for a dramatic pause, this was her deadpan response:

"*We* are here to make sure *you* understand that the purpose of the FDIC is to protect the *depositors* in a chartered organization. The FDIC will issue a charter to your organizing group when—and *only* when— we are satisfied that you are capable of protecting the *depositor*. Not the investor, not the borrower, but the *depositor*. We are concerned with how you *handle* deposits, we are concerned with how you *lend* deposits and we are concerned with how you *collect* deposits. The purpose of this meeting is to make absolutely clear that you understand the single most important element of our oversight. Number one is protecting the *depositors*. Got that?"

All heads nodded in ~~submission~~ agreement.

There were other questions and answers that followed, but that single message was no doubt the central purpose of the meeting. Our business plan, our internal controls, and all of our compliance efforts centered around keeping the bank "liquid"—capable of funding the transactions and withdrawal requests of our depositing customers. And if you think about it, that makes sense: everything about FDIC regulation is centered on the assurance that a depositor can get his or her money back when he or she wants it. Satisfy the FDIC that you're capable of doing so, and you'll be on the road to getting a charter and its insurance protection. But a long and winding road it is!

Risk Comes From Not Knowing What You're Doing (W. Buffett)

A few weeks after cleaning off Bill's pool table, we moved into temporary offices at 3740 Davinci Court in Norcross. Once the offices were serviceably furnished we began hiring our initial team to fill out the org chart. I took to keeping a bottle of good bourbon in my lower right drawer in order to celebrate our milestones (and to self-medicate when necessary).

Not long after we set up shop, the OCC came on-site to interview Bill and me as part of our application process. This occurred around mid-summer 2007. The purpose of the interview was to determine if we were both qualified to serve as executive officers of a "chartered institution." A favorable outcome would be critical: after all, it was one thing to be hired by the organizing group. It was another altogether to be deemed qualified by the regulator who would grant us permission to open for business! It was at this meeting that I first met Tom Wilson, who would serve as our lead field examiner for the first two years of de novo operation. Tom was responsible for overseeing two banks in Atlanta: us and The Banker's Bank.

Bill went first. His interview took nearly an hour. When at long last he and Tom emerged from our conference room, they were both smiling. That was good.

Next it was my turn. Bill nodded confidently as I walked past him and into my interview. Tom and I sat down and exchanged requisite pleasantries for a few minutes. Then he asked me a single formidable question:

"Bob, *what is your definition of risk*?"

I have an undergraduate degree in economics. I earned an MBA with a finance concentration. Graduated summa cum laude. I knew that the financial-academic definition of risk was nothing more than "the variability of possible outcomes." The definition means that until you know with certainty where the "top" and the "bottom" are, what the "best" and the "worst" might be, you really can't evaluate the prospects of a project—because you can't speak with certainty about the range of possible outcomes. It's a pretty deep question in the realm of statistical finance. But I also knew that *experience*—which I didn't have—enabled leaders to avoid stupid decisions. In the practical world, experience trumps "variability" by a mile. I didn't know Tom...but I sensed that he didn't plan to spend the same hour with me that he'd just done with Bill. The right answer could likely cut short my inquisition. Any attempt at wit could make me look like a smartass—and so I held back my natural inclinations. Parsing the question academically could only reveal me as a bore.

I stared at Tom for a moment and then answered like I knew what I was talking about. *"The variability of possible outcomes,"* I responded... and then I expanded a little more about what that meant. Tom paused...and then he smiled. It was the only substantial question that he asked me during our session. We spoke for another five minutes and then the interview was over. Tom was gone from our offices within ten minutes of my answering his single question.

As I walked out of the conference room, I recall feeling cheated— like I'd studied all night for an exam and then got passed just for having shown up. Bill, who was visibly relieved that the inquisition was over, told me I was crazy—and to visit my lower right drawer and get back to work. We were in.

Epiphany #7: Approach an opportunity with a champion on your side who knows players on the team that you want to join. If you're a stranger to the group, someone on the team has to validate your credentials—even if that person is himself is a newcomer.

Banking As A Small Business

Eighty-one percent (5,739) of the 7,083 FDIC-insured banks and savings institutions open for business on December 31, 2012 held less than $500 million in total assets. That means if you added up all of their outstanding loans, the value of their buildings, all of the furniture, coin wrappers and everything else the bank owned– the total would be $500 million or less. The 50th percentile of all those institutions—bank #3,541—held nearly $169 million of total assets. That means 3,552 were smaller than $169 million. At a 4 percent margin (the difference between the yield on loans and interest paid for deposits), a $169 million bank generates roughly $6.5 million in annual revenue. That bank may operate three or four branches and employ somewhere between twenty and thirty employees. The point of all these metrics is to demonstrate that community banking is essentially a highly regulated *small business enterprise*.

Like any start-up business, starting a banking company involves risk. The best way to mitigate risk is to have a well-devised plan, hire talented people, and keep tabs on how resources are being deployed. As noted earlier, everything about a banking plan—the types of loans, the markets to serve, the technology, job descriptions, and security procedures—is in place to insure and protect the *depositors* because that's where most of the money comes from to fund a banker's loan portfolio. Only after a bank *in organization* passes examinations of its strategic plans, policies, and projections, justifies demand for its services, passes background investigations on its proposed directors and officers, documents evidence of its controls for safety and soundness, and raises the necessary capital, can it expect to obtain clearance and be chartered by the FDIC.

It's a lot of work.

So *why* proceed with a start-up that has so many regulatory headaches on top of the "typical" perils of starting a business? Several reasons come to mind:

- In 2007, banking was (still) a noble enterprise—and was enjoying a prolonged cycle that was making investors a whole lot of money. Hey, it used to be downright prestigious to be a bank director!
- Everybody likes money.
- It's a white-collar endeavor. Ogden Nash put it best: "People who work sitting down get paid more than people who work standing up."
- It is a wonderful fraternity of professionals.

- If it's what you know, it's what you do. The margin begets the mission.

Banking is an intriguing business. Like the currency on which it is based, banking success is driven by trust and confidence in institutions and their leaders. *Trust* is driven by reputation and perceived experience. *Reputation* is driven by ambition, opportunity...and ego. Pride and greed are traveling partners of ego, and so you'll always find them in the mix. *Equity capital*—the underpinning of financial institutions—has always ebbed and flowed with confidence in the industry. Risk and uncertainly, alternately, are the bullies of these financial undertakings. And capital seeks refuge in confidence. From banks the size of Chase and Wells Fargo to tiny little Eureka Federal in Metairie, Louisiana, success in the long run relies on *trust, reputation,* and *capital.*

Banking also *requires* a higher degree of certainty and accuracy than any other business I can think of. Recall that on average, a bank's revenue is generated by the 4 percent differential between its loan yield and deposit expense—for example, charging 6 percent interest on loans and paying 2 percent interest on deposits. Flip that ratio on its head: *what other business do you know of will ultimately fail unless you make the right decisions at least 96 percent of the time?* On a typical $100,000 loan, a bank will earn roughly $4,000 per year ($100,000 x .04). If the bank makes a mistake and that loan can't be repaid, that bank will need to make another *$2,500,000* of *good* loans in order to replace the lost $100,000 from the deal that went bust ($100,000 / .04). It doesn't take long for weak lending standards (or changing economic circumstances) to bring many a banker to ruin! How do you feel about those odds?

Epiphany #8: Getting Chosen Makes All the Difference

In hindsight, I had meager experience to take on responsibilities as start-up CFO for an SEC-reporting national bank...on the eve of a global financial crisis. But this is America...and lots of things are still possible with chutzpah. The reality is that *I got chosen*. Totally inexperienced at leading what became a $35MM capital raise—one of the largest in Georgia banking history...but I got chosen. Completely unaware of how to structure a bank balance sheet or on what basis to select the thirty-four business partners with whom we ultimately contracted for technology and services—*but I got chosen*. I recall a passing concern that not a single one of our organizers really understood how to qualify me—or disqualify me—for the job. But I *was* chosen. I assumed that I could do it; I must have looked like I knew what I was talking about... and that (along with a healthy dose of divine intervention) seemingly made all the difference. The outcome of my odyssey ought to encourage anyone with a little ambition that the story of your career can be pretty interesting. Hey, you've read this far!

My single most valuable epiphany from this period of my life is as follows: you can be the most experienced dude on the block. You can be hot stuff technically and be brilliant and distinguished in your work. You can have connections, a pedigree, and expertise that will outshine the best of your rivals. But at the end of the day, if you don't get *chosen*, you have neither the opportunity for reward...or for regret.

Appendix: The Best Start-Up Advice Ever

The kind of advice you get in life depends on where you look for it. A stockbroker will always tell you that it's a good time to buy stocks—because he makes his money on the trade, not on the subsequent rise or fall of the stock price. In the eyes of a real estate agent, there will never be a better time than the present to buy a home—for the very same reason. There is nothing like personal enrichment to give a fellow sense of urgency in pushing for a close. But *whose opportunity is it really*? The capitalist world is reserved for the self-starters, those willing to take initiative— but you've got to stand on something by way of ideology—and the best place to stand is on a foundation of worthy advice. Discerning wisdom and *knowing where to find* it is a blessing, it is smart, and it just plain makes good sense.

In that regard, Robert A. Mason was a very fine place to start. When I began exploring the world of community banks, my friend Ross Mason suggested that I spend some time talking with his dad, who has managed a successful career in business—and has served both as a bank executive and a director in the process. At the time we spoke, Mr. Mason had managed through three bank mergers and two de novo start-ups. He and his family have long been associated with the successful United Bank franchise in central Georgia.

This chapter finishes with a summary of my gleanings from a phone conversation with Mr. Mason on December 21, 2006. After arranging a call through Ross, Mr. Mason caught up with me as I was driving home from a meeting in downtown Atlanta. I swung into a parking lot and scrambled for a pen and something to write on. I include his advice here because it turned out to be prescient in my formative banking experience—and because it has applications to just about any industry business start that I can think of. Some of this is stuff they don't teach you in business school because it has nothing to do with academics. It's the real stuff of wisdom and experience. Thank you, Mr. Mason—and thank you, Ross.

- "It is better to learn what is probable about important matters than to be certain about trivial ones."

- Ian Stevenson

The Best Bank Start-Up Advice Ever

- The three biggest priorities are the business model, board selection, and the asset portfolio (loans and investments). The board, the CEO, and the president have to work together to keep the business headed in the right direction. In most community banks, the president and the CEO are one and the same person—and so that one person is responsible for a lot of the foundation of the business. Keep in mind, though, that the roles of the president and the CEO are different. The president is responsible for running the business. The CEO is responsible for communicating with the board of directors and for driving the strategy of the business. The board of directors is responsible for choosing strategy and for maximizing shareholder return in a safe and sound manner. Regardless of banking booms and busts, this has been true for decades. It is a good idea to have separate individuals in these positions as early on as possible.

- Not all organizers should necessarily become directors. In fact, many of them would not want the job if they understood the responsibility.

- The board can change the business strategy if need be, but the business model is the framework for your company. Community banks tend to "take on all comers" and become unfocused. It's important to decide up front what your target market is and stick to it. Don't take on business outside of your expertise or outside of your market. The type of folks on your board should determine the kind of business you get—so long as you've got a good board. If they aren't committed to the bank and to bringing in new business, they won't be good board members. And you *will* be disappointed by how many of your directors won't bank with you unless you're intentional about making a point of it.

- The board as a whole should control 60 percent or so of outstanding shares, but no one individual should *ever* control more than 10 percent. Distribute the remaining 40 percent as widely as you can.

- Exceeding the maximum of s-corp shareholders will cost you at least $200,000 per year in increased regulatory requirements. (RDK note: SEC registration requirements were relaxed in 2012).

- Stay an s-corp as long as you can (fewer than one hundred shareholders) no matter what anybody says. You're better off proving your success as a private company before opening the door to more shareholders. There's always plenty of investment capital available to a successful business venture. Prove your model first.

- "It's a *whole lot* about the people!" Community banking is a relationship business. If you can't excel at meeting people's needs and crafting individual solutions, you're wasting your time with a community bank. Big banks will always offer commodity products better and cheaper than a community bank. You've *got* to provide exceptional service and advice.

- *The single most important thing about getting started* is to form the organizing group from people of known character in the community. Lots of people have money, but what you need in board members are people who will listen and offer advice rather than force direction. What you don't want are directors who are really just looking for a lending trough at the cheapest cost for their own business purposes. Such members will be poison to a board of directors, because they'll inevitably cause the other directors to become self-serving, too. Having a cooperative board of a common mind is the most important aspect of growing a successful business. If the board gets involved in anything outside of bank policy, bank strategy and business referrals, you're headed for trouble.

- Some start-ups will fail; that's the nature of all businesses. To maximize your chances for success, define your market and hire local, experienced talent with strong community ties. Pay more attention to demographics than to the actual number of bank competitors in your area: it is population density that determines if a market is overbanked—not the actual number of competitors. Know for certain which part of that demographic should want to become your customers—and have a solid plan in place to attract them. Businesses with a solid plan, good backing, and capable talent will succeed—because that's just how business works. Banking is an easy business to grow if you have good community contacts and good people in both the front and back offices. If you have even one bullheaded director, though, you're going to have trouble.

- Regarding Touchstone/Touchmark's Gwinnett County focus: "A good thing about Gwinnett is the Indian and Asian ethnic groups. In my experience, they tend to be knowledgeable and make wonderful clients because of their family-centered businesses and strong deposits. Asians and Indians tend to keep their balances liquid and aren't prone to buying stocks—they like small businesses. That's great for a community bank! Gwinnett is "growing like a weed," and a good bank model that focuses on these communities should succeed."

- Banking is cyclical like most businesses. Maintenance of key relationships, though, will see you through just about anything.

- Have a model that suits the service area. Know what your planned consumer versus commercial mix is and why. You will get what you pursue. If you pursue everything, you'll have poor customer service and an expensive model to maintain. You can never be good at everything, so be targeted and specific. Don't hire bankers without knowing what kind of business they'll bring with them.

- Bob Mason's CFOs have been former bank examiners (adequate) and a former poultry farm finance officer (better). A bank CFO needs good analytical skills and needs to be just as good at working with people. He or she also needs to be ready to learn—you'll be surprised at what comes at you!

- Lastly, find good partners. Your accountants, auditors, and lawyers will affect your community reputation more than you know. They'll get to know you, and their opinions will eventually be shared in the community.

Chapter 2

All In: A Brief History of Georgia's Banking Boom

"The National Association of Realtors released its monthly housing affordability index today. The April reading dropped 3.3 points from March to a level of 108.6—the lowest since July 1990. Although rising interest rates have played a role in recent months, making housing less affordable, it certainly is not the level of interest rates that has brought the April affordability index down to 1990 levels. In April 2006, the commitment rate on a 30-year fixed mortgage was 6.51%; in July 1990, the commitment rate was 10.04%. **In April 2006, the median price of an existing single-family home was 5.9 times the median family income; in 1990, it was 2.7 times the median family income."**

John Mauldin, *Thoughts from the Frontline* 6-2-06

"Booms do not merely precede busts. In some important sense, they cause them. Because people in markets make mistakes, tearing down is an indispensable part of the process of building up. The errors of the up cycle must be sorted out, reorganized, and auctioned off."

James Grant, *The Trouble with Prosperity*, 1996

I included the James Grant quote not only because of its poignancy, but also because of where I found it. This quote appeared at the opening of an FDIC research paper titled *Metropolitan Atlanta Construction and Development Lending Trends*. The paper was published in 1998.

Community bank start-ups had no better a hotbed than the state of Georgia between 1997 and 2007. Fully 152 new charters were issued over the period—149 of which were granted for 'de novo' or start up business ventures. By any measure, that's a lot of new banks—and an *enormous* amount of effort that was vested in their creation. What drove the velocity and volume of all these entrepreneurial start-ups? In short: population growth, changes in banking laws, and good ol'-fashioned American enterprise.

As recently as 1990, each of Georgia's 159 counties—some with populations less than ten thousand—existed as its own financial fiefdom on account of Georgia's antiquated banking laws (some of the smallest counties had no banking offices at all). While metro Atlanta counties housed numerous banking competitors, expansion limitations beyond county borders restricted banks from broadening into the outlying counties. As Georgia law began to accommodate statewide expansion in the early 1990s, a more favorable federal regulatory environment combined with growing population trends to engender a veritable banking boom across the great cities of the American South.

A robust regional economy and population growth fueled each other to build out metropolitan Atlanta between 1990 and 2010. The population across what is now a twenty-nine-county area amounted to a mere 2.96 million people in 1990. By 2000, the region had grown to 4.11 million—an astonishing 39 percent increase of 1.15 *million* people, putting Atlanta's rate of growth among the highest for any US city over that period. By 2010, the region reached a population of 5.73 million—a 39 percent increase of another 1.62 million people—despite the onset of the Great Recession of 2008. In all, a near doubling of Atlanta's population took place over the twenty-year period between 1990 and 2010. Fully 2.77 million people—nearly 12,000 per month, 140,000 per year, moved to or were born in and around the expanding metropolis of Atlanta, Georgia.

All of those people needed a place to live. All of them had, needed, or would soon be in search of jobs. They bought cars, ate at restaurants, shopped for clothes, and consumed education, energy, and health care. Every single one of those 2.8 million newcomers generated true-blue American *commerce*. And whether they cashed paychecks, took out mortgages or applied for small business loans, that burgeoning population had a variety of reasons on any given day to establish a banking relationship.

In the last chapter I cited some statistics to support the contention that banking is predominantly a small-business industry. Of the 7,083 FDIC-chartered institutions open for business across the United States at the end of 2012, 6,425 of them held assets of less than $1 billion, which is generally considered the threshold for "community" type institutions (above $1 billion are "super" community and small regional banks). Only 9 percent of banking institutions held assets of more than $1 billion as of December 2012—and of those, nineteen are "megabank" institutions with more than $100 billion each in total assets. To frame the industry from a majority perspective, *more than 90 percent of the 7,083 chartered institutions operating in this country are community institutions*. These community banks issue our debit cards, finance our cars, and sponsor our 4H clubs. They are owned by individual shareholders who live in our communities; they are staffed by community employees and managed by community executives. The "small-town" banking model, while declining in number and undergoing epic change, is still by far the predominant business model for depository institutions across the modern American landscape.

Chart 3

All Commercial Banks and Savings Institutions
12/31/2012

Asset Size	Count	%	Cumulative %
Under $100MM	2,207	31.1%	31.1%
$100-$300MM	2,697	38.0%	69.1%
$300-$500MM	836	11.8%	80.9%
$500-$1 Billion	686	9.7%	90.6%
$1B-$10B	560	7.9%	98.5%
>$10B	107	1.5%	
	7,093	100.00%	Source: FDIC

Compare the information above to the chart at the end of this chapter. The ten largest US banks held 49 percent of domestic deposits on December 31, 2012.

While boom and bust cycles have impacted regional trends, the total number of banking institutions has been in steady decline for decades. Chart 4 shows the declining trend of savings institutions and commercial banks since 1996.

Chart 4

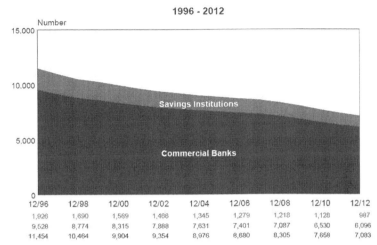

Number of FDIC-Insured Institutions

1996 - 2012

	12/96	12/98	12/00	12/02	12/04	12/06	12/08	12/10	12/12
Savings Institutions	1,926	1,690	1,589	1,488	1,345	1,279	1,218	1,128	987
Commercial Banks	9,528	8,774	8,315	7,888	7,631	7,401	7,087	6,530	6,096
Total	11,454	10,464	9,904	9,354	8,976	8,680	8,305	7,658	7,083

Source: FDIC

Note: the total count of 7,093 insured institutions in Chart 3 vs. 7,083 shown in the graph above relates to a slight distinction of how the FDIC counted charters at year-end 2012.

Historic Growth

According to the Federal Reserve, Atlanta held $37 billion in deposits in June of 1994. By June of 2000, balances had reached $56 billion. By 2005, deposit levels leaped to $94.5 billion. Incredibly, only two years later, in June 2007, deposits exceeded $113 billion—an increase of $76 billion or *more than three times the level of funds on deposit across the region only thirteen years prior*. That's a lot of money. And while the largest share of these deposits were concentrated at the biggest banks like Wachovia, Sun Trust and Bank of America, there was plenty available to new and aspiring community banks that were growing across the region. After all, consider the sheer scale of the Atlanta region: a deposit market share of a mere one quarter of one percent could fund a loan portfolio nearly twice the size of the median $169 million US institution! And as we'll cover shortly, all of those deposits begat a tremendous amount of lending.

Chart 5

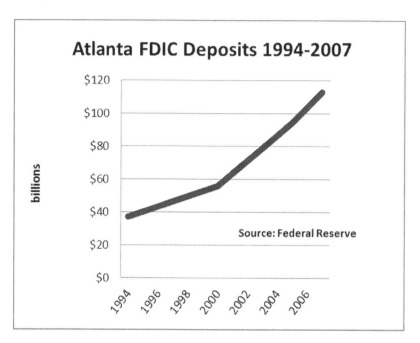

Population growth and productivity combine to generate output. The Atlanta metro area comprises two-thirds of Georgia's employment workforce. By the time of the 1996 Olympics, Atlanta was already the economic juggernaut of the South. By 2005, the gross domestic product of the region amounted to some $242 billion. Fundamental to that expansion was loan growth.

Friday, October 21, 2005
Atlanta's piggy bank fattens up
Atlanta Business Chronicle – by Jill Lerner, Staff Writer

Bank deposits in metro Atlanta grew at nearly twice the national average last year, remaining white-hot even as population growth here has slowed.

Deposits in metro Atlanta grew 17.2 percent to $94.5 billion through June 30, according to new data from the **Federal Deposit Insurance**

Corp. The upswing follows a modest 6.4 percent increase during the same period a year ago.

Atlanta was one of the top 35 fastest-growing metro areas for the 12 months ended June 30. Nationally, metro areas averaged a 9 percent increase in deposits during the period.

The increase stems partially from the shifting of deposits from other markets to Atlanta for bookkeeping purposes. **SunTrust Banks Inc.** (NYSE: STI) saw a big surge due partly to funds not generated locally.

But the local banking industry is nonetheless soaring as Atlanta continues to grow and bank organizers are still climbing over one another to start institutions here.

Despite the dominance of the top three banks, SunTrust, **Wachovia Bank** and **Bank of America Corp.**, which collectively tend 61.5 percent of deposits in the market, community banks are thriving in Atlanta.

For the year ended June 30, Atlanta saw the opening of six new banks, according to the FDIC. The metro area has been home to 73 new banks since 2000, according to Joe Brannen, president of the Georgia Bankers Association. That rate puts Atlanta on track to beat both the decades of the '80s and '90s in terms of new bank formation. Ninety-eight banks were created in Atlanta in the 1980s and 86 banks were formed in the 1990s.

"In general, the community banks feel they're doing quite well in terms of deposit growth in most markets," said Steve Bridges, CEO of the Community Bankers Association of Georgia.

Many community banks saw large deposit growth thanks to acquisitions and mergers, although several saw double- and even triple-digit percentage growth organically. Banks with the biggest increases in deposits included: Bank of North Georgia, up 56.5 percent; **United Community Bank**, up 60.2 percent; **Crescent Bank & Trust Co.**, up 60.5 percent; **Integrity Bank**, up 87.3 percent; and Georgian Bank, up 105 percent.

A key factor in the deposit growth has been Atlanta's continued population growth, which has led to another contributing factor, the region's real estate boom.

***

The ongoing population surge in Atlanta has begotten growth in construction – an industry that has become increasingly important to Atlanta banks. Real estate revenue accounts for more than half of all revenue at metro Atlanta community banks and has doubled over the last 15 years, said Jack Phelps, Atlanta-based regional manager in the FDIC's division of insurance and research.

National trends also have contributed to the health of the local banking industry.

Investors have continued their "flight to safety" following the stock market's woes earlier in the decade and generally are putting more money into safer investments such as bank products.

Another factor in the uptick is competition among banks in an increasingly crowded market. Competition between banks and by banks hoping to retain customers following a merger, has led to great incentives for consumers. The now-standard offer of free checking is one example.

"Anytime you have as much merger activity as we've had, there are an awful lot of promotions going on to maintain and attract customers," Brannen said.

"However," noted banking expert Chris Marinac, "banks are paying to play," which means they're offering better rates and thus spending more money to attract those deposits.

Still, interest in the Atlanta market continues unabated.

"Because of the growth in Atlanta, it gives [banks] opportunities you wouldn't have in Topeka, Kansas," said Marinac, managing principal and research analyst for **FIG Partners LLC**, who covers financial institutions.

"I think generally, it's been a very favorable time for bank deposits nationwide and Atlanta is riding that wave," he said.

Only California and Florida saw more bank starts than Georgia between 1997 and 2007. And while those states were economic engines in their own right throughout that period, it's worth noting that the populations of those states were *multiples* of the size of Georgia.

Chart 6

Select US Population Trends

	Florida	% US	California	% US	Georgia	% US	US Total
1995	14,166,000	5.40%	31,589,000	12.00%	7,201,000	2.70%	262,755,000
2000	15,233,000	5.50%	32,521,000	11.80%	7,875,000	2.90%	274,634,000
2005	16,279,000	5.70%	34,441,000	12.00%	8,413,000	2.90%	285,981,000
2010	17,363,000	5.80%	37,644,000	12.60%	8,824,000	3.00%	297,716,000

Source: U.S. Census Bureau

Chart 7

US Financial Institution Starts 1997–2011

Institution Starts	FL Count	CA Count	GA Count	Total US
1997	12	10	12	195
1998	16	18	15	213
1999	43	11	14	270
2000	18	10	17	218
2001	11	16	10	145
2002	6	10	11	93
2003	13	17	13	117
2004	15	11	14	127
2005	19	26	13	178
2006	23	23	21	191
2007	24	22	12	179
Total Starts 1997–2007	200	174	152	1,926
2008	10	9	10	94
2009	3	3	1	29
2010	2	1	1	11
2011	0	0	0	2
2012	0	0	0	0
Total Starts 2008–2012	15	13	12	136
Total Starts 1997–2012	215	187	164	2,062

Source: FDIC

November 6, 2007

Brookings Institution: Atlanta GDP worth $242B

Atlanta Business Chronicle

Metro Atlanta has come in as the No. 10 metro economy in a Brookings Institution survey of America's cities.

The Brookings Institution Metropolitan Policy Program, released Tuesday, identifies the economic assets of the top 100 metropolitan areas as measured by 2005 employment.

The metro area – defined as Atlanta, Sandy Springs and Marietta – had a population of 4,972,219 and 2,427,921 jobs with a gross domestic product (GDP) of $99,831 per job, which is 113.7 percent of the U.S. average. The average wage was $44,400 and the employment rate was 71.9 percent.

The report notes metro Atlanta's gross domestic product in 2005 was $242.4 billion, or 2 percent of the United States' total GDP.

The study shows 34.3 percent of metro Atlanta adults had a bachelor's degree in 2005, while 11.6 percent had a graduate degree.

So how could it be that a state with only 3% of the US population would give rise to such an outsized share of the nation's bank starts? (By way of comparison, the fourth highest state in bank launches over this period was Illinois with a count of 82—exactly half Georgia's total).

As noted at the outset of this chapter, a large part of the answer has to do with U.S. banking history and Georgia banking laws. As recently as 1975, no state in the U.S. permitted out-of-state banking companies to acquire in-state banks, and only 14 states permitted statewide branching (branching outside of an institution's county of origin or certain adjoining counties). By 1990, all states but

Hawaii had reversed course and allowed out-of-state companies to acquire in-state banks, and all but 3 states permitted statewide branching. In June 1997 The Riegle-Neal Act removed remaining national restrictions that kept banks from moving across state lines. The subsequent nationwide trend of banking expansion brought healthy competition to previously limited geographies, reduced borrowing costs, and fueled economic growth.

While Georgia had first moved to deregulate intrastate branching in 1983 and legalized interstate banking in 1985, it was the impact of Riegle-Neal in conjunction with the 1996 Atlanta Olympics that truly kick-started the state's banking fortunes.

Georgia has 159 counties. Compared to the average of the other forty-nine states, that's a lot of counties. In the early 1990s, Georgia's more populous counties were home to an assortment of banking enterprises. Many of the smaller counties, by comparison, had a single dominant financial institution...and some had no banking institutions at all. The onset of statewide banking enabled bankers to build branches wherever populations warranted or to acquire institutions in order to strengthen their networks across markets. This increased level of expansion and acquisition brought with it management buyouts and executive non-compete agreements, which promoted an even wider dispersion of start-up activity across the state.

Friday, October 8, 1999

Bank Cycle Starts Anew as Non-Compete Periods End

Atlanta Business Chronicle - by Mike Weiss, Contributing Writer

A year ago, Bill Butler was a top officer at a community bank.

In just a few months, he will be again. It has become a common scenario: Small bank grows, big bank buys small bank, officers from small bank start over again.

In the wake of several community bank buyouts in metro Atlanta in recent years, a slew of new institutions are springing up. In many of those cases, the new banks are headed up by experienced presidents or senior officers who made their name in the community before a larger institution, like Premier Bancshares Inc. or **Regions Financial Corp.**, bought their holding company.

Often, the officers at start-ups simply have waited until a non-compete clause in their contract runs out before opening a new institution in the same part of town, drawing on the same customer base they helped build at the old bank.

"Most community bankers you will find believe that people bank with people, not institutions," Butler said.

Wave of start-ups

At least 14 community banks have opened in metropolitan Atlanta since the beginning of 1998, according to the Community Bankers Association of Georgia. And more are planned, including Butler's own Futurus Bank, set to open soon on Windward Parkway near Georgia 400.

Many of these start-ups are led by bankers who have moved on to their second community bank in the area. Ed Mulkey, formerly of Cobb County's First Alliance Bank, now is with the new Southern National Bank in Marietta. The Peachtree Bank, just on the north Fulton County side of Duluth, is headed by former executives from First Gwinnett Bank.

Dennis Burnette was president of Pickens County Bank until the holding company was bought by Regions in 1996. Now, he runs Cherokee Bank in Canton.

"If you run a bank yourself and you enjoy doing it, it's likely you'd want to do it again," Burnette said. "And just because you sold the bank doesn't mean people don't still want to bank with you."

Discouraging competition

Realizing this, banks do not make it easy for former executives to compete. In many cases, the company buying the community bank requires that top officers sign non-compete agreements, which prohibit the officers from immediately jumping ship and starting a new bank, often taking employees and customers along.

Georgia case law requires such an agreement to be very specific, said Kathryn Knudson, an attorney at Powell Goldstein Frazer & Murphy LLP who frequently works on bank acquisitions.

Such agreements typically prevent an officer from working for another bank in the same county or service area for at least six months, with some agreements stretching as long as two years. Many specifically bar recruiting employees and customers from the old bank, Knudson said.

The company buying the community bank often insists on the restrictions to allow it a chance to convince customers inclined to shop around to stay, Burnette said. But the long process of chartering a new financial institution means that the officer likely would be unable to start a new bank before the time limit expires anyway.

Former officers are in demand, because they make it much easier for a new bank to succeed, said Julian Hester, CEO of the Community Bankers Association of Georgia.

"The most important thing a bank can do is find the right CEO with experience and contacts," Hester said. "There's nothing like contacts."

Starting fresh

Still, not every banker at a new bank wishes to draw on old customers.

Jimmy Walker, formerly of the Enterprise National Bank in Dunwoody, was barred from direct competition for two years after Regions Financial Corp. bought Enterprise in 1995. About two years later, he was applying for a charter for his new bank, North Atlanta National.

Instead of working in the same area, Walker moved a bit north to Alpharetta. That move made it tougher for him to build on old contacts, but the booming market near North Point Mall was more receptive to a new institution, Walker said.

"We didn't open with an immediate following," he said. "We're building it one brick at a time."

Bankers do not always open banks with the intention of selling them in the future. But bank officers ultimately are responsible for increasing the value to shareholders, and often selling the institution is the best way to do that, Burnette said.

"It can get to the point in time when you've grown all that you can grow, and you can do better by selling the bank to someone who can [grow it further]," he said. "Then they make you an offer you can't refuse."

Until its merger with First Union, Wachovia Bank was one of the grand and storied franchises of the American South. John Medlin, arguably the most highly regarded CEO in its history, famously described the old-school process of building a bank's balance sheet as "five yards and a cloud of dust," referring to the low-risk approach of advancing a football slowly down the field. Community bank starts in Georgia, by comparison, had developed a reputation by the early 2000s as wealth-building engines for bank organizers and the investors who'd thrown in with them. State banking laws were amended in the 1990s that reduced the required change of control period from five to three years. That meant bank organizers with aggressive business plans could launch an institution, gather deposits, and then strike an inviting pose for other banks looking to build market share in their service area. In fairness, this wasn't the attitude of all organizers—but banking is indeed a *business venture* just like any other, and business start-ups are undertaken by entrepreneurs with entrepreneurial mind-sets. Any bank executive prior to 2008 knew perfectly well that "three times book" was the brass ring for instant success and a liquidity event. The most fortunate of bankers took advantage of serial opportunities to launch, grow, sell...and repeat. Certainly the acquiring institutions were aware of this and took care to analyze a prospect's balance sheet. Indeed, while Wachovia's philosophy toward loan growth was slow-go, Wachovia was itself one of the larger Georgia bank acquirers over this period.

How Banking Works

The nature of community banking is pretty simple, but few outside the industry really understand how a bank makes money.

Most businesses are valued on the strength of their assets, which create earnings, a revenue stream, and an engine for performance and growth. In banking, however, it is the liabilities—or the bank *deposits*—that serve as the foundation of an institution's value. Banks have traditionally been valued and sold more on the basis of their 'core' deposit volume as opposed to the quality or yield of their assets: it's more the number of clients who do business with the bank, the number accounts that they hold, and the percent of deposits arising from the local market that make a bank an attractive acquisition. The logic behind this is simple, if not entirely intuitive: without deposits, there isn't money available to make loans...and no banker can make a loan without funding. Local or 'core' funding means the steady and repetitive deposits of local customers—local businesses and households from which to gather balances, make loans, and earn fees.

Like any business, a bank needs investors to get started. Those investors contribute capital in exchange for shares of bank stock, which provides the initial investment to get things going. In simplest form, a bank can leverage its capital roughly ten times. With $10 million of starting capital, a bank can underwrite about $100 million in customer loans...so long as it can attract $90 million of customer deposits in order to have funds on hand to lend. The difference between the rate that a bank charges for its loans and the rate that it pays to depositors is called *margin*. Margin is the revenue that a bank makes between its borrowers and its depositors. That revenue pays for all of the bank's expenses. When a bank first opens, it works hard to attract depositors—just as it also works to attract borrowers. By making good loans and attracting stable depositors, the bank increases the size of its balance sheet (and revenue stream) until it covers its expenses and becomes profitable.

Ever follow "the spread" in a sporting event (the payoff of winning versus losing)? It's pretty much the same thing as interest margin. While that's hardly a flattering comparison, your friendly neighborhood banker is in reality a highly regulated, highly leveraged...bookie.

Lending Basics: Asset Values, Cash Flow and Unnatural Acts

There are two types of lending in the commercial bank markets: loans that are made (underwritten) on the basis of *cash flow* and loans that are based on the value of *real assets* or *real property* collateral.

A *cash flow* loan is perhaps the easier to understand of the two, since it's the basis for almost all consumer lending: if your monthly take-home pay amounts to $4,000 and you have debt payments and other obligations amounting to $2,500 per month, then your available resources left over to support a new loan payment amounts to $4,000 minus $2,500, or $1,500 per month. If instead your documented obligations amount to $3,500 per month, chances are that no bank will lend you money—because it's unlikely that you can support another monthly payment (unless you can convince the banker that you don't need to eat). In using the cash flow approach of underwriting, a borrower qualifies for a loan based on his or her ability to repay the money from earnings within a monthly budget.

In contrast, collateral or *asset-based lending* is underwritten on the basis of a borrower's ability to purchase an asset, increase its value by some means, and then *sell* it—presumably at a profit—in order to pay back the loan. The asset is almost always real estate, and the increase in asset value is almost always commercial or residential property development (CRE). In order for a real estate developer to get a loan to build residential housing, for example, the lending banker must be confident that those finished houses will be purchased in short order by consumers at prices sufficient to pay back both principal and the interest that will accumulate on those loans. Without an active market of buyers and sellers, the borrower/developer has no way to repay the loan, unless other assets or cash reserves are pledged as additional collateral. This is a very important point: banks are *not* in the business of selling property—they are in the business of making *loans*. When a borrower is unable to sell a property that was acquired for development and sale, that collateral inevitably goes through a foreclosure process and becomes the property of the bank. The bank, then, must sell the property in order to recover its funds.

It is an unnatural act for a bank to manage real estate. The process of acquiring, rehabilitating and marketing property is cumbersome for a variety of reasons: an adversarial relationship with the borrower, costs and challenges associated with acquiring ownership, rehabilitation costs, marketing costs...all of which take time and effort in order to recover *principal* as opposed to anything that might resemble revenue or profit. Foreclosure sales are salvage and recovery operations, and banks are not staffed to handle such activities in ordinary times. Banks are skilled at financial management, not property management. As such, asset-based lenders much prefer to manage through problems with their developers than to take ownership of the properties themselves. It's simply a matter of working within an established expertise.

For example, if a developer wants to borrow $1 million to finance the construction of a ten-unit residential subdivision, both the developer and the banker have to believe that the added value of development will increase the attractiveness and selling price of the underlying collateral. If the developer can acquire real estate, build, and then sell ten resulting properties for $150,000 each, then cash will be freed up with each successive sale in order to pay back the loan. When all 10 units are sold, gross sales of $1.5 million less interest, fees and payback of the $1 million loan will leave the developer with a profit. Note that the primary difference between asset-based lending and cash flow lending is that *in order for the developer to pay back the loan, the properties have got to be sold.* Without the sale of an asset, the underlying collateral does not produce any income. Beginning in the early 2000s through late 2007, property values were soaring in many parts of the country—enabling "flipper" homeowners to trade up to larger properties every few years, enabling speculators to trade condominiums and commercial properties, and enabling developers to build homes, strip centers, and commercial buildings and sell out at sizable gains. This made for a vigorous real estate market and helped fuel a robust economy.

Without an *active market of buyers and sellers*, however, asset-based lending is a treacherous business. In the event that sales activity declines, sales prices fall or mortgages become difficult to acquire, there are fewer opportunities for a developer to repay principal back to the bank. Loan interest can be supported for a time...but should the value of the collateral decline, the developer must either find other sources of cash to support the loan, or default and turn the property over to the banker. I repeat a sentence from a few paragraphs ago: *It is an unnatural act for a bank to manage real estate.* More on this in later chapters.

Remember the 4 percent margin rule? A bank that makes bad loans more than 4 percent of the time will eventually and *inevitably* fail. A $100,000 loan at a 4 percent margin will generate $4,000 of annual revenue. Should that loan default and become uncollectable, the bank will suffer a $100,000 loss (in addition to the uncollected interest). The amount of *new* lending required to make up for this loss is calculated by dividing $100,000 into the 4 percent margin: such a loss requires another $2,500,000 of *good loans*—and a full year's time—to earn back the write-off on the single bad loan. Makes asset-based lending seem speculative by its very nature, huh?

As property values rose throughout the early 2000s, asset-based lending became a very profitable business. Both commercial and residential property values throughout metro Atlanta were appreciating at some of the fastest rates in the nation. According to John Hunt at Smart Numbers, the price of the median metro-Atlanta residential lot increased by 11 percent in 2003, then by 14 percent in 2004... and then by another 17 percent in 2005! And the increase in CRE lending was hardly just a Georgia phenomenon. As a percentage of capital, CRE lending for the community bank industry nationwide *doubled* between 1996 and 2008, as shown in the graph below. Increasing asset prices nationally caused a surge in investment and development activity for community banks during the period.

Acquisition, Development and Construction Loans (ADC) at FDIC-Supervised Institutions, 1991 to 2010

Chart 8

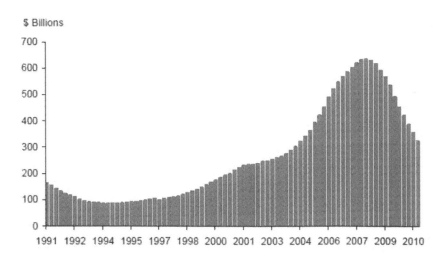

Source: FDIC's Division of Insurance and Research (DIR).

...while losses on these types of loans were almost nonexistent until 2008:

Chart 9

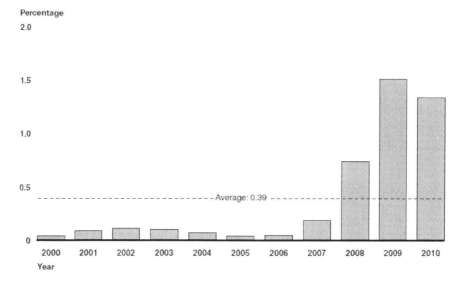

Figure 4: Average Charge-off Rate for Loans Secured by CRE at Community Banks (from 2000 through 2010)

Source: GAO Analysis Data from the FDIC

Rising property values made asset lending an easy play. For example:

If I were to lend you $400,000 on a property that appraises for $500,000 in a market rising at 5 percent each year, that property will be worth $525,000 just one a year from now. If you default after two years and I have to foreclose on the loan, the collateral should appraise for roughly $551,250. This is good, because I have to sell it in order to recover the money I lent to you. In reality then, so long as property values are rising, a lender doesn't worry much about defaults. If a developer started a project he couldn't finish, the banker could foreclose, find another developer capable of taking over the project, and then take it to completion at a profit. Life is good! During periods of brisk activity in a rising market, asset-based lending is an attractive proposition. But oh, those pesky boom and bust cycles!

As illustrated on chart 9, the rate of default on commercial real estate loans between 2000 and 2006---particularly in the Southeast, was essentially zero. Banks were printing profits.

The FDIC had long been taking notice. A 1999 FDIC circular raised an eyebrow to Atlanta's position as one of the fastest CRE-focused markets in the country. Anyone under the impression that the 2008 real estate bubble and banking downturn was the first of its kind for Georgia ought to read this report in full. Reader note: pay particular attention to the paragraph below Table 1. It's a little wonky, but the implications are clear.

July 1999
Excerpt from **FDIC, Bank Trends—Metropolitan Atlanta Construction and Development Lending Trends,**

Consistent with the rapid pace of growth and development across metro Atlanta, the percentage of local community institutions reporting high C&D loan concentrations is rising. Table 1 compares current C&D loan exposures to those measured during the high and low points of the past ten years—1988 and 1991, respectively. As of year-end 1997, fourteen institutions reported C&D loan concentrations of at least 20 percent of assets. This number is down from nineteen institutions in 1988 but represents roughly an equal percentage (17 percent) of the total peer group. Moreover, the percent-of-peer-group measure in 1997 was deflated by the opening of three de novo institutions in the fourth quarter that were included in the peer group but reported negligible C&D loans. When concentrations of 15 percent, 10 percent, and 5 percent of assets are compared across each time period, the current percentage of institutions with C&D loan concentrations is higher in each category than in 1988. Only at the 30 percent concentration level does the current distribution of institutions compare favorably to 1988.

Chart 10

	December 31, 1997		December 31, 1991		December 31, 1988	
Percentage of Community Institutions in Metropolitan Atlanta with High Construction and Development Lending Concentrations Is Increasing						
C&D Loans to Assets	# of Institutions	% of Institutions	# of Institutions	% of Institutions	# of Institutions	% of Institutions
30% or Greater	0	0.0	0	0.0	11	10.0
21% or Greater	14	17.1	4	3.5	19	17.3
15% or Greater	31	37.8	15	13.0	33	30.0
10% or Greater	46	56.1	34	29.6	53	48.2
5% or Greater	65	79.3	70	60.9	80	72.7

Source: Bank and Thrift Call Reports

Tracking the performance of the thirty-three institutions that reported 15 percent C&D loan concentrations in 1988, we find that those institutions performed rather poorly during the real estate market downturn that followed in 1990 and 1991. As shown in Table 2, *seven of the thirty-three institutions failed between 1989 and 1992.* This represents a 21 percent failure rate for institutions with high C&D loan concentrations, versus only 5 percent (four of seventy-seven) during the same period for metro Atlanta institutions that did not report high concentrations in 1988.

Dick Jackson, former CEO of First Atlanta (and author of the previously mentioned *Too Stupid To Quit,* AuthorHouse, 2005) told me over coffee one morning that Atlanta has seen four such cycles during his career, which began in the late 1970's. "You could see the next cycle building once you've been through a downturn. But that doesn't mean you could truly insulate your bank against the next one. Atlanta has been under construction to one degree or another for nearly the past forty years".

The Golden Age of Banking

In a region of the country with no natural geographic boundaries, an epic story began to unfold. Rising property values, pro-growth government, good demographics and strong population growth combined to create the most prosperous expansion in the history of the American South. Georgia was booming, and nothing was standing in its way. From a population of 7,353,000 at the outset of the 1996 Atlanta Olympics, the state grew to 8,186,000 by 2000 and 9,073,000 by 2005. The population had grown by 26.4 percent from 1990 to 2000, and then by 10.8 percent between 2000 and 2005. Metro area populations—predominantly Atlanta—grew by 29.2 percent between 1990 and 2000 and 12.3 percent between 2000 and 2005. The Atlanta metro region was characterized nationally as a contractor's paradise: if you had a hammer, an invoice binder and even a modest amount of initiative, construction prosperity was within your reach. The lack of any geographic boundaries only added to the scale of perceived opportunity. For its size, Atlanta has one of the lowest density populations of any urban area in the country. As such, the sheer volume of real estate development was among the highest of any city in the country.

The Golden Age of American Banking that began in 1992 was demonstrated by strong trends across all of the industry's primary metrics in the 14 years that followed. Allowance for loan losses (a bank's reserves against uncollectable loans) declined from 2.42% in 1992 to 1.09% in 2006. Net charge-offs amounted to 1.13% of loans in 1992. By 2006 charge-offs had declined to 0.37% of outstanding loans. Non-accruing loans amounted to $69.87 billion or 1.54% of outstanding loan balances in 1992. By 2006, nonaccruals had shrunk to $34.37 billion or only 0.37% percent of outstanding balances. Bank failures had averaged 167 per year between 1991 and 1993. Between 1994 and 2004, failures averaged only six per year. Not a single bank failed in either 2005 or 2006.

Profit Is an Opinion, Cash Is A Fact

Hundreds of studies have been undertaken to try and explain why humans can't see a "bubble" forming in vulnerable sectors of an economy. Further to James Grant's quote at the outset of this chapter, the answer seems straightforward to me: enjoying the party is just a whole lot more fun than watching out the window for mom and dad! The fact is, banks *always* lend "other people's money." And easy access to "OPM" became the driver of a nationwide real estate bonanza in the early years of our new millennium. Lending can prosper in a broad sense only during the expansion phase of a business cycle. But for an enthusiastic market of buyers and sellers, lending—both asset-based and cash flow lending—takes on a significantly greater risk of loss. Vigorous economic activity keeps currency flowing and asset values buoyant. Income statements can look great...and expenses can seem reasonable. But prudent management of all that activity requires balance, common sense, and one of the mightiest truisms in all of finance:

Profit is an opinion. Cash is a fact.

The essence of business success is keeping sufficient cash in the till. It doesn't matter how much profit a business generates until it can collect on its receivables and turn all of those invoices into cash. It can take a business years to build up a healthy level of sales, but the shop floor laborers still expect to be paid in in cash on Friday. *Every* Friday. The reality of the business owner is that invoices must be collected...or Thursday night will be a restless sleep indeed. It's only when the "music stops" and obligations are broken that the difference between profits and cash become clear.

When a player in a game of chance pushes all of his chips into the wager, he's "all in". And when the consumer inside each one of us becomes so confident in our ability to cash next Friday's paycheck that we neglect to make provision for what *could happen* should that check doesn't clear, we're running headlong down that same path of rising expectations. That's when we too are "all in."

"All in" for Georgia community bankers occurred during the second half of 2006. Merger and acquisition transactions for Southeastern banking companies peaked in the third quarter at a median of 3.05x tangible book (non-financial translation: a little more than three times the net worth of the company). Median price to previous year's earnings peaked in the fourth quarter at 28.06x.

Chart 11

Southeastern Community Bank M&A Transactions Median Price/Book

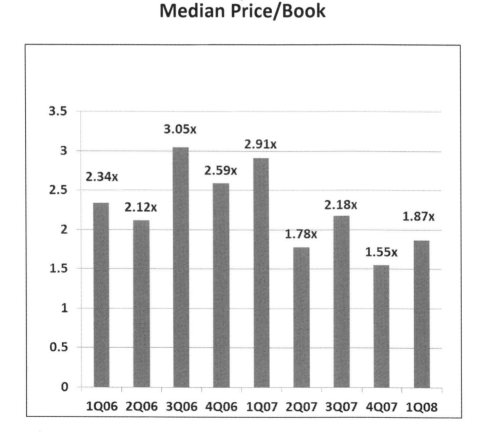

Chart 12

The year that was 2006 led up to a really, really good Christmas. Twenty-one new banking companies had opened across Georgia that year—most of them with a presence in metro Atlanta. There were 290 state chartered banks, 44 national banks, and 18 savings and loans (thrifts) operating across the great state of Georgia at the end of 2006. In all, the total amounted to 352 viable banking institutions. It would prove to be the high-water mark for the cycle.

June 11, 2004

Bank mergers, formations likely to grow

Atlanta Business Chronicle - by Meredith Jordan Staff Writer

The number of new banks being started in metro Atlanta has not kept pace with the number of banks being acquired over the past 12 years, but experts expect a lot more of both this year.

Since 1992 there have been 89 acquisitions of banks or savings institutions in metro Atlanta, and 64 de novos, or new bank startups, according to Charlottesville, Va.-based SNL Financial LC, an independent information provider for the bank and thrift industries.

"I think it's a pretty clear phenomenon that consolidation in the industry is outstripping the slower-paced de novos," said Bobby Schwartz, a partner in the banking practice at Smith, Gambrell & Russell LLP. "You can do an acquisition faster than you can form a new bank."

SunTrust Banks Inc. (NYSE: STI) completed its acquisition of National Commerce Financial Corp. (NYSE: NCF) in less than two months. The first meeting between CEO L. Phillip Humann and NCF CEO William Reed was March 19. The deal was announced May 9. That deal is valued at a little less than $7 billion.

Despite that high-profile acquisition, which still must be approved by regulators and shareholders, there have been relatively few mergers or acquisitions in the banking industry in Georgia in the past two years, according to SNL. There was just one in 2003 and one as of May 24. The number does not reflect any deals that have not yet closed.

De novos on the way

Meanwhile, 2003 saw a boom in de novos in Georgia, with 10 new banks started. Although SNL reports no de novos so far this year, bank consultants say there are numerous new banks in development.

"I know of at least six right now that I predict will come on board, and we're just at June," said Bob Calvert, president and founder of Calvert Consulting Co., a bank consultancy based in Alford, Fla. "We're looking at probably another six to eight from June through December," for a total of 12 to 14 this year, predicts Calvert, who has started 68 banks in the 22 years he has been in business.

Atlanta bank consultant T. Stephen Johnson also predicts an increased number of de novos this year.

"I know of about 10 banks that are getting started," said Johnson, president of T. Stephen Johnson & Associates Inc..

But consolidation also will continue, Johnson said. He predicted that Georgia's three most acquisitive banks will continue to look for banks to add, including Blairsville-based United Community Banks Inc., GB&T Bancshares Inc. of Gainesville, and Main Street Banks Inc. of Kennesaw.

"They've become the exit strategy" for the de novos of five years ago that have matured. Banks historically provide strong returns for investors willing to wait through the maturity process.

"After the fallout of Enron Corp. and all the other corporate and scandals, the idea that you can ride by and look at our investment is a neat thing," Johnson said.

Johnson also predicted that two relative newcomers could play big roles as acquirers in the second half of this year. The merger between Alpharetta-based CNB Holdings Inc. (OTC: CNBY) and First Capital Bancorp Inc., completed June 3, has created a $600 million asset bank under the CNB name. Meanwhile, Georgian Bank has climbed to $450 million in assets from about $71 million in less than a year. The bank was reborn with a $50 million equity infusion brought by Georgian's new CEO, Gordon Teel.

"I look for them to be pretty aggressive acquirers, as well," Johnson said.

Starting a bank is a long, involved process because of regulatory hurdles and the challenges of raising money from investors.

It takes a solid year, on average, to start a new bank, Calvert said.

"It takes about six months to get approvals and then another six months to raise the money," he said. "So you're really looking at a 12-month time frame."

"It's not that easy to form a new bank," said Schwartz of Smith Gambrell. "It takes time, expertise, effort and money."

***

Walt Moeling, a partner at law firm Powell, Goldstein, Frazer & Murphy LLP and head of its financial services practice, said supply and demand also could play a role.

"There are a lot of de novos out there right now," Moeling said. "And there are not a lot of obvious places where we need another bank out there."

Some markets, such as Alpharetta and Gwinnett County, are feeling crowded, he said.

"There are an awful lot of good small banks having to compete with each other [in those markets]," he said. "And that doesn't encourage yet another new small entrant."

Moeling predicts the banking market in metro Atlanta will see a lot of all types of activity in the second half of this year.

"Going forward, I think we'll continue to see some acquisitions and we'll continue to see some de novo activity," he said. "But we're probably at a stage where I would expect a little more consolidation before we see a lot of de novos."

Friday, August 25, 2006
Institutional investors hot to buy new banks
Atlanta Business Chronicle - by Joe Rauch Staff Writer

New community banks are opening at a record pace nationwide, including 16 in Georgia so far this year. The only thing keeping pace may be the institutional investors looking to buy into these banks.

There are so many bank funds and institutional investors popping up daily, Lee Bradley, managing director of Samco Capital Markets' Atlanta bank development group, has trouble keeping up, he said.

New bank creation is rivaling the last boom period in the late 1990s. On average, 128 new banks have opened since 2004, the highest since 1998-2000.

Samco is underwriting the initial stock offering of **Waterford Village Bank** in Buffalo, N.Y., and the bank received $650,000 from an Atlanta institutional investor.

"I didn't even know who the group was, that used to be unheard of," he said. "New funds are popping up every day."

Samco manages a $90 million bank investment fund with $50 million invested in community banks so far. A small portion of the fund, 15 percent, is dedicated to initial bank stock offerings.

The bank boom of the last few years is shifting the investment in organizing and nascent banks away from individuals and toward institutional investors.

As organizing and nascent banks are raising increasing amounts of investment capital, institutional investors are assuming a more prominent role as shareholders. Empirical data is scarce on the growth of institutional investors in banks, but anecdotal evidence from local industry observers suggests the field is growing along a similar track to the recent explosion in de novo bank growth.

"Five years ago I'd go to these funds with a de novo looking for capital, and they'd hang up the phone on me," Bradley said. "Now they're starting up funds left and right. It's like community banks are having their 15 minutes of fame."

Bank creation is booming, both locally and nationwide. SNL Financial projects 144 new banks and thrifts will be created by the end of 2006. That figure is the largest since the start of the decade, and rivals the last bank creation boom of the late 1990s, which peaked with 200 new banks in 1999.

Individuals still comprise the bulk of investors in smaller, more traditionally structured community banks. Industry analysts and observers said most new, or de novo, banks that look to raise up to $20 million are still funded primarily by private investors, usually the bank's board and local community investors.

"Those are the ideal investors in most community banks, because they want investors and someone locally who they can call on as a potential client to build deposits and loans," said Chip McDonald, head of the financial institutions group for **Alston & Bird LLP**.

But institutional investors – like private equity and hedge funds – are becoming shareholders in banks organizing large pools of initial capital.

One prime local candidate for institutional investment is the newly formed **Atlantic Capital Bank**, organized by several former executives from the city's largest regional and national banks. Atlantic Capital's management team hopes to raise $100 million.

That figure would triple the state de novo record of $34.2 million raised by Alpharetta-based **Alpha Bank & Trust**.

CEO Doug Williams said institutional investors would be involved as the bank sells stock, and confirmed that one institutional investor, Dallas-based **BankCap Partners Fund I**, has committed to investing in the bank.

He declined to state how large their investment would be.

BankCap Partners Fund I is a $200 million private equity fund. The fund was created earlier this year to invest in de novo banks, particularly those that followed a model to Texas Capital Bank, which emphasized business banking and service for high-net-worth customers.

Atlantic Capital's model will follow BankCap's investment strategy.

While institutional investors buy into banks at the de novo stage, industry observers said most institutional investors buy into banks slightly later in their life cycle. Those banks typically require the larger amounts of capital that are beyond the means of most individual investors.

"The smart institutional investors typically want to see a track record, both of the bank and the management team," McDonald said.

Institutional investment, particularly private equity investors, aren't a concern to state banking regulators yet. The Georgia Department of Banking and Finance began to field inquiries on institutional investment in banks six months ago, according to senior deputy commissioner George Reynolds.

"It's not been a phenomenon we've seen in this state, given some of the ownership requirement we have," said Reynolds.

State regulators do not publicly release statistics on a de novo bank's stock ownership in Georgia.

The state's banking regulations typically require that 50 percent of a de novo bank's stock owners live in the local market area, but that requirement can be waived by the department.

Federally chartered banks don't have a specific ownership requirement, beyond a charter and shareholder review by the relevant federal agencies.

Among the twenty-one members of the "class of 2006" was Creekside Bank, a state-chartered institution that opened in Woodstock, Georgia after raising $18 million from local organizers, their families and investor contacts. Tapped to become president and CEO of Creekside was Larry Peterson. Larry had stepped down as president of Atlanta-based Fidelity Bank in 2004. Fidelity at the time was a $1 billion Atlanta-based bank that Peterson managed to turn around after an ill-fated venture in the credit card business. Peterson had a reputation for diligence, administration, and regulatory compliance. Prior to Fidelity, Larry had built a successful career as a commercial lender at KeyBank in Ohio. As odd a fit as he may have seemed as a "big bank" CEO signing on for the de novo launch of Creekside, Larry was capable, willing and approvable. That made him a valuable catch. The market was hot, and the opportunity to build a franchise in the fast-growth northwest environs of Cobb, Cherokee, and north Fulton counties looked attractive—if not downright compelling.

Thirty miles east of Woodstock, another group of investors had been meeting informally for nearly two years to organize a bank in the northeast quadrant of the metro area. The group had set its sights on out-sized growth, and had plans for an out-sized capital base to match.

The Origins of Touchmark National Bank

An opportunistic businessman with a southern-fried physique sat in front of his computer monitor in the spring of 2004, reviewing a stream of merchant card payments. At fifty-four, the extent of Bobby Williams's financial industry experience consisted of selling merchant services to small Georgia businesses—the "swipe" boxes that customers use to pay retailers with credit and debit cards. But from his vantage point in Duluth, Georgia, Williams had become intrigued with the growing number of local bankers who were prospering by way of de novo community bank starts. Bobby's wife, Yuling Hayter, had found success in building their company by introducing Asian business owners to the convenience of accepting those credit and debit cards. As they built out a niche franchise business, Bobby came to believe that a bank charter could be a significant enhancement to their prospering operation.

Vivian Wong was already in her mid-sixties in 2004 when she was invited to join the organizing group for Independence National Bank in Greenville, South Carolina. Vivian had built a formidable reputation as the "dragon lady" of Greenville's Chinese restaurants and advanced her success even further with the launch of a successful trading company. Vivian saw advantage and profit in serving as a de novo bank organizer. Independence Bank had opened to moderate success in 2005. Greenville, however, was a small marketplace compared to the burgeoning economies of Charlotte and Atlanta. The successful launch of Independence interested her enough to seek a second opportunity in Atlanta, a city where she had hopes to expand in the next phase of her career.

By 2005, John Johnson had been a banker and a banking consultant for nearly thirty years. After early work as a bank CFO in the 1980s, John went to work at Bank Earnings International (BEI), a consulting and start-up advisory firm that provided services to community bank organizing groups. Now prospering in a real estate auction business, John still kept his fingers in the bank start-up realm by contracting with an ex-regulator-turned-consultant who helped bank organizing groups to navigate regulatory channels. Bill Crosby was a capable, if somewhat eclectic technician who had managed to assist with more than thirty bank starts in his own right over the years.

Williams first met with Johnson in July 2005 to discuss his interest in combining de novo banking with an Asian-focused merchant processing platform. Williams, who was more at home in a Tommy Bahama silk shirt than the button-down oxford of a community banker, was intrigued nonetheless at the prospect of partnering with a banking team to further his merchant card services businesses and to enter the fast-expanding prepaid card industry.

Organizing a community bank has always been about influence and the leveraging of commercial connections as much as it is about providing opportunity for longer term financial gain. The mainstream business case is that like-minded businesspeople with community ties join together, contribute seed capital, hire management and capitalize on their community involvement to bring business to the newly formed bank. Growth of the bank results from community development…and community networking enables the bank to prosper in the process. In that way, community banking is a natural outgrowth of local economic development in a "buy here, bank here" network of commerce.

By January 2006, John Johnson was under contract with Williams to coordinate the launch of a de novo bank in the northeastern quadrant of metro Atlanta. To house initial expenses, Bobby made use of an entity he had previously formed titled Formosa Rose LLC. Johnson in turn reached out to Bill Crosby, who was finishing up their joint Greenville, SC project that would become Independence National Bank. Equipped with Williams's concept to focus on Asian merchant deposits to fund a bank start, Johnson set up a meeting to introduce Bobby to Vivian Wong in March 2006. Over the next several weeks, Bobby and Vivian met several times to sketch out the opportunity.

John Johnson offered further introductions, and by April 2006 the group had grown significantly in number and diversity. Johnson proffered contacts from previous engagements that he knew were on the lookout for other start-up opportunities: Howard Greenfield, a technology sales manager—who brought with him Barry Culbertson, a technology distributor with Asian contacts. Hiluard Kitchens, a well-regarded residential contractor. Bill Butler, a commercial developer (unrelated to the Bill Butler referenced in the earlier ABC article). Butler invited Dan Cowart, an entrepreneur and son of the highly regarded community developer Jim Cowart. The Cowarts were known to have made investments in several recent community bank starts. Vivian invited Sudhirkamer Patel, a fellow organizer and director at Independence Bank. Patel, in turn, invited an acquaintance from Atlanta, Jayandrakuma J. Shah. JJ Shah and his wife, Meena, were owner/operators of the Gwinnett Clinic, chain of Atlanta-based primary care centers. While their demeanors were vastly different, JJ and Bobby shared a common ambition for profits and a community profile. Williams invited Emily Fu, an Atlanta real estate agent, who in turn invited Moon Kim, a Korean restaurateur. Greenfield invited Tom Persons, a retired ATT exec and a former director at Milton National Bank in Fulton County. Tom Persons knew that his childhood friend Dr. Dan Kaufman had recently moved to Atlanta, and Tom invited Dan to join the group. Brigadier General Dan Kaufman was of a significantly different stripe than the group assembled so far: Dan was an army officer who took an academic turn after a career of military service. Subsequent to serving as academic dean at West Point, Kaufman was awarded the opportunity to move back to Georgia and serve as president and first employee at Georgia Gwinnett College, a new four-year university that had recently been chartered by the Georgia legislature. Williams invited his wife, Yuling to the group. Vivian invited H.P. Rama, another Independence director and a hotel entrepreneur. She also invited Egerton Burroughs, a colorful real estate investor from Myrtle Beach. Finally, Vivian invited Larry Silver, a real estate developer from Virginia, Debra Wilkins, wife of a federal district judge, and Paul Lam, Vivian's brother-in-law. Of all the organizers, Persons, Johnson, and Cowart had previous bank board experience. Wong, Patel, and Rama had experience limited to the recently opened Independence National Bank.

The organizing group of Formosa Rose had its first meeting on April 26, 2006, at the 1818 Club in Duluth, Georgia. Over the following year and a half, the group met regularly to coordinate a plan and devise their search for an executive start-up team.

In 2006, Bill Short was winding up a thirty-year career with Wachovia Bank, having completed successful stints in correspondent banking, corporate lending, dealer financial services and wealth management. Bill was fifty-five, and while he had turned down several previous offers to try his hand at de novo banking, Formosa Rose looked different. The organizing group was now up to twenty-three members. Few start-ups had ever invited so many organizers with such varied backgrounds to the table. After considering his retirement options from Wachovia, Bill accepted the group's offer to sign on as the intended president and CEO. His first day on the job was December 22, 2006.

From Touchstone Bancshares' first SEC registration statement dated June, 18, 2007:

Why We Are Organizing a New Bank in Gwinnett County, Georgia

Our primary service area will center in Gwinnett County, Georgia, and the adjoining counties, with a focus on the Buford Highway corridor between the Cities of Chamblee and Buford. Located thirty minutes northeast of Atlanta, Gwinnett County has been one of the fastest-growing counties in the country for several decades. Between 1990 and 2000, Gwinnett County saw the largest net increase in population among the counties comprising the greater Metropolitan Atlanta area, and it continues to grow. The population of Gwinnett County is expected to grow from approximately 726,000 in 2005 to nearly 1.3 million by 2030. The area has three major shopping malls, as well as various financial, legal, professional, and technical services areas, which serve to attract customers and other businesses. Major employers in Gwinnett County include Gwinnett County Public Schools, Gwinnett County Government, Gwinnett Health Care System, Wal-Mart, Publix, the U.S. Postal Service, and the State of Georgia.

The ethnic diversity of Gwinnett County and the surrounding counties also provides an opportunity to reach a growing but underserved market. Gwinnett County also has one of the fastest growing Asian-American populations in Georgia, a demographic which we believe to be underserved at the present time. This population is expected to grow from 6 percent of the county's population to 15 percent of the county's population over the next thirteen years. Our organizers have extensive business experience, diverse ethnic backgrounds, and contacts in the market which we believe will create immediate business opportunities for the bank.

Monday, June 25, 2007

Touchstone Bank Joins Business-Focused Mix

Atlanta Business Chronicle - by Joe Rauch Staff Writer

When it opens later this fall, Touchstone National Bank will be the latest addition to a number of business-focused banks in Atlanta's northern suburbs.

Based in Duluth, the bank will target small to mid-sized Gwinnett County and northern Atlanta businesses as customers, and the area's Asian-American residents, according to a June 18 Securities and Exchange Commission filing announcing the bank plans to solicit investors later this summer.

"Indications are there's a lot of opportunity in that market right now," said Bill Short, Touchstone Bancshares CEO.

Short said the bank's organizing group, which includes Asian-Americans, will tap into that niche market to court clients for the banks. But with a commercial focus, Touchstone will be entering an increasingly crowded business bank market in the city's northern suburbs.

Other business-focused new banks in the same area include KeyWorth Bank, Alpha Bank & Trust and Rockbridge Commercial Bank.

All are business-oriented banks – KeyWorth is still organizing – and each sought similar amounts of initial capital. Touchstone Bancshares is raising at least $31 million before it opens, and has a fundraising cap of $42 million.

Industry observers have noted new banks, like Touchstone Bancshares, might face new challenges raising money, after waves of new banks in recent years – many with overlapping business models – drained local investors. Short said he had not started raising money yet, and couldn't comment on whether he expects difficulty in the investor market.

"We won't know until we start."

The bank's organizers tapped two local Wachovia wealth-management executives to run the new bank. Short, a 30-year veteran of Wachovia Corp. will be CEO and Bob Koncerak will be chief financial officer.

Short previously worked as a managing director for several local Wachovia wealth-management teams. Koncerak was Wachovia Wealth Management Division's Southeast region CFO.

But signs exist that Touchstone Bancshares will try to avoid getting lost in the mix.

Initially, the bank will open three branches in Norcross and Doraville, and a Duluth headquarters. Touchstone Bancshares has long-term plans to expand to Forsyth County and other north metro areas.

Short said the bank has no current plans to expand too deeply inside the Perimeter, but didn't rule it out either.

Bill Short wryly recollects that during his initial interview with the search committee, JJ Shah asked him how long it would take before this new de novo undertaking would be larger than Sun-Trust Bank (at $105B, SunTrust is the largest bank chartered in Georgia). As he tells it, Bill responded to Shah that "so long as we're always the acquir*or* and never the acquir*ee*, we may have chance one day to make that claim." Indeed, anything seemed possible.

The twenty-four organizers each seeded $20,000 of starting capital along with a commitment to purchase a minimum twenty thousand shares of the company's stock at $10 per share (a total contribution of $200,000). To support the effort with additional liquidity, the organizers also guaranteed a $2.5 million line of credit from The Banker's Bank based in Atlanta. That seed capital combined with a large credit line lent considerable credibility to the undertaking.

The Rise of The Correspondent Lender And The Banker's Bank Model

Two hundred thousand dollars is fairly large ante. For most people, it's more than they have available to invest—and certainly more than they want to commit to a single enterprise. Fortunately for de novo bank organizers, another entrepreneurial banking channel stood ready to finance their investments as de novo banks sprung up across the region in the early years of the millennium.

The Banker's Bank was organized in Atlanta, Georgia in 1986 with a so-called "special-purpose" charter. Correspondent banks are a specialized group of institutions that serve as intermediaries to the community banking industry, providing such services as organizer credit lines and stock loans to groups in the formative stage, and a variety of settlement and accounting services after a new bank opens for business. The Banker's Bank and other correspondents like Nexity in Birmingham and Independent Banker's Bank near Orlando thrived as community banks signed on for their services. By 2007, The Banker's Bank counted nearly 1,500 institutions as clients across 44 states.

What distinguished The Banker's Bank among its correspondent peers was its aggressive pursuit of commercial real estate lending beginning in 2001. In addition to bank stock and holding company loans, The Banker's Bank developed a significant business in underwriting deals that were too large for smaller institutions to originate on their own. By leveraging its capital base to structure large (primarily CRE) loan facilities, The Banker's Bank would then sell portions of the loans to its banking clients, a practice known in the industry as loan participations or syndicated lending.

Near the peak of the cycle in 2006, The Banker's Bank celebrated the opening of four loan production offices in Boston, Cincinnati, Los Angeles, and Seattle, and a full-service branch in Maryland.

By the end of 2007, the Banker's Bank had originated $1.1 billion in real estate loans, and sold off $600 million of that production across its client base. At the end of 2008, half—or about $1 billion—of its $2.1 billion loan portfolio was composed of residential construction and development lending. Its portfolio ballooned by 61 percent in the last two years of the housing bubble. Indeed, there was no better a cheerleader—or enabler—for the community banking industry than The Banker's Bank of Atlanta, Georgia, which changed its name to Silverton Bank in January 2008.

A bank organizer without a ready source of cash (or one who preferred not to commit personal funds to the enterprise) could apply for a loan at a correspondent bank, put up 20 percent of the investment as cash and borrow the remainder by pledging the stock as collateral for the loan. In this way, an organizer looking to acquire, say, $100,000 of a de novo stock could pony up only $20,000 in actual cash—and borrow the rest at an attractive interest rate. Common terms for financing were two years of interest-only payments at prime minus half a percent, followed by a term loan of three years on a ten-year amortization schedule. The balance of the note would come due after five years. Such favorable terms came with an implicit quid pro quo, whereby the organizing group would be expected to house escrow funds, guarantee a borrowing line and in other ways contract with the correspondent bank for services once the institution was open for business.

For the organizer or "insider" of a start-up (non-organizing executives sometimes qualified as insiders, too) the investment of seed capital and personal guarantee of a credit line carry with them a potentially lucrative leveraging opportunity. Because bank organizers put their personal funds at risk (organizers are legally obligated to pay back other investors if the start-up fails to receive its FDIC charter and open for business), organizers are eligible to issue themselves warrants (stock options by another name), which can vest upon the opening of the bank, thereby leveraging their ownership position. Some organizing groups issued themselves two or three warrants for each share of stock that they purchased (or financed)...which in some cases stood to significantly dilute other shareholders if and when those warrants were eventually tendered.

Consider this example of such leverage: an organizer puts up $20,000 cash for ten thousand shares of bank stock priced at $10 per share. The stock is pledged as loan collateral to a correspondent bank, which enables the organizer to borrow $80,000 to complete the purchase of the shares. The $80,000 loan is structured with interest-only payments for two years. Warrants are issued at ratio of two per each share purchased: so far that's a three-to-one leveraged position using only 20 percent of the organizer's personal funds. Now let's imagine that the bank is sold after four years of operation for two times book value—and book value is determined to be no more than the original $10 issued share price (three times book was the target to shoot for, but hey, let's not be greedy here). After netting out the strike price of the warrants, the organizer would collect tidy the sum of $400,000. The organizer's only expense would be a few thousand dollars of accrued interest over the term of an $80,000 loan. The gross cash on cash return in this example amounts and enviable 2,000 percent! It was the leverage play of the decade.

Strategic Organization and Seeds Of Conflict

You may have noticed in the previous chapter that the organization of Touchstone (ultimately Touchmark National Bank) stood at odds with one of Bob Mason's most important de novo start-up rules. Every bank CEO that I have ever spoken with on the subject has stressed the importance of screening organizers for their suitability to serve as directors in the cooperative execution of an adopted business plan. In hindsight, this makes complete sense and would prove to be portentous to the early management of Touchmark, and in ways that none of us imagined. Through the lens of experience, it now seems clear that the success of *any* enterprise is reliant upon the execution of a viable and *uniformly adopted* business plan. In the case of Touchmark, however, it was the organizers who came together first…and then went about recruiting an executive team. The only real "vetting" that took place came by way of invitation...and an adequate checkbook. There was no experienced bank CEO in place to evaluate the suitability of a national charter, or to opine on the appropriateness of a public stock offering. It was instead the collective organizers who decided that an SEC-registered offering would be best, that a national charter was preferable to a state charter, and that all willing organizers would ultimately be suitable to sit as bank directors.

I make note of these conditions not out of criticism or judgment, but merely as a record of choice in the telling of this story.

While the perspective of hindsight is valuable, it is a poor substitute for even minimal foresight. Every one of Touchmark's organizers was a successful and capable individual. Each member shared a common aspiration for creating a prosperous and successful community bank. And all were excited about the opportunity for success that lay ahead. What we could not know, though, was that we *individually* held very different notions about a business plan that would bring vision and clarity to our aspirations—and in so doing, support the highest probability for success. As result of this, the coming years would prove to be a remarkable adventure for us all.

A Side Note: Everything You Need to Know About "Too Big To Fail" On One Page

Of the 7,083 FDIC-insured institutions operating on December 31, 2012, the top ten—which comprise *fourteen one-hundredths of one percent* of the total—control nearly 49 percent of all US domestic deposits and 56% of banking assets. The largest 70 institutions—or the "top 1%" of all banks controlled fully 77 percent of banking assets and 86 percent of domestic deposits at the end of 2012. Change your opinion about "too big to fail"?

Chart 13

Rank	Bank Holding Company	Assets of Insured Subsidiaries 12/31/2012 (millions)	Domestic Deposits of Insured Subs 12/31/2012 (millions)
1	JPMORGAN CHASE	2,026,976,000	946,321,100
2	BANK OF AMERICA CORPORATION	1,689,264,900	1,195,373,300
3	CITIGROUP INC.	1,315,288,000	416,474,900
4	WELLS FARGO & COMPANY	1,332,554,100	969,713,000
5	U.S. BANCORP	351,306,300	235,030,900
6	PNC FINANCIAL SERVICES GROUP	295,026,400	211,846,000
7	BANK OF NEW YORK MELLON	301,383,900	143,162,400
8	CAPITAL ONE FINANCIAL CORPORATION	331,560,500	231,650,600
9	STATE STREET CORPORATION	218,655,000	67,329,000
10	TORONTO-DOMINION BANK	219,011,500	182,668,600
	Group Total:	$8,081,026,600	4,599,569,800

Total Assets of Banks and Savings Institutions 12/31/12:	$ 14,451,000,000	
Total US Domestic Deposits at 12/31/12:		$ 9,447,000,000
Percent Held by Top 10:	55.9%	48.7%
Total Banks and Savings Institutions at 12/31/2012:	7,093	
Top 10 % of Total Banks and Savings Institutions:	0.14%	

	Total Assets	Total Deposits
Top 70 US Banks $ Holdings at 12/31/12	11,105,114,600	8,142,291,900
Top 70 US Banks % Holdings at 12/31/12	76.8%	86%
Top 70 Banks as % of US Total at 12/31/12	1.0%	

Even so, American megabanks are considerably smaller than their European and Asian counterparts—primarily because the US has numerous other intermediaries in the financial marketplace: think credit cards, PayPal and Wal-Mart's new Bluebird debit cards.

The point to be made here is that community banking—while the predominant American business model, commands only a small fraction of the US deposit base, and had little to do with investment decisions that brought about the 2008 financial crisis. The graph below, reprinted from the FDIC's December 2012 community bank study, charts the disparity that has created megabanks now deemed "Too Big To Fail".

Chart 14

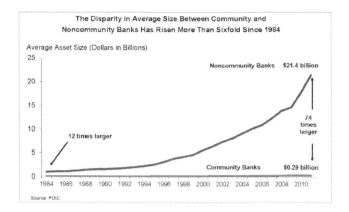

In contrast, 2012 FDIC data reveals that community banks are responsible for some 46% of small business lending. As such, the contrast of industry size versus economic importance is nothing short of astonishing. Community banking is a business that—for reasons of systemic economic support rather than market share—is "too important to fail". Any long-time community banker can point to businesses in their markets that are here today because the bank took a chance on them. The *Occupy Wall Street* movement that captured the nation's attention in the fall of 2011 painted the financial services industry with a broad, unruly brush.

Community banks are the "other 99%" of American banking!

List 1

Georgia State and OCC De Novo Charter Openings
1997 - 2012

Includes bank-level capitalization only. Total including holding company capital may be higher

		Open Date	Name	County	Bank Capitalization	Total Bank Capital
1997	1	2/3/1997	The Citizens Bank of Forsyth County	Forsyth	$6,500,000	
	2	3/3/1997	Peoples Bank of West Georgia	Carroll	$6,000,000	
	3	4/21/1997	Gateway Bank & Trust	Catoosa	$6,000,000	
	4	5/29/1997	Sapelo National Bank	McIntosh	3,694,000	
	5	6/12/1997	Rivoli Bank & Trust	Bibb	$7,392,200	
	6	9/2/1997	Decatur First Bank	DeKalb	$8,000,000	
	7	9/8/1997	First Georgia Community Bank	Butts	$6,500,000	
	8	10/14/1997	Liberty National Bank	Rockdale	6,000,000	
	9	10/22/1997	HomeTown Bank of Villa Rica	Carroll	$7,203,740	
	10	10/31/1997	Gwinnett Banking Company	Gwinnett	$9,000,000	
	11	12/2/1997	Eagle National Bank	Henry	5,971,000	$72,260,940
1998	12	4/15/1998	First Piedmont Bank	Barrow	$6,800,000	
	13	4/27/1998	InfiBank	Fulton	$15,000,000	
	14	5/15/1998	Chestatee State Bank	Dawson	$9,500,000	
	15	6/15/1998	First Community Bank of Georgia	Crawford	$5,000,000	
	16	6/29/1998	American Century Financial Services	Henry	$7,424,460	
	17	7/1/1998	BB&T Bankcard Corporation	Muscogee	$3,625,000	
	18	7/27/1998	Chattahoochee National Bank	Fulton	9,600,000	
	19	8/31/1998	Atlantic National Bank	Brunswick	8,100,000	
	20	9/8/1998	Citizens Bank of Effingham	Effingham	$5,000,000	
	21	10/5/1998	The Peachtree Bank	Fulton	$7,753,750	
	22	11/16/1998	North Atlanta National Bank	Fulton	6,241,000	
	23	11/30/1998	Unity National Bank	Bartow	7,930,000	
	24	12/21/1998	Southern National Bank	Cobb	6,000,000	$97,974,210
1999	25	1/4/1999	Southern Heritage Bank	Hall	$8,000,000	
	26	2/10/1999	North Georgia National Bank	Calhoun	8,954,000	
	27	4/28/1999	AB&T National Bank	Dougherty	7,500,000	
	28	5/3/1999	Belk National Bank	Gwinnett	2,000,000	
	29	7/26/1999	Cherokee Bank, National Association	Cherokee	6,000,000	
	30	8/2/1999	Community Bank of the South	Cobb	$8,458,000	
	31	8/31/1999	Bank of Terrell	Terrell	$9,758,000	
	32	8/31/1999	Commercial State Bank	Seminole	$6,877,000	
	33	9/1/1999	First National Bank of Johns Creek	Gwinnett	9,594,000	
	34	9/16/1999	Dalton Whitfield Bank	Whitfield	$14,300,000	
	35	9/16/1999	FSGBank, National Association	Whitfield	14,157,000	

		Open Date	Name	County	Bank Capitalization	Total Bank Capital
	36	9/20/1999	United Americas Bank, NA	Fulton	11,000,000	
	37	10/1/1999	Cumberland National Bank	Camden	4,000,000	
	38	10/18/1999	Gwinnett Community Bank	Gwinnett	$7,059,600	
	39	10/18/1999	GlennSouth Community Bank	Tattnall	$4,000,000	
	40	10/25/1999	Alliance National Bank	Whitfield	8,673,000	$130,330,600
2000	41	1/24/2000	Horizon Bank	DeKalb	$7,000,000	
	42	1/31/2000	First Intercontinental Bank	DeKalb	$7,305,000	
	43	2/18/2000	The Bank of Georgia	Fayette	$11,000,000	
	44	4/17/2000	Security Exchange Bank	Cobb	$7,857,175	
	45	4/17/2000	North Georgia Bank	Oconee	$5,366,220	
	46	4/20/2000	Newnan Coweta Bank	Coweta	$9,000,000	
	47	5/8/2000	The National Bank of Georgia	Clarke	7,312,000	
	48	5/15/2000	First Bank of Gwinnett	Gwinnett	$11,672,000	
	49	5/26/2000	United National Bank	Grady	6,733,000	
	50	6/2/2000	Southern Community Bank	Fayette	$8,109,830	
	51	6/26/2000	pointpathbank, National Association	Muscogee	13,125,000	
	52	6/29/2000	Century Bank of Bartow County	Bartow	$7,900,350	
	53	7/12/2000	Centura Card Bank	Gwinnett	$5,004,000	
	54	10/2/2000	Community Bank of Pickens County	Pickens	$5,700,000	
	55	11/1/2000	Integrity Bank	Fulton	$10,000,000	
	56	11/4/2000	First National Bank of Gwinnett	Gwinnett	7,726,000	$130,810,575
2001	57	2/20/2001	CornerstoneBank	Fulton	6,730,000	
	58	5/1/2001	Guardian Bank	Lowndes	$4,500,000	
	59	5/2/2001	Futurus Bank, National Association	Fulton	7,500,000	
	60	10/9/2001	Piedmont Bank of Georgia	Fulton	$9,700,000	
	61	11/1/2001	Georgia Banking Company	Fulton	$8,250,000	
	62	11/14/2001	Georgian Bank	Cobb	$8,362,034	
	63	11/19/2001	Douglas National Bank	Douglas	5,800,000	
	64	11/20/2001	Satilla Community Bank	Camden	$5,053,270	
	65	12/4/2001	CompuCredit Bank	DeKalb	$19,884,000	
	66	12/10/2001	New South Bank	Bibb	$7,694,354	83,473,658
2002	67	1/23/2002	Citizens & Southern Bank	Chatham	$10,000,000	
	68	1/28/2002	First Bank of Henry County	Henry	$7,633,550	
	69	2/5/2002	First Southern National Bank	Bulloch	6,700,000	
	70	3/5/2002	Omni Interim, National Association	Whitfield	6,000,000	
	71	3/5/2002	First Century Bank, NA	Hall	6,000,000	
	72	3/25/2002	First National Bank West Metro	Paulding	11,500,000	
	73	7/22/2002	Piedmont Community Bank	Jones	$7,783,400	
	74	8/5/2002	Southern Horizon Bank	Clayton	$10,000,000	
	75	9/3/2002	United Commercial Bank	Fulton	$10,407,750	
	76	11/5/2002	McIntosh Commercial Bank	Carroll	$10,500,000	$86,524,700
2003	77	1/27/2003	Generations Bank	Union	$9,100,920	
	78	2/24/2003	Homestead Bank	Gwinnett	$12,000,000	
	79	3/4/2003	First Commerce Community Bank	Douglas	$10,000,000	
	80	3/25/2003	Community Bank of West Georgia	Carroll	$7,000,000	

		Open Date	Name	County	Bank Capitalization	Total Bank Capital
	81	4/15/2003	Mountain State Bank	Dawson	$10,025,169	
	82	6/17/2003	Lanier Community Bank	Gwinnett	$10,000,000	
	83	7/1/2003	Georgia Commerce Bank	Cobb	$12,000,000	
	84	8/11/2003	American Trust Bank	Fulton	$9,100,000	
	85	8/26/2003	Oglethorpe Bank	Glynn	$8,308,310	
	86	9/19/2003	Neighbors Bank	Fulton	$10,800,000	
	87	10/30/2003	Midtown Bank & Trust Company	Fulton	$10,500,000	
	88	11/3/2003	1st Georgia Banking Company	Heard	$17,000,000	
	89	11/10/2003	Mountain Heritage Bank	Rabun	$9,624,470	$135,458,869
2004	90	2/17/2004	Freedom Bank of Georgia	Jackson	$7,543,996	
	91	3/11/2004	NorthWest Bank & Trust	Cobb	$13,511,370	
	92	4/5/2004	First National Bank of Forsyth County	Forsyth	10,000,000	
	93	4/5/2004	First National Bank of Decatur County	Decatur	6,000,000	
	94	5/4/2004	Mountain Valley Community Bank	White	$7,244,000	
	95	5/11/2004	Community Bank of Georgia	Appling	$5,645,097	
	96	5/21/2004	New Horizons Bank	Gilmer	$8,000,000	
	97	7/12/2004	First Coweta Bank	Coweta	$13,866,540	
	98	8/30/2004	Highland Commercial Bank	Cobb	$12,567,710	
	99	9/8/2004	Flint River National Bank	Mitchell	5,300,000	
	100	9/20/2004	Hamilton State Bank	Gwinnett	$13,217,500	
	101	10/4/2004	Peoples Community National Bank	Harrelson	8,232,000	
	102	10/12/2004	Tifton Banking Company	Tift	$7,578,000	
	103	12/20/2004	American United Bank	Gwinnett	$10,120,000	$128,826,213
2005	104	2/9/2005	Cornerstone Bank of Georgia	Walton	$11,750,000	
	105	3/15/2005	Legacy State Bank	Gwinnett	$17,852,040	
	106	3/30/2005	First Madison Bank & Trust	Madison	$10,000,000	
	107	4/27/2005	Peach State Bank & Trust	Hall	$12,499,290	
	108	5/9/2005	Community Bank of Rockmart	Polk	$7,836,430	
	109	5/16/2005	Georgia Trust Bank	Gwinnett	$12,500,000	
	110	8/1/2005	Hometown Community Bank	Jackson	$10,300,000	
	111	8/30/2005	American Southern Bank	Fulton	$11,000,000	
	112	9/26/2005	Northside Bank	Bartow	$10,000,000	
	113	10/3/2005	State Bank and Trust Company	Dooly	$7,674,370	
	114	10/5/2005	Sentry State Bank	DeKalb	$35,000,000	
	115	10/26/2005	Georgia Heritage Bank	Paulding	$12,007,680	
	116	11/1/2005	Eastside Commercial Bank	Rockdale	$12,000,000	
	117	11/7/2005	Signature Bank of Georgia	DeKalb	$17,402,220	
	118	12/6/2005	Southern Bank & Trust	Habersham	$9,500,000	$197,322,030
2006	119	2/3/2006	Flint Community Bank	Dougherty	$10,500,000	
	120	2/6/2006	Hana Bank	Gwinnett	$12,000,000	
	121	2/9/2006	Jefferson State Bank	Forsyth	$12,368,160	
	122	2/28/2006	Century Security Bank	Fulton	$14,978,000	
	123	4/3/2006	Bank of Ellijay	Gilmer	$11,374,510	
	124	4/4/2006	Metro City Bank	DeKalb	$14,410,000	
	125	4/10/2006	Providence Bank	Fulton	$14,885,050	

		Open Date	Name	County	Bank Capitalization	Total Bank Capital
	126	5/5/2006	One Georgia Bank	Fulton	$23,553,240	
	127	5/8/2006	Alpha Bank & Trust	Fulton	$34,159,590	
	128	5/23/2006	River City Bank	Floyd	$16,342,968	
	129	6/12/2006	Covenant Bank & Trust	Walker	$9,000,000	
	130	6/13/2006	Liberty First Bank	Walton	$11,000,000	
	131	6/21/2006	Sunrise Bank of Atlanta	Fulton	$8,000,000	
	132	6/21/2006	Bank of Valdosta	Lowndes	$6,000,000	
	133	7/3/2006	Patriot Bank of Georgia	Forsyth	$16,175,000	
	134	7/24/2006	CreekSide Bank	Cherokee	$13,640,370	
	135	8/8/2006	WestSide Bank	Paulding	$12,979,067	
	136	9/18/2006	First Covenant Bank	Cherokee	$15,940,000	
	137	10/16/2006	Columbus Community Bank	Muscogee	$12,062,660	
	138	10/27/2006	Gold Hills Bank	Lumpkin	$10,000,000	
	139	11/6/2006	Republic Bank of Georgia	Gwinnett	$24,000,000	
	140	11/13/2006	RockBridge Commercial Bank	Fulton	$27,000,000	
	141	12/11/2006	Private Bank of Buckhead	Fulton	$12,500,000	$342,868,615
2007	142	3/5/2007	First Citizens Bank of Georgia	Dawson	$12,400,000	
	143	3/5/2007	Embassy National Bank	Gwinnett	10,500,000	
	144	4/9/2007	First Choice Community Bank	Paulding	$18,000,000	
	145	5/15/2007	Atlantic Capital Bank	Fulton	$119,314,004	
	146	7/9/2007	Vinings Bank	Cobb	$16,394,160	
	147	8/14/2007	Brookhaven Bank	DeKalb	$23,407,958	
	148	10/15/2007	KeyWorth Bank	Fulton	$36,000,000	
	149	10/22/2007	Georgia Primary Bank	Fulton	$18,045,060	
	150	11/5/2007	State Bank of Georgia	Fayette	$13,292,690	
	151	12/5/2007	Security Bank of the Coast	Glynn	$14,000,000	
	152	12/12/2007	American Pride Bank	Bibb	$26,080,000	$307,433,872
				Total capital 1997-2007		$1,713,284,282
2008	153	1/22/2008	Community Business Bank	Forsyth	$16,490,890	
	154	1/23/2008	LaGrange Banking Company	Troup	$13,723,650	
	155	1/28/2008	Touchmark National Bank	Fulton	27,741,000	
	156	1/28/2008	Metro Bank	Douglas	$22,000,000	
	157	3/24/2008	First Landmark Bank	Cobb	$20,435,990	
	158	6/9/2008	Resurgens Bank	DeKalb	$12,350,000	
	159	9/15/2008	Chattahoochee Bank of Georgia	Hall	$20,832,200	
	160	10/15/2008	Independence Bank of Georgia	Barrow	$18,919,690	
	161	10/27/2008	Verity Bank	Barrow	$20,856,934	
	162	11/6/2008	NOA Bank	Gwinnett	$15,498,680	
	163	12/22/2008	Milltown Banking Company	Lanier	$10,000,000	$198,849,034
2009	164	1/6/2009	North Metro Bank	Forsyth	$22,000,000	
	165	6/22/2009	First Milton Bank	Fulton	$16,250,000	
	166	9/11/2009	Regional Bank of Middle Georgia	Bibb	$8,000,000	$46,250,000
2010	167	1/29/2010	Community & Southern Bank	Fulton	$110,000,000	$110,000,000
				Total capital 2008-2010		$355,099,034
2011			none			
2012			none			

Listing not inclusive of the following non-community institutions

First Union Direct Bank, NA
Bank of America Georgia, NA
Wachovia Card Services, NA
Silverton Bridge Bank, NA
Deposit Insurance NB of McDonough
First Retail Bank, N.A.

Chapter 3

Caveat Emptor

"When you aren't hampered by experience that could help you to see the risk in moving forward, sometimes things get accomplished that would otherwise never have gotten done."

Bud Carter

"Given the right circumstances, from no more than dreams, determination and the liberty to try, quite ordinary people consistently do extraordinary things."

Dee Hock

From ***Facts About Chartering A State Bank in Georgia***

Georgia Department of Banking and Finance, October 2007

Q. WHAT IS THE MINIMUM CAPITAL NECESSARY TO CHARTER A STATE BANK?

A. Minimum capital requirements are set forth in the Official Code of Georgia as follows: Capital stock of a newly chartered (de novo) bank should total not less than $3,000,000. If the main office is to be located in a county with a population of less than 200,000 as of the most recent United States census, the minimum shall be $2,000,000. In practice, greater amounts of capital (stock) have historically been required by both DBF and the OCC depending upon the location of the bank, the number of locations proposed at

---

> start-up, and the strategic direction and scope of operations of the bank as set forth in the business plan. The amount of start-up capital required by the state and national bank regulator will normally be in a comparable range for banks located in similar markets and having similar business plans.

Business associates, friends, family and an assortment of venture funds capitalized newly minted Georgia banks with more than $1.6 billion dollars between 1997 and 2007. That's not a deposit figure—that is total invested *start-up shareholder capital*. It's the kind of capital that comes from hearing a sales pitch, placing faith in a management team, deciding it's a good investment opportunity...and then writing a check to buy stock in a start-up business. The opportunity presented itself 149 times in Georgia over the ten-year period covered in this book. In some years the opportunity, as well as the appetite, was greater than others...

Friday, November 17, 2000

Capital crunch hurting small community banks
Atlanta Business Chronicle – by Rajiv Vyas

William Butler's recent experience shows that bankers aren't immune from the difficulties of raising capital. Butler and other organizers of Futurus Bank in Alpharetta are several months behind schedule in raising $9 million in start-up funds.

Futurus Bank is the latest local community bank to find investors shying away from equity investing because of stock market gyrations. Local banks **Southern Bank** and Ebank.com Inc. also have recently canceled stock offerings due to difficult market conditions.

"In Atlanta, raising funds for a new bank is a 50-50 type venture," said Nancy LaFoy, senior vice president of T. Stephen Johnson & Associates.

Failed attempts to raise money are not particularly new. In a volatile stock market such as the current one, where major indices fluctuate by as much as 15 percent in a week, investment banks have not been successful in raising money for many dot-coms and other high-risk companies.

Investors passing over banks

Banks, on the other hand, typically are considered a safe haven when markets gyrate. But the poor performance of bank stocks and concerns about an economic slowdown are prompting investors to seek shelter elsewhere.

Futurus Bank tried to raise funds in June, but without much success because investors are avoiding community bank stocks with limited demand. Futurus retreated from its IPO schedule in the middle of June, after Wachovia Securities Inc. – its lead underwriter – did not complete the "firm commitment" offering. Wachovia Securities is the investment banking arm of Wachovia Corp. (NYSE: WB).

After the failed attempt, Butler and other organizers are giving an initial public offering one more try. This time, though, the bank's IPO will not have any underwriter or a lead manager. Organizers are selling the shares themselves and through Wachovia Securities, which is acting as a sales agent.

"Since July, we have been trying to raise money on our own, and we think this time we will be successful," said Butler, president and CEO of Futurus Bank.

Butler said that Futurus already has received commitments of a little over $5.1 million since July.

The bank is targeting a minimum of $9 million.

"When we officially called off the deal with Wachovia, they had commitments of up to $3 million," said Butler, who has 17 years of banking experience, most recently as senior vice president and senior lender at Charter Bank & Trust in Marietta.

Other banks' difficulties

To fund its Internet-only bank ambitions, Ebank.com came out with its secondary offering of $45 million this past January. The offering was managed by Surto & Co., Scott & Stringfellow Inc. and Wachovia Securities.

Because of failure to garner funds, Ebank.com had to change its original business model – from an Internet-only bank, which requires deep pockets, to that of a community bank.

Southern Bank, which tried to raise money with Wachovia Securities as the lead underwriter, has given up its attempt to open a community bank near the Mall of Georgia. The bank was trying to raise around $10 million.

***

John Moore, senior vice president and banking analyst with Wachovia Securities, said that market conditions make it very difficult for community banks to raise money. "It was a lot easier last year to raise money," he (Moore) said. "There is a lot of concern on growth and profitability."

The stock of Ebank.com (OTC BB: EBDC), for instance, has fallen by almost 70 percent from its initial offering price of $10 in July 1998. The stock is trading at around $3. "A great number of [community banks] that were formed last year are trading below their offer price," Moore said. He also said that stocks of community banks that raised funds in 1999 are trading 20 percent to 25 percent below their offering price.

In 1998, 15 community banks commenced operations in Georgia. That number fell to 10 in 1999, according to SNL Securities. In 2000, 11 community banks have begun operating in the first half.

"Bank stocks have been poorly performing since April 1998," said Leonard Seawell, senior vice president at Morgan Keegan. Seawall said the BKX banking stock index fell from a high of 913 on April 17, 1998, to a low of 635 on March 17, 1999. The index is currently around the 850 level after gaining ground in recent months, though it still lags its 1998 high.

Seawell said that since the beginning of this year, stock markets have been very volatile and investors are reluctant to invest in stocks of community banks, which are illiquid, meaning they are traded less frequently.

***

If Futurus Bank gets the required funding and final approval from regulators, it will then start its banking operations in the Windward Parkway area of Alpharetta. Butler expects the bank to open next March. He estimated that the bank would have $28 million in deposits and $21 million in loans within a year. Butler said that although there are three community banks in Alpharetta, the Windward Parkway market still is untapped by community banks. Butler expects the bank to be profitable within 36 months.

"The market is still very healthy for community banks," said Jon Burke, principal of Brown Burke Capital Partners. "Raising funds depends a lot on the management."

Given the momentum conveyed in the previous chapter, the November 2000 *Atlanta Business Chronicle* article above may seem out of place. The point of including it, though—in addition to the context it provides—is that it clearly relays *how fast* the spigots can turn on and off for the funding of "illiquid" industry start-ups. Despite a groundswell of momentum in the late 1990s, the US economy was stalling in late 2000—and so was the momentary enthusiasm for community banks.

Investment Versus Speculation
Decisions of Trust And Decisions of Knowledge

To a serious investor, evaluating a stake in a community bank start-up is no different than considering the same for a silicon valley IPO, a municipal bond or seed capital for a neighborhood Laundromat. An *investor* places capital only after a thorough analysis and a high degree of certainty for the security of *principal* and *gain* over a determined period of *time*. An investor knows how a venture will make money, and is confident of both the exit strategy and the forecasted return on capital employed. With confidence and certainty, an investor knows when he strokes a check that the term of an investment will be x, the gain can be as much as y, and that the return of both principal *and* gain will occur at maturity z. The exit strategy, time frame, and expected return are defined elements of the transaction. *Without these essentials in place, an opportunity may be compelling...but it is something other than an investment.*

Now I realize the above is an exacting description, but that's just the point—and it's an important point. In the classic sense, risk and return take a backseat to certainty when *investing* is the objective at hand.

As an example of this methodology, I recall speaking with an "old time" credit manager in Atlanta who contended that when done right, there is *no risk* in a bank's loan portfolio. Now that's not just a method, that's attitude!

In contrast, a *speculator* places capital into a venture after a thorough analysis of *potential gain by way of an exit strategy* without certainty for the security of principal, return, or time frame. *Speculation* is the placement of capital on the premise that *at some point in the future*, the vehicle into which capital has been deployed will be worth more than the original wager. Something about the *limited and exclusive opportunity* of the venture leads a speculator to believe that an underlying event or trend will ultimately provide a gain. The initial contribution may have limited resale value—in other words, it is probably an *illiquid* vehicle. The speculator is confident, however, that a trend or change (either existing or forecast) will bring about a "liquidity event" that will create both an exit opportunity *and* a satisfactory return. Sounds a little like construction lending, doesn't it?

Investing and speculating are both worthy pursuits, but they are *not* the same thing—and it is perilous to confuse one with the other.

Finally, the placement of capital *without* a clear understanding of how the venture is going to make money, *without* the security of principal, *without* the certainty of a return in a defined time horizon and *without* an exit strategy is not investing. It is not speculation. It might be gambling, though I know gamblers who would take offense at such a distasteful comparison.

The reality is that most decisions to place capital for a prospective return involve some degree of *both* investment and speculation, don't they? The wise thing to consider, then, is the amount of *each* involved in the decision.

Beyond the question of investing versus speculation, there is a second factor to consider: is the willingness to put capital at risk based on knowledge and experience...or is it based on trust? Do we *know* for a fact how our capital is going to generate a return—or are we trusting instead that someone else is going to make the right decisions on our behalf? Isn't that what mutual fund managers are for?

The point of all this exactitude is that most people who believe they are *investors* are really just speculators...or worse. Speculators don't really understand, for example, how a bank makes money, *but they know that it happens when the conditions are right.* And because banking is above all else a confidence game, those with the most confidence are the ones that you'll find at the tables.

Allow me to contend that capital placed in a community bank start-up is illiquid, prospective, and at best a speculative venture (that's shorthand for the multi-page disclosures that you'll find in the pages of any de novo offering memorandum). To call it an *investment* to my way of thinking, is not just optimism...it's plain wrong. After researching this industry and making my living in this arena for the past several years, I've concluded that the wagering of community bank capital is by and large a decision of *trust* as opposed to a decision of *knowledge*—and I am both mindful and grateful for the distinction. People *trust* entrepreneurs to make money for them—either because the entrepreneur has done it before, or because he/she seem capable of doing it the first time. That's both an awesome privilege and a fairly heady distinction. Unfortunately, it's also why so many community bank shareholders ultimately lost their shirts in this past boom-bust cycle. The hope of many bank investors in 2013 is not for a return *on* their investment...but for an eventual return *of* their investment.

My apologies, gentle reader, if the paragraphs above have given you heartburn. But if you'll mind those distinctions and take them to heart,

I believe that they alone are worth the price of this little book. The distinctions between investing and speculation are certainly among the most important lessons that *I've* learned in the past five years.

Lo, Those Many Years Ago...

A.D. 2000—the year of the new millennium (and those clever 20-Oo glasses) was a long time ago. Here are a few news headlines from November of that year—the same month that the Atlanta Business Chronicle article at the opening of this chapter went to press:

Layoffs mount as US economic slowdown continues 11/1/2000

Clinton Asked to Apologize for Agent Orange 11/17/2000

FOUR GYPSIES FOUND DEAD IN KOSOVO 11/14/2000

Americans ready to accept Gore or Bush as president, poll says 11/13/2000

BAKING ALASKA; AS WORLD LEADERS BICKER, GLOBAL WARMING IS KILLING A WAY OF LIFE 11/28/2000

Those headlines conjure up some distant memories, don't they? Here are a few mile markers for the finance-types among us:

- The US prime rate was 7.50% in November 2000
- Three-month LIBOR stood at 6.735%
- Fed Funds was 6.50%,
- and the US unemployment rate stood at 4.0%—up from 3.9 in October

Now, to a banker, *that* was a long time ago! In November 2000, "9/11" was still shorthand for an emergency phone call, George W. Bush was a popular Texas governor, and IndyMac, Bear Stearns and Wachovia were thriving centers of American financial commerce.

Despite some national headwinds, the economic fundamentals in Georgia were looking comparatively strong in November 2000. Businesses were expanding, the number of days that a listed house stayed on the market was just beginning to level out (locals will recall the bidding wars) and entrepreneurial start-ups, while tentative, were clicking along at robust levels across many industries in the state.

"What do you plan to do with all that money?" The question spoke volumes about expectations for community bank performance prior to the 2007 downturn. After all, the more relative capital a business holds, the lower its return to shareholders. Raising a *lot* of capital, then, meant laying out bold plans for putting that capital to work. Touchmark's 2007 capital plan called for a minimum equity raise of $31,250,000 in order to accommodate aggressive lending growth along the northeast corridor of I-85. An upper bound of nearly $40 million placed Touchmark at the high end of the range among banks planning to open in that year's class of de novo institutions. Indeed we got questioned about capital planning a lot—but in every case those questions were geared toward our growth plans rather than our level of capital sufficiency. My, how times have changed!

Average starting capital for a Georgia community bank that opened between 1997 and 2000 amounted to $7.6 million (limited-purpose charters not included). The largest raise among the fifty-two starts of those four years was $14.3 million for the Dalton Whitfield Bank in September 1999. By the 2001- 2004 period, average starting capital had grown to $9.0 million, with 1st Georgia Banking Company topping the group of forty-six banks with a $17 million raise in November 2003. By the final period of that ten-year stretch, average starting capital between 2005 and 2007 amounted to $17.3 million, with Atlantic Capital Bank topping out the forty-nine members of that group with $119.3 million. Even with the exclusion of the outsized Atlantic Capital, average capital raised for a new bank in the 2004–2007 period amounted to $15.2 million—fully 69 percent higher than the preceding three years and *double* the average of the 1997–2000 period.

Chart 15

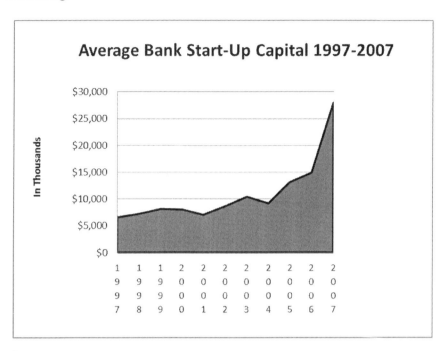

Chart 16

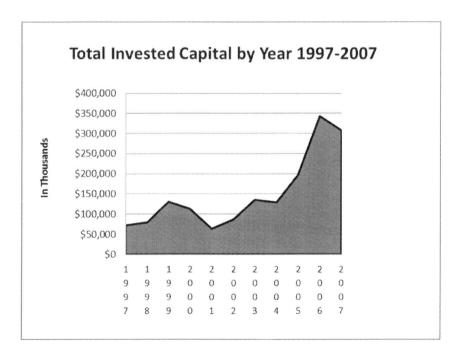

Chart 17

Total Invested Start-Up Capital in Georgia Community Banks 1997-2007*		
Year	Avg. Invested Starting Capital	Total Invested Starting Capital
1997	$ 6,569,176	$ 72,260,940
1998	$ 7,213,565	$ 79,349,210
1999	$ 8,145,663	$ 130,330,600
2000	$ 8,048,684	$ 112,681,575
2001	$ 7,065,518	$ 63,589,658
2002	$ 8,652,470	$ 86,524,700
2003	$ 10,419,913	$ 135,458,869
2004	$ 9,201,872	$ 128,826,213
2005	$ 13,154,802	$ 197,322,030
2006	$ 14,907,331	$ 342,868,615
2007	$ 27,948,534	$ 307,433,872
	Total 1997-2007:	$ 1,656,646,282

* excludes limited purpose charters and other non-community starts

Expected gains for community bank stocks have shifted in dramatic cycles over the past several decades. Independent of those cycles, though, community bank establishments have predominantly been locally owned and run, with solid but reasonable returns anticipated over some indeterminate horizon. Because most are small companies, stock trades are infrequent and are often negotiated transactions. In the majority of cases, though, community banks have been founded for the purpose of fostering local growth and building local wealth over a long horizon—regardless of the cycle. While there is *always* an entrepreneurial component to a start-up business, prospects for a fast buck only enter the picture when economic conditions spawn over-anxious enthusiasm.

Build for the Long Haul, Build for the Exits

The dramatic growth of the Atlanta's population from the mid-1990s through the early 2000s created just that sort of enthusiasm. John Medlin's "five yards and a cloud of dust" philosophy was increasingly supplanted by a more entrepreneurial focus on fast loan growth coupled with a short-term sale–the speculative exit strategy. While the discipline of building a local deposit base to fund community-centric lending has *always been* the foundation of a successful community bank strategy, other funding sources found their way onto bank balance sheets when loan demand outpaced the availability of local deposits. "Wholesale" funding by way of broker deposits (CDs from brokerage houses and other institutional sources) and Federal Home Loan Bank advances (funding secured by bank assets) were easy ways to juice the capacity for loan growth and put a new bank on a faster track to profitability. While customer deposits could be attracted over time by paying above-market rates on CDs and money market accounts, the attraction of low-cost institutional funding was hard to resist—and when used in moderation, these funding sources provided an additional layer of liquidity for a new bank. Lending opportunities were plentiful—especially in the real estate markets. It was the *funding* for loans that required intentional planning and strategy. Despite the robust level of deposit growth moving into the Atlanta metro market in those years, community banks still had to work hard to attract depositors to their institutions. Touchmark's focus on Asian and Indian depositors throughout its development was key to our strategy for a stable funding base.

Some bankers were more aggressive with their planning and strategy than others. As the more opportunistic class of bankers worked quickly to build out their balance sheets, they also kept the door open to acquisitive institutions eager to build market share across their service area. After all, selling a business after only three years of operation at a healthy multiple of book value (leveraged by options and warrants!) could fund a luxury vacation, provide for a prestigious club membership...and still leave leftover funds to the seed the next de novo opportunity!

A respectful note: the characterization of "built-to-sell banks" in the paragraph above is in no way intended as a criticism of that business plan. There is nothing inherently "good" or "bad," "right" or "wrong" with building out a balance sheet in order to attract the attention of a suitor; it happens in business all the time. Some banks remain closely-held companies for generations. Others could indeed change control after three years and a day. *Planning* for one scenario versus the other, though, requires very different strategies in regard to shareholder expectations, personnel and contracts. In other words, if you're "building to sell," the planning and strategy ought to look markedly different than an institution that is building for the long term. In reality, most shareholders outside of the director group are rarely a party to such discussions. And that *is* a criticism of build-to-sell.

Starting capitalizations, then, increased rapidly through the early 2000s as investors were drawn to the "entrepreneurial model" of growing and selling charters for significant returns. I think it's fair to say that some organizing groups started out with little thought of ever serving as long-term bank directors. Some may cringe at such a contention, but those familiar with the industry won't deny that it's true. I'll just go ahead and type it: some start-up groups were better characterized as "organizing investors" as opposed to "organizing directors." Such banks are (were!) more prone to have boards filled with inexperienced and professionally uninvolved members, and the learning curve for such groups became really, really steep at the beginning of 2008. The judgment of history speaks loudly through *Atlanta Business Chronicle* articles that pepper remaining chapters of this book.

In May 2006, Georgia's largest-yet community bank capital raise was accomplished by Alpha Bank & Trust, which opened for business in Alpharetta, Georgia after having raised $36 million (a mere twenty-nine months later, Alpha Bank would distinguish itself again by becoming the shortest lived banking enterprise in Georgia history). A year later, in May 2007, Atlantic Capital Bank topped out the all-time-largest list with a whopping $119 million de novo launch, followed by Keyworth Bank in Johns Creek in October 2007, which matched Alpha's $36 million raise. Touchmark National Bank opened a few months later in January 2008 with $34.5MM of shareholder capital...and in so doing became the last $30+million de novo launch of the biggest community banking cycle in Georgia's history.

The starting capital balances on the remarkable roster that precedes this chapter abridges *thousands* of individual "investors". Local brokerage houses followed the progress of bank organizing efforts and contracted to assist with underwriting wherever they could find a willing client. Broker-dealers like Samco Capital Markets and Wachovia Securities organized receptions and dinner parties for start-up groups wherever investors could be found. Organizers themselves held gatherings where the proposed CEO and his executive team would discuss business plans and stump for stock subscriptions. Some enthusiastic individuals placed significant sums in multiple de novo start-ups, amassing multi-million dollar bets on the prospect for outsized returns in community banking. On the other side of the market, the capital markets arms of banks like SunTrust and First Tennessee issued trust preferred securities by the billions that enabled bank holding companies to fund acquisitions and mergers. While chart-topping de novos like Atlantic Capital Bank took on $38 million from Texas investment fund BankCap Partners, the overwhelming majority of start-ups accepted only family and individual subscriptions, often amounting to $10,000 or less. The premise was to invest locally, but the attraction during boom periods was decidedly in favor of larger capital bases and larger enterprises.

$1.7 billion dollars of cumulative start-up capital is surely a lot of money, and regardless of whether it was invested, speculated or worse, all of it was placed in the hands of community bank organizers amidst extraordinary performance expectations between 1997 and 2007.

Friday, November 14, 2003

Bank investors find rewards worth wait

Atlanta Business Chronicle - by Jim Molis

A story in this week's edition shows that banks keep drawing more money from consumers. What the story doesn't show is that banks, at least smaller ones, also keep drawing money from investors.

The Federal Deposit Insurance Corp. had granted insurance to 10 new Georgia banks as of mid-October, after approving 11 banks in 2002 and 10 banks in 2001. Another seven applications were pending as of last month, making it the busiest year since 2000, when the FDIC granted insurance to 17 banks.

All of these banks have substantial backing from investors. Most banks raise $7 million to $12 million before opening.

Like consumers, investors are drawn by the security that banks offer, particularly when compared with the volatile stock market. Banks are a tangible asset that investors can see each day.

Banks also are better managed and regulated than they were in the late 1980s and early 1990s when some failed in the Atlanta area, said T. Stephen Johnson, chairman of T. Stephen Johnson & Associates Inc., a local bank consulting firm.

"Nobody has lost any money in a bank in a long time," he said.

Some investors may put $10,000 or more in as many as 30 banks, Johnson said.

There may not be much of a market for shares of small banks. But early investors who hold on to their shares often reap long-term rewards when a bank is acquired by a larger competitor.

In the largest deal in recent years, in 2002, RBC Centura Banks Inc. paid $153 million in cash, or $26 a share, for Eagle Bancshares Inc., the holding company for Tucker Federal Bank.

Tucker Federal had amassed more than $1 billion in assets over more than 40 years. At the time of its acquisition, it was one of the largest community banks based in Atlanta. Thus, it was an attractive target that allowed RBC Centura to enter the market as one of the largest players.

There could be a series of bank acquisitions ahead as community banks look to trim overhead to improve profit margins, Johnson said. Historically low interest rates make it difficult for banks to make money on the difference between the deposits they take in and the loans they make, while still paying personnel and funding loan loss reserves, for example, he said.

A change in state regulations that allows banks to sell after three years instead of five years also could hasten consolidation, Johnson said.

First National Bank of Johns Creek sold for a strong premium, of three times book value, just three years after it started, Johnson said. Main Street Banks Inc. acquired First National Bank of Johns Creek for $26.2 million in 2002.

"We used to tell banks starting out not to expect to talk to anyone for seven to eight years," said Johnson, who has been a consultant since 1986. "Now it's being reached in half the time."

Similarly, it used to take 10 to 15 years for banks to reach $100 million in assets. "Now you're following the pack if you haven't done that in two years," Johnson said.

If area deposits continue to grow as they have, that time frame may be reduced further; and the rewards for early investors will follow.

Anybody who has ever done it will agree: there is little in life that compares with the exhilaration of starting a business. Even the smallest of full-time ventures requires vision, strategy, excitement, good partnerships...and capital. If you get the first four elements right, you're likely to find plenty of the fifth in even the choppiest of markets. The jubilation of completing a capital raise (successfully and alive) is almost certainly what gives rise to the "serial" entrepreneur. There is just something deliciously primal about the cunning and the teamwork that gets those entrepreneurial juices flowing. A bold opportunity excites the soul and drives ambition—perhaps blind ambition sometimes (!), but hopefully an ambition fostered by opportunity, strategy, and a capable team.

I Refuse To Join Any Club That Would Be Willing To Have Me As A Member

- Groucho Marx

A personal reflection: no group in its right mind would have chartered a community bank in 2008 had they caught a glimpse of the shitstorm that was gathering in the larger economy. In hindsight, the launch of Touchmark National Bank stands as stark testimony to how *little* the business and investment community understood about the calamity that awaited the U.S.— and metro Atlanta in particular. The timeline of the global financial crises that accompanies this story (List 3) cascades in astonishing contrast against the timeline of the Touchmark Bancshares stock offering. For example, as our organizing group began innocently distributing investor prospectuses over Labor Day weekend 2007, Northern Rock in the UK was appealing to the Bank of England for a lifeline. As we were winding down our stock offering in late March of 2008, we did so in tandem with the astonishing implosion of the legendary Bear Stearns franchise. The backdrop of the gargantuan financial implosion that unfolded during our organizing period makes the launch of Touchmark National Bank look not just implausible—it makes it look like sheer insanity. In my mind's eye, I see our little organizing group as something akin to either a pride of lions—or a troop of monkeys—calling out plays on the open savannah; we were following a plan, caught up in the moment...but glancing occasionally over our shoulders at those curious and ominous clouds amassing on the horizon.

And I admit that I personally had good reason to turn a blind eye to the ominous weather forecast. After all, getting this bank open was now my *job*—and it was the only job that I had! Had any one of our organizers gotten cold feet and begun to reverse course on Touchmark's prospects, surely the whole undertaking would have been at risk—and I'd have gone wanting for a paycheck. For the organizers, after all, this was "merely" a business project—an undertaking to leverage their discretionary capital and available time. For me and the other employees who had signed on to the effort, however, this was our employment livelihood! While writing this section I thought about the other start-ups that had opened along-side Touchmark...and I wondered if the employees of those start-ups ever harbored similar thoughts to what I had at the time. My interests in getting the bank open were really not in alignment with the organizers. *Regardless* of circumstances, I *needed* the bank to open! There was *no reason* for me not to go forward—I had no backup plan! It's like that old adage about the chicken and the pig when it comes to preparing breakfast: the chicken is involved (eggs), but the pig is *committed* to the enterprise in the form of bacon and sausage.

Opportunity Finds A Name

What is now Touchmark National Bank began in earnest in April 2007 as what my family used to refer to as the *First National Bank of BillyBob.*

After mulling over potential bank names since 2006, it was Bill Short who first suggested using "touchstone" to our organizing group, which was an idea he came across while reading Wachovia Bank's annual report. While runners up like "Liberty Bank" and "Atalanta" got short consideration, the board eventually coalesced around *Touchstone National Bank* and *Touchstone Bancshares, Inc.* for the holding company when we filed our first SEC registrations on April 6, 2007. Within a few months, though, we were alerted that our chosen name was being contested by an Ohio-based insurance company that claimed trademark rights for the name "touchstone" in anything related to financial services. After several unsuccessful appeals for use of the name, we altered our handle to "Touchmark" National Bank...and so that's how we finally proceeded.

A touchstone is actually a measuring device. In history, metallurgists would use a dark, uniform stone to test the quality of precious metals by scraping them across its surface and then assessing the quality of the streak they left behind. On the day that we settled on the name "Touchmark", I lobbied Bill with what I though was the perfect marketing "spin" for making the required announcement to our investors: the Touch*mark*, I told him, was the streak that a precious metal left behind. The Touch*stone* was merely the backdrop for creating that streak. So I suggested he posture the change with this question: *Would you rather be the streak...or would you rather be the stone?* Bill sent me away and decreed that I wasn't allowed to offer marketing advice ever again. To this day, I *still* think it was a good idea.

As mentioned at the end of the last chapter, the Formosa Rose organizing group had made two strategic decisions before Bill and I ever came on board. The first was that the new bank would have a national bank charter, issued by the Office of the Comptroller of the Currency. An OCC charter would enable Touchmark to open branches anywhere in the country. The second was that the bank would aspire to the largest capital raise possible—and as such was open to draw from a substantial base of investing shareholders from across the Southeast and beyond. This would require a public company registration and "blue sky" approvals across any number of states. Touchmark's initial public offering (IPO) would be executed under the aegis of the Securities and Exchange Commission (SEC)—along with all of the trappings and regulation (and expense) that went along with it. Both of these decisions were highly unusual for a Georgia bank start; most sought a state charter from the Georgia Department of Banking and Finance (a known quantity with local regulators) and a nonpublic offering to a small group of shareholders in order to limit expense, regulatory interference, and reporting requirements. But we were moving forward at the very crest of a cycle that had propelled so many previous efforts to success...

The regulatory application process in itself is a lot of work, but it's an important preparatory experience for running the bank. A good job with the regulatory application demonstrates that the organizing group has done its homework in developing a strategy that includes the business plan, forecasts, and director/officer investigations. It took hours to draft components like the product set, community development plans, the service model, risk management...the list goes on. The process of e-mailing files and developing background information on twenty-two organizers in itself took several weeks: fingerprints, credit checks, and biographies. Five sets of each were required for the OCC, three for the FDIC, and two for the attorneys and auditors. Eventually, 105 pounds of paperwork were crated at the UPS store and mailed off to the OCC—along with a $25,000 application check that was taped to the table of contents on top of the document pile. We were as likely to have given birth to a hernia as we were to a new bank as those documents were hoisted into Bill Crosby's truck.

Application for Charter
Table of Contents

The following confidential submissions are separately bound:

> **Background check forms**
> **FBI fingerprint cards**
> **IRS Tax check waivers**
> **FDIC form 6510/05**
> **Directors' Oaths**

Filing Fee payable to Comptroller of the Currency—$25,000

Cover letter
<u>Application Table of Contents</u> *(this document)*
> Application Cover Page
> Publication Notice
> Branch Application
> Table of Contents for Interagency Application
> > Interagency Application
> > OCC Signature Page
> > FDIC Signature Page
> > Compact Disc containing pictures of Market Area Map

<u>Confidential Section:</u>
> CD with Excel Files containing the various pro forma financial projections
> Confidential Section Cover Page
> Table of Contents for Business Plan
> > Business Plan Narrative
> > > Table of Contents for Pro forma Financial Projections
> > > > Pro forma Scenario A—Consolidated BHC
> > > > Pro forma Scenario B—Bank Only
> > > > Pro forma Scenario C—Bank Only-Worse Case

> Management Contracts and Agreements—CEO and CFO
> Bylaws and Articles of Association for Bank and Parent
> Organizational JV Agreement
> Contracts/Agreements with Accountants, Attorneys, Consultants, and Executive Placement Firms
> Main Office Lease
> Branch Leases and supporting insider documentation
> Market Feasibility Study

> Confidential Interagency Biographical and Financial Reports for all Organizers and the Chief Financial Officer to include:

> **Credit bureau reports and explanations/additional supporting documentation**
> **Confidential Interagency Biographical and Financial Reports**
> **Explanations/additional supporting documentation**

Taking Stock in Draperies

After hauling our application to the post office, we turned our attention next to the preparation of our stock offering prospectus—which is fundamental to starting the capital raise. While much of what we used to prepare the OCC application was useful in building the offering circular, it was quite a project to work on the prospectus while at the same time continue with preparations for organizing the bank.

The abundance of bank starts across Georgia in the early 2000's generated plenty of white-collar work for the law firms and audit practices that are critical partners to the process. Prosperity and press coverage over several robust years gave rise to an odd celebrity for personalities in the trade. Walt Moeling of the former Powell, Goldstein (now Bryan Cave) developed a deserving reputation as the ultimate go-to attorney on all manner of community bank issues—and as such became the go-to resource for media quotes as well. A near second to Walt was Bobby Schwartz at Smith, Gambrell, Russell (SGR). Bobby had built a very successful career and led a legal team that catered to all manner of capital raises, acquisitions, and negotiated sales. He, too, was worth his reputation—and had the billing rate to prove it. Others like Chip MacDonald at Jones Day, CPA Tim Keadle at Porter, Keadle & Moore, and start-up consultants like T. Steven Johnson, John Johnson, and John Kline were sought out for their expertise with engagements, projects, and press quotes. These professionals and the teams that worked for them made good money for good reason: the skills, documents, and project paths from start to finish are complicated, tedious, and expensive.

The stock offering had its own share of rigorous documentation. The extensive financial projections that I was responsible to prepare had to conform to a litany of standardized templates used by the OCC and the FDIC for purposes of regulatory reporting. As such, *every* item of revenue and expense was codified in tedious, exacting detail. My days of budget-fudging returned to help me quite a bit in this part of the process! Crosby and I developed a running joke that we incorporated throughout the application: "draperies" was our code word for the padding I felt might be necessary to cover unforeseen expenditures in my projections. We ultimately budgeted for some fairly high-end "draperies" in several areas of the financial projections. After all, every budget needs some "dressing up", right?

Reese Porter, our attorney at SGR, was appalled when he came across the term in our draft prospectus. "Draperies," so it happened, was *not* an approved Securities and Exchange Commission budgeting category. As such, Reese insisted (with no small level of indignation) that "draperies" had no respectful place in an SEC registration statement.

Well, gentle reader, you can judge for yourself. If you ever have reason to look up the final Touchmark Bancshares, Inc. prospectus, look on page 18 under "Use of Proceeds." I can only hope that the janitorial staff have them steam-cleaned every once in a while.

One aspect of Touchmark's capital raise that was unlike any of its de novo brethren was an uncapped shareholder limit. Public-company status, after all, was anticipated to provide team Touchmark with ready access to the capital markets for a follow-on capital raise within five years (*ahh, those glory days of 2007!*). Among *all* the other bank starts in Georgia over the previous ten years, *not a single one* had been launched with the intention of opening as a publicly traded company. But Touchmark's aspirations for growth outweighed any concerns that the organizers might have had for registration fees, compliance requirements and regulatory reporting. The organizers were convinced that Touchmark was going to be different. Despite incredulous looks from the auditors and accountants that we interviewed, our organizer group was undeterred. While Bill and I had our doubts, this was an area where the organizers were fully in the driver's seat—and the majority were resolute that public company status would be a necessary driver of our success. After all, how else could we maintain ready access to Wall Street in order to fund our growth? It all seemed plausible in those heady days of 2007.

While SGR was helpful in pulling our OCC application files together, their primary role was in preparing our group's application with the Securities and Exchange Commission. In tandem with developing the business plan, the OCC application, financial models and hiring a team of employees (as if we weren't busy enough), Bill and I were working simultaneously with Reese Porter to construct the offering circular for Touchstone's prospectus, known in the industry as a red herring. All of that took time, money, and a fair number of highly caffeinated evenings.

Friday, September 1, 2006

State regulators studying costs of forming banks

Atlanta Business Chronicle – by Joe Rauch Staff Writer

State banking regulators have begun to examine the costs associated with creating new community banks, particularly the fees paid to third-party consultants and stock underwriters.

The informal examination comes in the midst of one of the state's largest new, or de novo, bank booms.

This is the state's first broad examination of the banking industry's startup cost trend, several longtime Atlanta banking consultants said.

The review could lead to a more formal analysis and potentially to new rules, analysts said.

Banking and Finance Commissioner Rob Braswell said the department's mission to charter banks requires that the department review anything that could impact the safety and soundness of a state bank.

For a typical community bank, costs before the bank opens can range from $800,000 to $1 million, according to banking attorneys and consultants.

Banks can take up to a year to navigate the various application processes, and the bank's organizers have to cover costs for hiring the executive team, securing branch locations and paying attorneys and consultants.

That upfront expense is paid through the initial private offerings to shareholders and other bank insiders.

Those external costs have remained largely fixed because of the competitive pressure between new bank consultants, they said. "It's a remarkably competitive market here for some of the consultants who work here," said Walt Moeling, banking attorney for **Powell Goldstein LLP**. "That tends to have kept consulting fees and prices low."

But a few areas, such as salaries for new bank executives and the percentage payments to stock underwriters, have increased in the latest flurry of de novo bank creation. Precise data on a typical de novo bank's startup costs – what it spends to open its doors – was not available through state or federal banking regulators.

But anecdotally, local attorneys said the typical bank CEO's salary has increased $30,000 to $50,000 since 2004, the first year of the latest de novo bank boom.

Estimates of underwriter fees are less precise.

As the sponsor and agent for a community bank's private stock offering, an underwriter's fee is usually percentage payment based on the size of the private stock placement. Industry observers said underwriters usually receive 5 percent to 10 percent of the total funds raised in the stock offering.

Their compensation hasn't increased as a percentage of the overall capital raised by banks. Instead, the amount of capital sought by de novo banks is increasing.

"It appears to be an easier thing to get into," said Byron Richardson, senior consultant at Marietta-based **Bank Resources Inc.**

"There's a perception that there are a lot of people who are consulting, like myself, who are making a lot of money. But I remember when I was doing two de novos a year in this business."

From April 6, 2007, when we first established Touchstone Banc-shares, Inc., until we opened for business on January 28, 2008, total expense associated with opening the bank amounted to roughly $1,600,000. One of our goals from the start had been to avoid the offering expenses associated with hiring an outside stock sales group. Standard underwriting expense involved not just a monthly retainer approaching $10,000 a month but also a fee of 6 to 7 percent on every dollar raised (as a reference point, 6% of $30 million is $1.8 million). Because Touchmark ultimately brought in a sales agent late in the process to help close out the offering, roughly $512,000 of our total start-up expenses were related to stock issuance costs (only part of the $512,000 was for stock sales commissions---and that's a heck of a lot better than $1.8 million!). In all, given the size of our initial capitalization, we were a very cost-effective start-up.

There's an accounting issue that is worth noting here: a change was instituted in late 2006 that significantly affected the time that it took for a de novo bank to show a financial profit. Prior to 2006, the value of organizer warrants didn't have to be expensed upon the opening of the bank. With the institution of a new accounting rule, however, warrants were required to be expensed over their vesting period (typically three years). The change significantly delayed the profitability horizon of de novo institutions. In comparison to banks that had opened earlier, the newer start-ups appeared to show a slower and longer track to profitability. By regulatory statute, a bank can't pay a dividend to shareholders until retained earnings becomes positive (cumulative profitability), which means that the bank has earned enough in profits to recoup all of its start-up expenses. As of January 1, 2007, it was going to take a lot longer for a de novo institution to show a return for shareholders. Just my luck.

From an operational perspective, a community bank is really just a collection of third-party technology contracts...with lenders, tellers and staff people stacked on top. A new banking enterprise doesn't have nearly the resources or budget to handle functions like clearing checks, delivering on-line banking services and restocking ATM machines. Those functions in practice are handled through service bureaus and technology providers that make up the internal plumbing of the entire banking industry. The process of vendor selection in opening a new bank is meticulous—and it's really where experience plays a critical role in hiring the right people for a start-up. In January 2007, I had no idea what a "core processor" was. By January 2008, though, I could argue technology, parse the pricing plans and articulate the strengths and weaknesses of at least five major industry providers (I did refer to myself as a geek earlier, didn't I?). From start to finish, I reviewed, negotiated and ultimately executed thirty-four separate service agreements as part of the opening of the bank. I was spectacularly unprepared for such an assignment. If it wasn't for my good fortune in hiring the remarkable operations team of Ellen Eigel and Dana Wallace, it is not an overstatement to write that the bank would never possibly have opened for business. The meticulous process of coordinating the electronics and implementing the technology—what I came to refer to as "connecting the hoses"—was a months-long adventure that I wouldn't recommend to the faint of heart.

Dana Wallace passed away just as this book was being finalized for publication. She was a fine lady with an outrageous laugh. I enjoyed her dearly. She is missed by many.

On Filing Applications and Avoiding Opposition

The SEC doesn't ask questions: they provide "interrogatories"—which are pretty much the same thing. You see, like most of the financial regulatory authorities, the SEC never actually "approves" anything...they just stop asking questions when you've met their expectations. Put another way, reading "We do not object" in a response letter is the ultimate objective of the process.

And then there's the NASD (National Association of Securities dealers) organizer interrogatories...*detailed* applications for those who aspire to public scrutiny for the privilege of becoming a bank director. A personal note: the invasive nature of these applications is a significant reason why the number of public institutions will continue to decline. They're just too darned complicated and intrusive.

Yet a *third* application process was required because of our plan to establish a bank holding company. A holding company is the entity that owns the bank and can "hold" other companies as well. Holding companies provide flexibility for organizations that envision a larger franchise under the umbrella of a single-stock company. Another regulatory application...another process to manage. Because we actually sold stock in our holding company as opposed to the bank, our stock offering represented shares in Touchmark Bancshares, Inc. rather than Touchmark National Bank.

The organizers pulled together their network of contacts to build out a mailing list for our offering. Elaine Barnes dedicated hours to typing and categorizing the names. The final prospect roster spread across thirteen states, each with its ensuing regulatory applications and filing requirements! By August 2007, the SEC registration paperwork was nearing completion. Our plan called for a minimum capital raise of $31,250,000 ($30 million after estimated expenses) to be in escrow by October 31, 2007, which put us on a sixty-day time line. Given the experience of similar de novos at the time, two months seemed to be entirely reasonable. Of course we still weren't much paying attention to those ominous storm cloud formations...

Weeks of training, interviewing, editing and hiring ensured. While I'm sure that I could bore even the most enthusiastic reader to tears (and I may already have!) with details of the time and effort that it took to shepherd regulatory applications to conclusion, instead I'll just include here a definitive filing that queues the Hallelujah Chorus in the heart of every aspiring SEC registrant: it's called the effectiveness statement:

UNITED STATES
SECURITIES AND EXCHANGE COMMISSION
Washington, D.C. 20549
Notice of Effectiveness

Effectiveness Date:	August 31, 2007 1:15 P.M.
Form:	SB-2
CIK:	0001403008
Company Name:	Touchstone Bancshares, Inc.
File Number:	333-143840

Once a registration statement becomes *effective*, then and *only* then can an organizing group accept checks from prospective shareholders. Because Touchstone organizers had primary residence addresses spread from Virginia to Florida, the legal and regulatory matrix for subscriptions was complicated, but one by one, requirements were met and address lists were refined for mailing.

In spite of the self-confidence that inspired us to limit our stock offering to the sixty-day period between September and October of 2007, SGR wisely provided for extensions of the offering to as far out as March 2008. For that, Reese, you get a gold star!

At 1:15 p.m. on Friday, August 31, 2007, our stock offering became "effective." Before then, I suppose, we were "ineffective." Regardless, what began over Memorial Day weekend moved into high gear on Labor Day weekend as an avalanche of 2,367 prospectuses were bundled into the mail for first-class delivery to our prospect list.

Friday, February 9, 2007

Bank buyout market may be beginning to cool

Atlanta Business Chronicle - by Joe Rauch

Atlanta's bank buyout market continued to boom with the purchase of **Gwinnett Commercial Group Inc.** by **United Community Banks Inc.**

United Community (Nasdaq: UCBI) paid a premium for Gwinnett Commercial's First Bank of the South, and the deal fills a glaring hole in the bank's "surround Atlanta" strategy.

But local industry insiders are saying the deal could mark the beginning of a cool-down after nearly half a decade of furious bank creation and consolidation.

Local bank attorneys declined to be named because of their client relationships. But each said the market for local bank sales is slowly cooling.

One local attorney said the first three months of this year are already "an inflection point" in bank sales. Several banks on the auction block, they said, are not finding buyers eager to pay the premium sale prices of the past few years.

Data from United Community's own presentation on its latest purchase tells the story.

Atlanta banks, compared with the rest of the Southeast, are relatively inexpensive, with declining overall prices. Since Jan. 1, 2005, acquiring banks in Atlanta have paid, on average, 2.4 times book value in a deal. Some local banks have paid well above that average, but the window on these types of deals appears to have closed. In August 2005, Synovus Financial Corp. paid 3.6 times book value for **Riverside Bancshares Inc.**

Alabama National BanCorp. paid 3.4 times book value for **PB Financial Services Corp.** last May. No bank in Atlanta has gone for more than three times book value since the PB Financial Services sale. United Community's data also shows prices cooling in 23 bank sales across the Southeast since 2005. Southeastern buyers have paid an average of three times a selling bank's book value, according to United Community's data.

Acquiring banks, locally and regionally, typically have paid about 23 times the selling bank's annual earnings to close a deal.

FIG Partners LLC analyst Chris Marinac cautioned that the market for new, or de novo, banks is not bottoming out – state banking regulators have previously projected as many as 15 new community banks this year – but turning more toward a buyer's market.

United Community's $216.6 million purchase is broken into 85 percent stock and 15 percent cash; the deal pays Gwinnett Commercial's shareholders at 2.7 times the bank's book value, and only 18 times its earnings per share.

"This won't calm de novo activity that's already out there in the pipeline," Marinac said. "But investors can't expect three to four times book value anymore for a bank."

The timing of our offering would prove to be dramatic. In hindsight, we couldn't help but be naïve. While few souls in the fall of 2007 could say that they truly had a premonition of the nightmare about beset the economy, we went about our business with the expectation that some remnant of retail investors still believed that *"Nobody has lost any money in a bank in a very long time."*

It's a bit of a challenge to convey on these pages the enthusiasm (and perhaps the imprudence) that existed for de novo banks during the time that Touchmark was assembling its IPO. As Bill and I would subsequently recall, there was only one individual at the outset of our offering who suggested that Touchmark should abort its opening and avoid what he said was a serious economic downturn on the way. Wayne Mason, the legendary Gwinnett county real estate developer, had initially expressed interest in our project, but ultimately deferred on a larger investment. Prescience is a gift—and I am amazed by his foresight. It is for Wayne that I included the Bud Carter quote at the outset of this chapter.

The filing to the right is used to make the acrylic "tombstones" souvenirs you tend to find on the credenzas of surviving IPO executives (ironic, huh?) and relevant information from our June 2007 SEC registration statement. I include it here because this filing recites the essential business case for the stock offering, presents the officers and directors responsible for the deal, and how we intend to use shareholder funds. I decided to include the background of each organizer that follows these pages to demonstrate the genuine diversity that existed across this group.

As filed with the Securities and Exchange Commission on June 18, 2007

SECURITIES AND EXCHANGE COMMISSION

WASHINGTON, D.C. 20549

FORM SB-2
REGISTRATION STATEMENT UNDER
THE SECURITIES ACT OF 1933

TOUCHSTONE BANCSHARES, INC.

(Name of small business issuer in its charter)

Georgia	6021	20-8746061
(State or Jurisdiction of Incorporation or Organization)	(Primary Standard Industrial Classification Code Number)	(IRS Employer Identification Number)

3740 Davinci Court, Suite 150

Norcross, Georgia 30092

(770) 407-6700

PROSPECTUS

TOUCHSTONE BANCSHARES, INC.

A Proposed Bank Holding Company for

(Proposed)

4,156,250 Shares of Common Stock

$10.00 per share

We are conducting this initial public offering of common stock of Touchstone Bancshares, Inc. to raise capital to fund the start-up of a new community bank, Touchstone National Bank, a national bank to be located in Duluth, Georgia. We are currently obtaining regulatory approval for the bank and expect to open the bank in the fourth quarter of 2007. Touchstone Bancshares will be the holding company and sole owner of the bank. The minimum purchase requirement for investors is 1,000 shares and the maximum purchase amount is 200,000 shares, although we may at our discretion accept subscriptions for more or less. Our officers and directors will be marketing our common stock on a best efforts basis and will not receive any commissions for sales they make.

This is our first offering of stock to the public, and there will be no established public market for our shares following the offering. Shares sold in this offering will not be listed on Nasdaq or any other national securities exchange. The common stock is a new issue of securities for which there is currently no public market. We do not believe that an active trading market will develop for the common stock after this offering. As a result, you may be unable to resell your shares of common stock or you may only be able to sell them at a substantial discount.

Our organizers and executive officers intend to purchase at least 675,000 shares in this offering, for a total investment of $6,750,000. They may purchase more, including up to 100% of the offering amount. All shares purchased by the organizers and executive officers will be for investment and not intended for resale. In recognition of their service and the financial risk they have undertaken, we are also offering our organizers, which include our directors, an aggregate of 470,000 organizer and director warrants to purchase shares of our common stock for $10.00 per share. Each organizer and director warrant will have a term of 10 years. If each organizer exercises his or her warrants in full and we do not issue any other shares, our organizers and executive officers will own 32% of our outstanding stock based on the minimum offering of 3,125,000 shares and 25% based on the maximum offering of 4,156,250 shares. We describe the warrants in more detail in the "Management—Organizer and Director Warrants" section.

The offering is scheduled to end on October 31, 2007, but we may extend the offering until March 31, 2008, at the latest. This offering will be conducted on a best efforts basis. All of the money that we receive from investors will be placed with an independent escrow agent that will hold the money until (1) we sell at least 3,125,000 shares and (2) we receive preliminary approval from our bank regulatory agencies for the new bank. If we do not meet these conditions before the end of the offering period, we will return all funds received to the subscribers promptly without interest

Touchstone Bancshares, Inc. and Touchstone National Bank

We formed Touchstone Bancshares on April 3, 2007 to organize and serve as the holding company for Touchstone National Bank, a proposed new national bank to be headquartered in Gwinnett County, Georgia. From March 31, 2006 to April 3, 2007, we operated as Formosa Rose, LLC which we had formed to facilitate the organization of Touchstone National Bank. All activity and agreements of Formosa Rose, LLC were assigned to Touchstone Bancshares, Inc. as of the date of incorporation. Upon successful receipt of required regulatory approvals, the bank will engage in a general commercial banking business, emphasizing personal service to individuals and businesses primarily in Gwinnett County and the surrounding areas. We have filed applications with the Office of the Comptroller of the Currency to open the new bank and with the FDIC for deposit insurance. Once we receive preliminary approval from the Office of the Comptroller of the Currency and FDIC, we will file for approval by the Federal Reserve Board to become a bank holding company and acquire all of the stock of the new bank upon its formation. We expect to receive all final regulatory approvals and open for business in the fourth quarter of 2007. Until we receive these regulatory approvals, we cannot commence banking operations and generate any operational revenue. During this offering process, we have been, and will continue to, incur start-up expenses. We incurred a net loss of $509,815 for the period from our inception on March 31, 2006 through May 31, 2007. For more detailed information regarding the risks of investing in our company, see "Risk Factors" beginning on page.

Why We Are Organizing a New Bank in Gwinnett County, Georgia

Our primary service area will lie in Gwinnett County, Georgia, and the surrounding areas, with a focus on the Buford Highway corridor between the Cities of Chamblee and Buford. Located 30 minutes northeast of Atlanta, Gwinnett County has been one of the fastest-growing counties in the country for several decades. Between 1990 and 2000, Gwinnett County saw the largest net increase in population among the counties comprising the greater Metropolitan Atlanta area, and it continues to grow. The population of Gwinnett County is expected to grow from approximately 726,000 in 2005 to nearly 1.3 million by 2030. The area has three major shopping malls, as well as various financial, legal, professional and technical services areas, which serve to attract customers and other businesses. Major employers in Gwinnett County include Gwinnett County Public Schools, Gwinnett County Government, Gwinnett Health Care System, Wal-Mart, Publix, the U.S. Postal Service, and the State of Georgia.

Touchstone Bancshares, Inc.
Touchstone National Bank (Proposed)
Primary Service Area

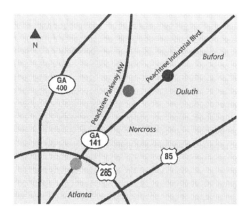

Peachtree Pavilion Branch	Davinci Branch	Main Office
6100 Peachtree Road	3740 Davinci Court	3170 Peachtree Industrial Blvd.
Suite C-121	Suite 150	Suite 100
Doraville, Georgia 30341	Norcross, Georgia 30092	Duluth, Georgia 30097

The ethnic diversity of Gwinnett County and the surrounding counties also provides an opportunity to reach a growing but underserved market. Gwinnett County also has one of the fastest growing Asian-American populations in Georgia, a demographic which we believe to be underserved at the present time. This population is expected to grow from 6% of the county's population to 15% of the county's population over the next 13 years. Our organizers have extensive business experience, diverse ethnic backgrounds and contacts in the market which we believe will create immediate business opportunities for the bank.

Our Board of Directors and Management Organizers

We were founded and organized by 22 business leaders, many of whom have lived in Gwinnett County for many years and have substantial business and personal connections in our proposed market area. We believe our organizers' long-standing ties to their communities and their significant business experience will provide Touchstone National Bank with the ability to effectively assess and address the needs of our proposed market area. The board of directors includes several members that have many years of hands on banking experience. The organizers believe that our experienced board will combine with the equally extensive management experience of William R. Short, our president and chief executive officer, to deliver high quality banking services to the community. Our organizers include the following:

J. Egerton Burroughs, director, has been a real estate developer in Conway, South Carolina and Myrtle Beach, South Carolina for over 35 years. Mr. Burroughs is chairman of the board of Burroughs & Chapin Company, and president of Burroughs Brothers Properties. In addition, he is a director and organizer of Crescent Bank, Myrtle Beach, South Carolina, and a past director of The Anchor Bank, Myrtle Beach, South Carolina. Mr. Burroughs is a graduate of the University of the South, Sewanee, Tennessee.

J. William Butler, director, is an Atlanta native and a graduate of Georgia State University. Mr. Butler is a licensed real estate broker and the owner and president of JWB Realty Services, LLC, a commercial brokerage, property management and leasing company. He previously served as president and director of AFCO Inc., an investment company, whose subsidiary AFCO Realty Services, LLC., is a full service commercial brokerage company.

Daniel B. Cowart, director, owns and operates Dan Cowart, Inc., a commercial and residential real estate development company located in Norcross, Georgia. He is a native of Atlanta and a graduate of the University of Georgia with a B.A. in real estate. During his 25 years in real estate, Mr. Cowart has developed over 1,700 residential lots in North Fulton, South Forsyth and Gwinnett Counties. In addition, Mr. Cowart served for seven years on the board of directors for Peachtree Bank, Peachtree City, Georgia. He is involved in various community groups and currently serves on the board of trustees of Wesleyan School and the King's Ridge Christian School.

Barry A. Culbertson, director, is president and co-owner of Power Products Unlimited, Inc., a distributor of wireless device accessories since 1995. He has also been an active real estate and community bank investor for over a decade. Mr. Culbertson is a graduate of Florida Atlantic University and has resided in the Atlanta area for over 20 years. He previously volunteered in the Metro Atlanta Big Brothers/Big Sisters program and currently promotes teen driving safety in Georgia through the Joshua Brown Foundation.

Emily M. Fu, director, is an owner of RE/MAX Greater Atlanta, a realty firm with 13 offices in the greater Atlanta area and the largest franchise in the RE/MAX global network. Born in Indonesia, Ms. Fu received her M.B.A degree from Georgia State University, and has resided in the Atlanta Metropolitan area since 1977. Ms. Fu is also the founder and chief executive officer of Capital Investment International Inc., an investment company with offices in Beijing, China, and Jakarta, Indonesia.

Howard Greenfield, director, has been a real estate developer and investor in Georgia, Florida and North Carolina since 2006. Previously, Mr. Greenfield served as regional vice president of Mercury Interactive, a software company in Atlanta, from 1996 to 2005. From 2005 until July 2006, he served as vice president of sales for Witness Systems, a software company based in Roswell, Georgia, until he left to focus full-time on his real estate investments. Mr. Greenfield received his B.A. in finance from Florida Atlantic University.

Yuling R. Hayter, director, is a native of Taipei, Taiwan. She received her M.B.A. from the University of West Georgia in 1997.

Ms. Hayter has been the co-owner of E.Z. Pay, Inc., a credit card processing company headquartered in Duluth, since 1997.

John L. Johnson, director, is the founder and president of Interstate Auction Company, which also operates under the name Interstate Brokers, a financial services consulting firm and national real estate auction company. Mr. Johnson has helped organize over 30 de novo banks. He is also the founder and president of Sperry Van Ness, a commercial real estate brokerage company in Atlanta. Mr. Johnson has lived in Atlanta for over 30 years and is actively involved in various charitable organizations in the community. In addition, he has served on the boards of directors of the Atlanta Chamber of Commerce, the Gwinnett Chamber of Commerce, Leadership Atlanta Board of Trustees, Leadership Gwinnett Board of Trustees and the University Yacht Club Board of Governors. Mr. Johnson graduated from the University of Tennessee, and received M.S. degrees in industrial management and accounting, respectively, from the University of North Dakota, while serving as an officer with the United States Air Force.

Daniel J. Kaufman, director, retired from the United States Army, holding the rank of Brigadier General, in 2005. In September 2005, Mr. Kaufman became the charter president of Georgia Gwinnett College, the first new state college in Georgia since 1970. Previously, he served as dean of the academic board and chief academic officer at the United States Military Academy, West Point, New York. Mr. Kaufman graduated from the United States Military Academy and obtained a M.P.A. degree from Harvard University and a PhD from the Massachusetts Institute of Technology.

Moon Kim, director, is a real estate agent with RE/MAX Greater Atlanta, the largest franchise in the RE/MAX global network. Prior to joining RE/MAX, he was president and chief executive officer of Grace Medical Resources, Inc., a recruiting and placement firm specializing in the placement of foreign nurses in United State's healthcare organizations, since 2002. Mr. Kim is also the president and chief executive officer of International Products Unlimited, an import and export firm based in Suwanee, Georgia.

C. Hiluard Kitchens, Jr., director, founded Hiluard Kitchens Homes, Inc., to develop and construct custom homes in the northeast Metropolitan Atlanta area, in 1991. His firm is a preferred builder for the Sugarloaf Country Club and The River Club in Gwinnett County. In addition, Mr. Kitchens is a founding member of Air & Energy Products, LLC, a manufacturer and distributor of indoor air quality products head-quartered in Acworth, Georgia.

Robert D. Koncerak is our chief financial officer. He has over 20 years of experience in the financial services industry. He was most recently employed by Wachovia Bank, N.A., as SVP and regional CFO of the Wealth Management Division from February 2002 until February 2007, when he left to assist in the formation of the bank. While with Wachovia, N.A., Mr. Koncerak was responsible for the financial management of 19 Wealth Management Teams located throughout the south and western United States. From January 2000 until February 2002, he served as capital markets controller for Wachovia Bank, N.A. Mr. Koncerak graduated from Penn State University and received his M.B.A. from Duquesne University. He is actively involved in the community and serves on the boards of the Georgia Free Clinic Network and the Coverdell Leadership Institute.

Paul P. Lam, organizer, has served since 2000 as the production manager for SMW Corporation, an import/export firm headquartered in Honk Kong, China. Mr. Lam was an organizer of Independence National Bank in Greenville, South Carolina. He currently resides in Greenville, South Carolina and is active in various charitable organizations in the community.

Sudhirkumar C. Patel, director, has been a practicing physician and partner of Carolina Internal Medicine in Greenville, South Carolina since 1990. Born in India, Dr. Patel graduated from the Baroda Medical College in India and completed his residency at Coney Island Hospital in Brooklyn, New York. In addition, Dr. Patel was an organizer and is a board member of Independence National Bank in Greenville, South Carolina. He currently resides in the Greenville, South Carolina area, and is actively involved with the Indian community in South Carolina. Dr. Patel is also a member of the Rotary Club of Greenville, the American College of Physicians, and the American Association of Indian Physicians.

Thomas E. Persons, Sr., director and chairman of the board, retired in 1996 as senior executive and general manager of the South Atlanta area for AT&T, the telecommunications company. While at AT&T, Mr. Persons was one of only two executives to serve for five years in AT&T's Leaders Council, and was honored as AT&T General Manager of the Year for six years during his tenure. He is the cofounder and chief executive officer of the South Carolina Technology Alliance. From 1991 to 1994, he was the business advisory chairman and member of the board of directors of Milton National Bank. He is a Leadership Georgia graduate, a life member of the Atlanta Chamber of Commerce, where he served on the board of directors, as well as president of SME-A and was recognized as one of the five outstanding young leaders in Atlanta. Mr. Persons currently resides in Columbia, South Carolina, and is active in various charitable organizations and serves on numerous business boards and served as the chairman of the Greater Columbia, South Carolina, Chamber of Commerce and is Chairman Emeritus of the Capital City Club. He served as a Trustee of Columbia College for twelve years. He completed Emory University Graduate School's Executive Management Program and the MIT Cambridge Institute's AT&T Executive Program, and is also an Aspen Institute Fellow.

Hasmukh P. Rama, director, is the chairman of the board and chief executive officer of JHM Hotels, Inc., in Greenville, South Carolina, which owns and operates 29 hotels with over 4,000 rooms in six states. Mr. Rama has been in the lodging industry for over 30 years and has received several awards for his leadership in the industry. He is the former chairman of the American Hotel & Lodging Association. He obtained his M.B.A. from Xavier University and was awarded a Doctor of Business Administration in hospitality management, honoris causa, from Johnson & Wales University. Mr. Rama serves as an advisor to a number of hospitality schools including the mentorship program at Cornell University. In addition, he is a director and organizer of Independence National Bank in Greenville, South Carolina.

J.J. Shah, director, has been an orthopedic surgeon and president and owner of Gwinnett Clinic, Ltd., in Lawrenceville, Georgia, a multi-practice group with over 30 licensed physicians in 13 locations, since 1984. He received his M.S. from the Baroda Medical College in India in

1978 and received his Georgia state medical license in 1983. Dr. Shah is licensed by the American Board of Orthopedic Surgery and is a fellow in the American Academy of Orthopedic Surgeons.

Meena J. Shah, director, is an owner of Gwinnett Clinic, Ltd., in Lawrenceville, Georgia, where she has practiced family medicine and has been medical director for over 22 years. She obtained her M.D. in 1978 from the Baroda Medical College in India and completed her residency at the Medical College of Georgia in Augusta, Georgia.

William R. Short, director, is our president and chief executive officer. He has more than 30 years of banking experience in Metropolitan Atlanta having held various positions with Wachovia Bank, N.A., since 1976. He was most recently senior vice president/group executive and managing director of several highly successful Atlanta Wealth Management Teams from 2001 until he joined our bank in December 2006. While at Wachovia, Mr. Short also led the banks significant retail and business banking growth in Gwinnett County in the 1980s and 1990s. Mr. Short is actively involved in the community, serving as a board member and chairman of both the Finance and Investment Committees of the Community Foundation for Northeast Georgia, and is a member of the Peachtree Corners Rotary Club. He is a past officer and director of numerous civic organizations including the Gwinnett Children's Shelter, the Gwinnett Chamber of Commerce, the Gwinnett Convention & Visitor's Bureau, the Gwinnett Council for Quality Growth, the Cobb Community Foundation, the Gwinnett Council for the Arts and the Atlanta Athletic Club. Mr. Short graduated with a bachelor's degree in industrial management from Clemson University, obtained his M.B.A. degree from Duke University and has completed management development programs at the Tuck School of Business at Dartmouth and the Kenan-Flagler Business School at the University of North Carolina at Chapel Hill.

Larry D. Silver, organizer, has been the owner of the Silver Companies, a real estate and investment company, for the last 35 years. Under his leadership, the Silver Companies have grown from a local development company in Fredericksburg, Virginia, to a national organization with offices in Washington, D.C. and Boca Raton, Florida, specializing in commercial and residential development and organizing real estate investment funds.

Debra D. Wilkins, organizer, has been a judicial assistant with the United States Court of Appeals for the Fourth Circuit, Greenville, South Carolina, for the past 20 years. She is married to the Honorable William W. Wilkins, Chief Judge of the United States Court of Appeals for the Fourth Circuit. Mrs. Wilkins has offices in Greenville, South Carolina and Richmond, Virginia. She and her husband reside in Greenville, South Carolina.

Bobby G. Williams, director and vice chairman, has been the president and chief executive officer of E.Z. Pay, Inc., a credit card processing company headquartered in Duluth, since 1997. He is also the chief executive officer of Innerspace Ads, Inc., an indoor advertising company. From 1987 to 1993, Mr. Williams was the Mayor of Duluth, Georgia, having served three complete two-year terms. He is a member of the advisory board of the National Processing Corporation and a former member of the advisory boards for Retriever Payment Systems and First National Bank of Omaha's Merchant Processing Division. Mr. Williams resides in Suwanee, Georgia.

Vivian Wong, director, has been a real estate investor and developer for over thirty-two years and has developments throughout the Southeast. In 2001, Ms. Wong formed Pacific Gateway Capital, LLC, a company specializing in new United States/China trade including development of United States retail franchises in China and attracting Chinese investment to South Carolina. She is a co-founder and organizing director of Independence National Bank in Greenville, South Carolina. Ms. Wong currently resides in Greenville, South Carolina and is active in various charitable organizations and sits on several community boards and committees.

Among the twenty-two organizers, four were not interested in becoming board members: those were Burroughs, Silver, Lam, and Wilkins. By being organizers, though, the four qualified to receive warrants. Emily Fu bowed out early in the process, and her

$20,000.00 was returned. Moon Kim stepped down in December 2008 and sold his shares and warrants. That left sixteen directors at the end of our first year in business.

The Raise (Race) Is On!

The organizers compiled their prospect lists over the summer of 2007: family, friends, business associates, and anyone else we could think of who might have an interest in purchasing community bank stock. The strategy for filling the capital bucket was straightforward: the first level of capital would be provided by the directors themselves; fully 43.2 percent of the stock or $15,364,000 of starting capital would ultimately come from our enthusiastic directors and officers. The second tier would come from close friends and business associates. Lastly, a shotgun mailing was sent to sundry prospects identified across thirteen states.

The "capital crunch" cited in the ABC article at the outset of this chapter was bearing down with force again in the fall of 2007. The sixty-day subscription period that we'd planned for ourselves between September and October didn't anticipate the dismal developments that began to barrage the headlines. During the spring and summer of 2007, Touchmark received several inquiries from venture capital funds. One group in particular, Starboard Specialty Funds, reached out to us on several occasions with an offer to take a 9.9 percent stake based on our final equity tally. The organizers, however, viewed institutional investors as dilutive and held firm to the notion that only individual subscriptions would be considered as worthwhile shareholders.

By mid-September, subscriptions were behind schedule, and we were reconsidering the desirability of those private equity subscriptions. By that time though, most fund managers weren't even returning our calls. One interesting PE conversation I recall from the period perfectly characterized the turn of the tide: "*Why should I invest with a start-up like you, a bank that will burn through capital until it grows to profitability, when I can buy shares in banks that are* already *profitable at a fraction of their book value?"* Ouch. The market had moved that fast...

We had a ready answer to that question, though. And it was a good one: *"Yeah, well, there's a* reason *those banks are suddenly selling at a fraction of book. Commercial real estate is in a nose-dive, and the market is forecasting losses in the loan portfolios of all those banks."*

It really was a good reason not to invest in the other guys...just not a good enough reason to invest in us! The institutional door had closed.

Looking back, it is painful to recall how the financial markets burst into flames just as our 2,357 prospectuses were posted in the mail. From September on, the drumbeat of financial bad news became relentless. On October 9, 2007, the Dow Industrials closed at an all-time high of 14,164. But with the onset of the recession that began early in 2008, equity markets began a gradual decline. As weeks rolled on, interest in equities of all stripes waned rapidly. By the time Bear Stearns collapsed in April 2008, the Dow had dropped to 11,000.

- **October 5**: Merrill Lynch reported a $5.5 billion third-quarter loss
- **October 9**: The Dow 30 Industrials closes at an all-time high and begins a historic decline
- **October 15:** Citicorp announces a $6.5 billion third-quarter loss
- **October 31:** The Federal Open Market Committee of the Federal Reserve votes to reduce fed funds by twenty-five basis points to 4.5 percent and the prime rate by twenty-five bps to 5.0 percent. Merrill Lynch restates its third-quarter loss at $6 billion.

Stories abound as to the causes and excess that led to the implosion of 2008. Some market professionals claim that they saw it coming. Personally, I can recall only three moments that stood out as markers along that wide road paved with good intentions:

1. I was in Fort Lauderdale in May 2004, looking over loan production forecasts for our Florida Wealth Management division. The regional executive, Mike Dyer, had incorporated a good-sized loan loss reserve against residential mortgages that had some possibility of default. I thought he was sandbagging his budget. I asked Mike how there could possibly be losses on any of our mortgage loans, since we were only working with "high net worth clients"...and we were dealing in first position mortgages. "Well, you don't get to go after *both* the borrower *and* the collateral anymore," he told me. "Most residential mortgage documents now cite that if the lender forecloses on a property, that lender sacrifices the personal guarantee—and so the ability to pursue the borrowers for any deficiency if the property is sold at a loss." *Huh?* As it happens, 11 states—most with strong areas of residential growth, had made it illegal to pursue a defaulted borrower's personal assets in the event of a foreclosure.

So...if a mortgage borrower defaults, the bank can take back the property—but it then loses any ability to recover remaining losses from the borrower's personal assets, even if the borrower strips or trashes the house on the way out the door (what, you think that only happens in lower-income neighborhoods?). For the record, that's where the term "jingle mail" came from: jingle mail is named for the sound that all those envelopes make that began showing up on mortgage bankers' desks once homeowners decided that they no longer wanted to own houses with "underwater" mortgages. Treacherous.

2. I was watching television in January 2005 when I first saw a commercial that offered me the ability to borrow 125 percent of what my home was worth. I wondered how borrowing 125 percent of the value of my home could be a good idea under any circumstance.

3. I again was in South Florida in August 2006, talking with a banker who was himself in the process of applying for a mortgage loan. The banker was amused by the fast progress of his application and was looking forward to closing on a $650,000 home mortgage...even though his annual income was $115,000 and he cited numerous other debts that he was supporting at the time. "And they never even asked me to provide evidence of my income," he told me. "All they wanted was for me to put down a "good" number on the application!" *Huh?*

So-called liar loans marked the final phase of the mortgage boom. Underwriters also called them fog loans: if you could *fog* a mirror, you qualified! Such were the underpinnings of the economy in which we had chosen to open a bank.

Capital is the fuel that drives a market economy. Everything about a capital raise draws excitement and enthusiasm: the presentations, the phone calls, the buzz. Everyone wants to open the mail, everyone wants an update on the tally, and everyone wants to hear about the latest subscription "score." It was a drama, and it made everyone look forward to coming in to work. Opportunities like that don't come around often—and it was surely a lot of fun. It would have been nice, though, to have been launching a little earlier in the cycle. As it turns out, we had our own version in 2007 of what has since become known as a fiscal cliff.

E-Mail as Drama

Bill developed a routine of e-mailing weekly updates to the directors and start-up team in order to relay our progress. In pulling together the materials for this book, I was grateful to receive a series of communications that were shared with former organizers throughout the process. These e-mails were provided to me by an ex-director. Collectively, they help tell the story of our dramatic success in a way that both documents the times and conveys the increasing urgency of our progress.

From: Bill Short
Sent: Friday, September 28, 2007 1:34 PM
Subject: Weekly Subscription Receipts—Important

The following chart represents our receipts through noon on Friday, September 28th. This represents only the organizer/directors' commitments and the checks received by me from other investors. The organizer commitments at this point are now $10,450,000. As you can see, we had 14 new investors for the week, totaling $517,000. Our cumulative number is $12,914,500. This means that our receipts from non-organizers total $2,464,500. Our minimum to open is $31,250,000, leaving us a **balance to collect of $18,335,500.**

We have had a number of very good meetings and many people have committed to purchase shares, but the flow of checks is a little worrisome. I spoke with Tom Persons and John Johnson this morning to see if we should re-engage the organizers to begin their personal solicitation of their prospective investors. John suggested that we call a meeting via conference call for Monday afternoon at 3:00 p.m. to discuss our marketing efforts. I think this is appropriate and will send out an email invitation later today.

We also need for the board to get their funds in–to date, only 5 organizers/ directors have all of their money in, while another 3 have part of their money in.

While we have a full month to get this money collected, I would like to create a sense of urgency around this process. I would greatly appreciate any feedback.

Thanks.

Week Ended	Weekly	Cumulative	% of Minimum	% of Maximum	Total # of Investors *
9/14/2007	$ 10,700,000	$ 10,700,000	34%	26%	26
9/21/2007	$ 1,697,500	$ 12,397,500	40%	30%	61
9/28/2007	**$ 517,000**	**$ 12,914,500**	**41%**	**31%**	**75**

* includes organizers and directors

Bill

By early October, Bill and I were growing concerned that our prospectus would be out of date ("stale" in market terms) long before our escrow account had reached its minimum. We'd hoped to reach $20 million by the end of September...and we were barely approaching $13 million. The drumbeat of bad news continued in the headlines, and the flow of subscriptions was ebbing. The organizers began to discuss extending the offering from October 31 until later in the year.

From: Bill Crosby
Sent: Friday, October 19, 2007 3:35 PM
To: Bill Short
Subject: RE: Weekly update

Sweeeet.....!!!

Reese said that the extension of Oct 31 can go all the way thru March 31 without FS revisions, unless there are material events that affect it. Good thing you didn't blow the budget on draperies!

From: Bill Short
Sent: Friday, October 19, 2007 3:27 PM
Subject: Weekly update

Organizers and Directors,

Attached is the update for the week ended 10/19. Good activity, but we will need a strong push to get to $31,250,000 by 10/31. Please don't forget to send me an update of your calling efforts by next Monday afternoon. Thanks.

Bill

Week Ended	Weekly	Cumulative	% of Minimum	% of Maximum	# of Investors *
9/28/2007	$ 517,000	$ 12,914,500	41%	31%	75
10/5/2007	$ 2,905,000	$ 15,819,500	51%	38%	115
10/12/2007	$ 725,000	$ 16,544,500	53%	40%	134
10/19/2007	$ 1,880,000	$ 18,424,500	59%	44%	161

* includes organizers and directors

Bill

We knew by the second half of October that getting to our minimum at all was going to be a struggle. We weren't expecting, though, that it would turn into the fight of a lifetime! I began stressing to our organizers that unless we could reach our minimum by the first week of December, there was little hope of getting the bank open before year-end. Nobody was buying bank stocks for Christmas that year.

It was around this time that I began to sense that our organizers had varied capacities when it came to supporting our capital raise. While most had willingly contributed names and addresses for the prospect list, few showed a willingness to personally solicit subscriptions.

As the highest-ranking non-organizer employee, I was uniquely unsettled by this. After all, Bill had *retired* from Wachovia. The organizers had their day jobs. I, however, was a *pig* in this game and not a chicken! A few of the organizers—namely JJ Shah and John Johnson—actively demonstrated that they were "working" their lists; others seemed to be bringing no investors to the table at all. Because the process was new to me, I didn't realize that among organizing groups this was typical (it seems the 80/20 rule applies to everything!). I found the apparent lack of participation by some of the organizers to be disappointing—and I allowed it to frustrate me. Bill Short shared with Chairman Persons the apparent disparity regarding director participation, and Persons in turn tried to stoke some enthusiasm across the group. The drumbeat of e-mails continued. By late October, we began to realize that with the coming year-end holidays, reaching our regulatory minimum by year-end would be all but impossible. Taking advantage of the flexibility in our capital-raising time line, we filed to extend the deadline for our raise.

From: Bill Short
Sent: Wednesday, October 31, 2007 8:49 AM
Subject: Capital Raise Update

Organizers and Directors,

Here are the numbers regarding our capital raise through Tuesday, October 30th. I know that today will be a big day based on many conversations, but it will not get us to our minimum of $31,250,000. We had contemplated this in our prospectus and we can actually extend through March 31, 2008, at the latest. We will file an extension this morning with the SEC through December 15, 2007. There is no limit to the number of extensions we may file up to March 31, 2008. The offering can be closed at any time up to December 15th if we hit our benchmarks.

While it is disappointing not to have achieved our goal at this time, we have in fact raised a significant amount of money over less than 2 months in a fairly turbulent economy. We will continue to market the stock, though we are now in conversation with several brokers to understand how they might assist us and what the parameters of a contract might look like. In the meantime, we are still looking to get open in early December and the staff is working diligently to make this happen.

Many of you still have personal contacts who have expressed an interest in Touchstone. Please continue to market to these folks and let me know how I can help.

Week Ended	Weekly	Cumulative	% of Minimum	% of Maximum	Cumulative # of Investors *
10/19/2007	$ 1,880,000	$ 18,424,500	59%	44%	161
10/26/2007	$ 1,677,000	$ 20,101,500	64%	48%	197

Day	Daily Total				
10/29/2007	$ 1,259,980	$ 21,361,480	68%	51%	230
10/30/2007	$ 197,000	$ 21,558,480	69%	52%	244

* includes organizers and directors

Bill

The following filing was sent to the SEC on October 31, 2007:

Filed pursuant to Rule 424(b)(3)
SEC Registration No. 333-143840

TOUCHSTONE BANCSHARES, INC.
OFFERING OF A MINIMUM OF 3,125,000 AND A
MAXIMUM OF 4,156,250 SHARES OF COMMON STOCK

SUPPLEMENT NO. 1 TO PROSPECTUS
DATED AUGUST 31, 2007

This document supplements our prospectus, dated August 31, 2007, pursuant to which we are offering a minimum of 3,125,000 shares and a maximum of 4,156,250 shares of our common stock at $10.00 per share.

Extension of the Offering

The offering was originally scheduled to expire on October 31, 2007, subject to our right to extend the offering for one or more periods up to March 31, 2008. We have decided to extend the offering through

December 15, 2007. We still reserve the right to extend the offering until March 31, 2008, or to terminate the offering earlier.

Subscriptions to Date

As of the date set forth below in this supplement, we have received subscriptions for 2,160,848 shares and subscription proceeds totaling $21,608,480. We have not obtained the required minimum amount of subscription proceeds nor received the final regulatory approvals, which will permit us to break escrow and begin banking operations.

Preliminary Approval from the FDIC

On October 12, 2007, we received preliminary approval from the FDIC for deposit insurance. Now that we have received preliminary approval from the Office of the Comptroller of the Currency (which we received in August 2007) and the FDIC, we have filed an application with the Federal Reserve to form a bank holding company. We expect to receive all final regulatory approvals during the fourth quarter of 2007.

The date of this Supplement No. 1 is October 31, 2007

Touchstone had set a goal of accomplishing the capital raise on its own—without the assistance of a fee-based underwriter. But by early November of 2007, the organizers were reaching a consensus to engage with an outside firm to help reach our established regulatory minimum of $31,250,000.

Knowing as I did that only a few of the organizers were actively working to raise capital, I fumed. Up to this time I'd had no substantive conversations with Chairman Tom Persons...and I was feeling a need to *share*. Tom lived in Columbia, South Carolina, and it was becoming apparent that his distance from Atlanta was going to present some challenges in the long run of this offering. I approached Bill about calling Tom to vent my concerns, and he encouraged me as a professional to do so.

I phoned Tom and left word with his office on November 1 that I wanted to speak with him, but for some (likely very good) reason, he didn't return my call. That didn't help my temperament one bit. While I'm grateful to write that Tom and I have since become good friends, on November 3, 2007, I was steamed.

Saturday, November 3, 2007

Tom,

Hope you are well. Now that Penn State has whomped Purdue, I can turn my attention to the other matter that's been on my mind this weekend!

Sorry we didn't have opportunity to speak Friday. I had left msg. with your secretary at about 11:30 a.m. that I wanted to relay some "talking points." I present them below as Bill, Ellen, James, and I will be training in Orlando all day Monday—and I hope that TBI will have a conference call at earliest opportunity (Tuesday?) after we get back to Atlanta Monday night.

I remain as enthusiastic about Touchstone today as I was in January when Bill first relayed to me his excitement about our organizing group. Everything about this company is important to me; Touchstone is the largest challenge I've yet taken on in my career.

As the highest-ranking "non-organizing employee" of Touchstone, I would like to share some candid insights and observations that I hope are helpful and that I hope you will consider as we plan the next steps on the path to opening our bank.

While I realize that all organizations have some members that "pull the load" more than others, I was astonished to learn this past week that several members of our board have yet to bring a single investor to TBI and its $41MM capital raise. The record goal that $41MM represents has been a point of pride for our group since I joined the start-up team. I hope you will recall that *my* first question during the interview process was "What do you plan to do with all that money!?" The consistent response was that the size and scale of this organizing group made such a goal a foregone conclusion...on our own—with no help from outside underwriters. Please know that, as a proud officer of this team, it was deflating for me to participate in 2 meetings this past week with our employees in order to relay that: 1) we are significantly shy of our minimum goal and 2) we are pursuing engagement with an underwriter.

Tom, the most compelling aspect of our offering has been that this group said that it intends to raise its significant capital via the strength of its organizer network. Some 2,400 prospectuses have been mailed in this effort. That we have seen a spotty follow-through from our directors on this strategy distresses me. *Every* member of our board has an obligation to the employees that have joined us (read: trusted us) to contribute toward a successful capitalization. If we are seen to be "struggling" in this critical phase, it will be difficult—if not impossible—to attract superior talent. I was concerned to hear secondhand Friday morning that a very influential Gwinnett businessman was heard to say that Touchstone was "having problems" raising its capital. Such opinions will destroy our momentum.

Keyworth Bank http://keyworthbank.com/index.asp opened for business on October 15 near our PSA with a $36MM raise (see attached Georgia de novo report). *Without* an underwriter, this group planned for an initial raise of $15MM early this year and was oversubscribed by millions, finally more than doubling their expected take-in. It concerns me greatly that Touchstone may well decide to pay an outside party for such duties as making the *first* follow-up call to prospective investor names provided by *our* organizing group. Such a decision stands in stark contrast to the vision that was presented to me in January. In this challenging market, investors are far more apt to respond favorably to a friend's invitation than to a professional fundraiser. Our employees are heartily involved in the investor effort. Charlene Fang and Vitra Darden have enthusiastically phoned and met with their contacts, raising over $1.5MM. Though far more modest, my investment is the largest such commitment I've ever made—and I, too, have worked to bring investors to the table. How will our folks feel to find that some of our organizers have been less engaged?

I had expected that beginning November 1, my primary roles would be implementing technology, establishing and refining policies, and hiring/training with remaining team members. I did not imagine that Bill and I would be consumed with the considerable distraction of driving the capital raise into November. Please know that the ongoing requirements of this capital raise—especially on Bill—will cause significant stress on our opening time line. The regulators will not schedule our preopening exam until convinced of a satisfactory capital raise. If marketing Touchstone becomes the responsibility of a professional underwriter, Bill will be expected (and rightly so) to participate intensely in the capital raise until the job is done. Please realize, Tom, that this will overwhelm Bill's other responsibilities unless the full board steps up to help finish the job. Bill has done outstanding work representing our effort. He should be acting in concert with the board…and not for it.

My request: with an assertive push from our chair and vice-chairs, I would like to see Touchstone meet its minimum of $31MM+ via internal efforts by November 10. With such an accomplishment, we can proudly represent that Touchstone raised its required capital through the diverse interests of its organizers. If we choose to engage with an underwriter *beyond* the minimum, we can say that our reserve capital or "dry powder" was raised with outside support. Our primary investors—up to the regulatory minimum—will have been sourced by our directors—and we should hope that those primary investors have the highest probability of becoming clients of Touchstone National Bank.

Know that I am having the time of my life in getting this bank off the ground—and I trust that you find my remarks constructive. I am excited for our opportunity. My greatest hope is that we'll all be "committed like the pig"…and not just "involved like the chicken" (ask me if you haven't heard this before). Thanks for your very important role in leading our efforts.

Bob

Tom never responded to me regarding that memo. By November 20, an engagement agreement had been signed, and Commerce Street Capital was working our subscription list out of our temporary offices at Davinci Court.

In the opening chapter, I offered that this book was written as "part documentary, part biography, part life lesson, and part cautionary tale." As such, I included the letter above as part of the documentary...and perhaps as a part of the cautionary tale. More than anything, it helps to convey the dependence that we as employees had on the ultimate success of the organizing group—as well as the unintended risk that we would be suddenly facing if the effort fell short and disbanded!

The documentary part: As I've written previously, the organizers of Touchmark National Bank were all accomplished, capable businesspeople. In completing the IPO, however, it became clear that expectations had not been established for minimum participation in the capital-raising process. Because no threshold had been set for bringing investors to the table, participation was anything but uniform. As noted in the memo above, some organizers invested considerable time in working prospects, while the effort of others was patently disappointing. While the networking capacity of the group no doubt varied from member to member, a minimum set of expectations would have enabled our leadership team to respectfully press and enforce those expectations.

The cautionary tale part: Should you, gentle reader, ever have opportunity to participate in an offering such as this, I recommend that you tie the eligibility of warrants (options) not only to the organizer's minimum contribution, but also to the amount of investor capital that an organizer must bring to the table. Had each Touchmark organizer been expected to source a minimum $1 million of shareholder investment before qualifying for warrants in the offering, I dare say that participation would have been much more equal across the group.

From: Bill Short

Sent: Tuesday, November 20, 2007 5:33 PM
Subject: Capital raise update

Touchstone Officers, Organizers, and Directors,

A little bit of a slow start to the Thanksgiving week but we have now surpassed the $26 million mark. The good news is we have Commerce Street Capital on the ground working, and they are contacting a number of people on our mailing list as well as others with good early results.

We have a luncheon for prospective investors scheduled for Tuesday, December 4th, at Berkeley Hills Country Club at 12:00 noon, as well as a cocktail reception on Wednesday, December 5th, at the 1818 Club from 6:30 to 8:30 for anyone interested in learning more about Touchstone. Reference the attached flyer that you can use to invite guests. Please feel free to invite as many of your prospects to either of these meetings. It would be helpful for planning purposes if you would let me know who might be attending.

We have challenged Commerce Street Capital to get us to our minimum by December 10th, and they have accepted the challenge. We will then keep the offering open to get to the $41.5 million maximum. We are still hoping to open before year-end if the fundraising and regulatory approvals are forthcoming.

Thanks for your continued hard work on our behalf.

Bill

The flyer that we used for our December 2007 receptions:

TOUCHSTONE
B A N C S H A R E S, I N C.

Board of Directors and Organizers
Cordially invite you for a lunch or dinner reception

or

December 4, 2007 at 12:00 pm	December 5, 2007 at 6:30
2300 Pond road	6500 Sugarloaf Parkway
Duluth, GA 30096	Duluth, GA 30097

RSVP
770 407 6718

Enjoy a brief presentation about Touchstone National Bank (IO) and the Investment opportunity for shareholders

Board of Directors and Executive officers

Thomas E. Persons, Sr.	Bobby G. Williams	Vivian A. Wong	William R. Short
Chairman of the Board	Vice Chairman & Founder	Vice Chairman & Founder	President & CEO
	Robert D. Koncerak	James E. Lebow	
	CFO	CCO	

John I. Johnson	Daniel J. Kaufman	Moon K. Kim	J. Egerton Burroughs	J. William Butler
Director	Director	Director	Director	Director
Daniel b. Cowart	C. Hiluard Kitchens, Jr.	Paul P. Lam	Sudhirkumar C. Patel	Hasmukh P. Rama
Director	Director	Organizer	Director	Director
Barry A. Culbertson	Emily M. Fu	Howard R. Greenfield	Yuling R. Hayter	J.J. Shah
Director	Director	Director	Director	Director
Meena J. Shah	Larry D. Silver	Debra D. Wilkins		
Director	Organizer	Organizer		

From: Bill Short
Sent: Thursday, November 29, 2007 3:03 PM
Subject: Conference Call—Commerce Street Capital

Organizers and Directors,

Our flow of investments has slowed with the holidays, and we are now in our push to get to our minimum of $31,250,000 within the next several weeks in order to open prior to year end. We have engaged Commerce Street Capital to assist with this portion of our capital raising activities. This firm and these people are extremely competent in raising capital for banks, and they would like the opportunity to discuss the process with our Board on a group basis. To that end, we would like to schedule a brief conference call for **Friday, November 29th at 11:00 a.m.**

Several of you have indicated a desire to contact your list without any assistance and that is fine—please join the call anyway as it is important that you understand what we are doing. Representing Commerce Street Capital will be Shaun Dalton and Jeff Amershadian.

Just a reminder that we have scheduled a luncheon for Berkeley Hills CC for **Tuesday, December 4th, at 12:00 noon**, and an evening presentation at The 1818 Club on **Wednesday, December 5th, from 6:30-8:30 p.m.**—please feel free to invite as many prospective investors as possible.

The following represents our capital fundraising activity through today:

Week Ended	Weekly	Cumulative	% of Minimum	% of Maximum	Cumulative # of Investors *
11/23/2007	$ 30,000	$ 25,828,480	83%	62%	329
11/26/2007	$ 50,020	$ 25,878,500	83%	62%	332
11/27/2007	$ 100,000	$ 25,978,500	83%	63%	333
11/28/2007	$ 35,000	$ 26,013,500	83%	63%	334
11/29/2007	-	$ 26,013,500	83%	63%	334

* includes organizers and directors

Bill

As late as December 13, we were still hoping to open by year-end. On December 14, 2007, we filed a painful second offering extension with the SEC—this time through March 31, 2008. Notice that by now that we had become Touchmark National Bank (also by this time, Bill insisted on opening all of the mail to be sure that he'd counted all the checks!).

From: Bill Short
Sent: Thursday, December 13, 2007 10:27 AM
Subject: Capital Scorecard Update

Organizers and Officers,

We had a very nice collection day on Wednesday with **$565,000** and we have now exceeded **$27 million.** There was a lot of good conversation during yesterday's board meeting, and several of you have already updated me regarding your personal fundraising efforts. Please keep your sense of urgency around the capital raise as we strive to open by year-end.

Thanks.

Week Ended	Weekly	Cumulative	% of Minimum	% of Maximum	Cumulative # of Investors *
11/30/2007	$ 215,020	$ 26,043,500	83%	63%	336
12/7/2007	$ 403,000	$ 26,446,500	85%	64%	345
Day	**Daily Total**				
12/10/2007	$ 10,000	$ 26,456,500	85%	64%	345
12/11/2007	$ -	$ 26,456,500	85%	64%	345
12/12/2007	$ 565,000	$ 27,021,500	86%	65%	351
Goal			$ 31,250,000	$ 41,562,500	

* includes organizers and directors

Bill
Bill Short
President & CEO
Touchmark Bancshares, Inc. (formerly Touchstone Bancshares)

By mid-December, we were getting realistically close to reaching $31,250,000 in escrow. After discussion with our primary regulator, the OCC came on-site for our preopening examination. We passed with no notable exceptions. Our regulators explained, however, that due to the remaining holiday calendar, opening prior to year-end would be unlikely, regardless of funds in escrow. As such, we resolved to make the best of the holiday, continue on course, and work to wrap up the final escrow raise after the New Year. Little did we know that the final push to $31,250,000 would come by way of a pivotal surprise development...

From: Bill Short
Sent: Friday, December 21, 2007 1:58 PM
Subject: Capital Raise Update

Organizers, Directors, and Officers,

Below is our progress to date in our fundraising—an exceptional week this week with $1.4 million. However, since we did not hit our minimum today, we will have to push our opening into early 2008. The fact that we have raised $28.4 million in this market is remarkable, particularly in light of having received no institutional money. We continue to receive commitments and make presentations, and I feel confident we will get to our minimum over the next several weeks, and hopefully our maximum or beyond by March 31.

Attached is a letter that was mailed out today to all of our existing subscribers describing where we are in the process and what they should expect going forward. I have also attached a copy of the December 14, 2007 Supplement filed with the SEC.

It is critical to our success that we maintain the momentum—otherwise the achievement of our minimum will push out even farther. To that end, Tom Persons will be hosting a prospective investor event in Columbia on Thursday, January 10th, at 6:30 p.m. at the Capital City Club. See the attached invitation that was previously sent to you. Should you have any associates in the Columbia area who might benefit from attending this event, please let me know so that we can add them to the invitation list.

Again, thanks to everyone for your support as we **complete our fundraising** and **open our Bank!** Best wishes to everyone for a Merry Christmas, Happy Holidays, and a healthy and prosperous 2008.

Week Ended	Weekly	Cumulative	% of Minimum	% of Maximum	Cumulative # of Investors *
12/21/2007	$ 1,407,000	$ 28,438,500	91%	68%	378
					Balance to open
		Goal	$ 31,250,000	$ 41,562,500	$ 2,811,500

Bill

That same day we finalized a letter to our prospective shareholders that noted our progress and notified them as well of our name change:

December 21, 2007

Dear Subscriber,

Thank you again for investing in Touchstone Bancshares, Inc. We would like to take this opportunity to update you on the status of our stock offering and to inform you of our decision to extend the offering through March 31, 2008. Enclosed you will find a supplement to our prospectus dated

December 14, 2007, which we filed with the Securities and Exchange Commission. This document, which supplements our prospectus dated August 31, 2007 and supplement dated October 31, 2007, contains additional information regarding the status of the offering and our decision to extend it. Your subscription will continue to be binding pursuant to the terms of the Subscription Agreement and the prospectus.

We are pleased with the demand and the enthusiasm that we are experiencing for our stock and for the bank. As of December 20, 2007, we have received subscriptions for 2,843,850 shares and subscription proceeds totaling $28,438,500. We continue to receive new subscriptions daily, and are confident that we will reach our minimum offering of 3,125,000 shares in the coming weeks.

We have just completed our pre-opening examination with the Office of the Comptroller of the Currency (OCC), our primary regulator. The examination went extremely well, and upon reaching the offering minimum we will notify the OCC, make final arrangements to secure our FDIC insurance, capitalize the bank and open for business. Investor registration will begin once we reach our minimum capitalization and share certificates will be issued to our investors.

In the enclosed supplement to our prospectus, you will note that we have extended the offering date to March 31, 2008 for the purpose of raising additional capital. You will recall from the prospectus that we have set a maximum of 4,156,250 shares and we hope to achieve our maximum prior to March 31. There will be no further extensions beyond March 31, and we reserve the right to close the offering earlier if we achieve our maximum.

Additionally, you may have noticed our letterhead above showing Touchmark Bancshares, Inc.

Our use of the names Touchstone Bancshares, Inc. and Touchstone National Bank were challenged during the summer by a mutual fund company headquartered in Cincinnati, Ohio. While our legal counsel advised that there was a chance we could prevail in keeping this name, legal fees to do so could have ranged from $500,000 to more than $1,000,000. Given our responsibility to create the most value for our shareholders and build the strongest institution possible, we considered it most prudent to rename our organization.

We have thus decided to change our name from Touchstone Banc-shares, Inc. to Touchmark Bancshares, Inc. The latter will serve as the parent company of Touchmark National Bank. The Touchmark name was selected to reflect our core values of service, honesty, passion and leadership. Alongside our clients, shareholders, and staff, we look forward to creating ***the new standard in banking*** under our new name.

Thank you again for your confidence in our company. Should you have questions regarding the enclosed supplement, please contact Bill Short at (770) 407-67xxx-xxxx. We appreciate your investment in Touchmark Bancshares and look forward to completing the offering and having you as a shareholder and as a client.

Sincerely,

Bill Short

From: Bill Crosby
Sent: Friday, December 28, 2007 4:15 PM
To: Bill Short
Cc: Bob Koncerak
Subject: RE: Capital Scorecard

It's all downhill now! **The toughest feat I have seen since 1987**. A good story for your grandchildren. Call me when Bob opens the Scotch.

Happy New Year!

BC

Headline: Dog Catches Car

The following is a pivotal communication in the history of Touch-mark's organization; it documents a capitulation on maximum percentage of ownership in the bank. Recall earlier that institutional ownership was initially frowned upon because of the outsized voting strength that would come with concentrated ownership. But despite an initial intention limit on shareholder ownership, two crucial accommodations were made on account of the painfully slow pace of subscriptions:

1. An allowance for concentrated individual ownership was permitted, and

4. Two husband/wife teams were accepted on the board.

These accommodations would ultimately enable a leadership turnover as the bank navigated its way through challenging times in the coming year.

From: Bill Short
Sent: Thursday, January 17, 2008 4:36 PM
Subject: FW: Capital Fundraising Update

Team Touchmark,

Please see my note below to the Board of Directors–the finish line for fundraising will turn into the starting line for the Bank very soon. Let's get ready to ramp up our efforts for the premier community bank in the industry!! I'm excited–I hope you are.

Bill

From: Bill Short
Sent: Thursday, January 17, 2008 4:25 PM
Subject: Capital Fundraising Update

Touchmark Organizers, Officers, & Directors,

I am extremely pleased to report that we received investments today totaling **$1,072,000** to include significant investments from Dr. JJ and Meena Shah and Dr. Raja. We are now only **$498,250** from our minimum. The regulators have all been notified of our progress and are working with us to get open as soon as possible. Please continue to work with your prospects to help get us over the top. Also, several of you have made additional commitments, and the receipt of these dollars will go a long way towards helping us break escrow and open the Bank. Thanks again to everyone for your support—we are ready to take the next big step.

Week Ended	Weekly	Cumulative	% of Minimum	% of Maximum	Cumulative # of Investors *
12/28/2007	$ 636,250	$ 29,074,750	93%	70%	389
1/4/2008	$ 300,000	$ 29,374,750	94%	71%	393
1/11/2008	$ 180,000	$ 29,554,750	95%	71%	399
Day	Daily Total				
1/14/2008	$ 15,000	$ 29,569,750	95%	71%	400
1/15/2008	$ 10,000	$ 29,579,750	95%	71%	401
1/16/2008	$ 100,000	$ 29,679,750	95%	71%	406
1/17/2008	**$ 1,072,000**	**$ 30,751,750**	**98%**	**74%**	**409**
					Needed to open
	Goal	$31,250,000	$41,562,500	**$ 498,250**	

Bill

Then finally, on January 18, 2008...

From: Bill Short
Sent: Friday, January 18, 2008 12:24 PM
Subject: We made it!!

Team Touchmark,

We will have $31,250,000 in our escrow account on Tuesday morning. All of the regulators are working to get us open on Monday, January 28, 2008.

A heartfelt thank you to each of you for all you have done in getting us to this point, and all that you will do to make us the premier community bank in the industry.

Tighten up your chin straps – it's game time!!!

Bill

From: Bill Short
Sent: Friday, January 18, 2008 5:24 PM
Subject: A Red Letter Day

Touchmark Organizers, Officers, and Directors,

Tuesday, **January 22** will be a red letter day in our history as we will make a deposit that puts us at **$31,250,000**. Thanks primarily to Dan Cowart and several others, we deposited $388,000 today bringing our weekly total to $1,585,000. This puts us within $130,250 of our minimum. Vivian Wong has graciously agreed to fund the gap, and we will make that deposit on Tuesday morning–Monday is a Bank holiday, and our escrow agent will be closed. At this level we will meet the minimum established in our public offering and will be able to break escrow. We will pay off the Organizational line of credit, thus extinguishing the guarantees of the Organizers. We will capitalize the Bank with $25,000,000, and we will also pay off the real estate loan on the 10 acres we purchased for our headquarters site, extinguishing that guaranty as well. The regulators are all aware of our status, and we are tentatively scheduling a very soft opening on **Monday, January 28**[th], another red letter day.

As you are aware, the office at Davinci Court is really not set up to be a full-service branch. We are not in a position to service a number of retail accounts as we do not have a teller line, and office space is limited. We will start by opening employee and director accounts and will make sure all of the systems are working and all of the reporting meets our standards. We will then roll out Touchmark to the public.

This is a remarkable time in our history, and there is a great deal of credit that should be passed around to each of you. I look forward to gathering in the near future to toast each of you and to toast Touch-

mark in the beginning of a very special opportunity for all of us. A sincere thank you to everyone. Have a great weekend–I know I will.

Chart 18

Week Ended	Weekly	Cumulative	% of Minimum	% of Maximum	Cumulative # of Investors *
9/14/2007	$ 10,500,000	$ 10,500,000	34%	25%	26
9/21/2007	$ 1,697,500	$ 12,197,500	39%	29%	61
9/28/2007	$ 517,000	$ 12,714,500	41%	31%	75
10/5/2007	$ 2,905,000	$ 15,619,500	50%	38%	115
10/12/2007	$ 725,000	$ 16,344,500	52%	39%	134
10/19/2007	$ 1,880,000	$ 18,224,500	58%	44%	161
10/26/2007	$ 1,677,000	$ 19,901,500	64%	48%	197
11/2/2007	$ 3,691,980	$ 23,593,480	75%	57%	288
11/9/2007	$ 1,285,000	$ 24,878,480	80%	60%	308
11/16/2007	$ 900,000	$ 25,778,480	82%	62%	326
11/23/2007	$ 30,000	$ 25,808,480	83%	62%	329
11/30/2007	$ 215,020	$ 26,023,500	83%	63%	336
12/7/2007	$ 403,000	$ 26,426,500	85%	64%	345
12/14/2007	$ 585,000	$ 27,011,500	86%	65%	352
12/21/2007	$ 1,407,000	$ 28,418,500	91%	68%	378
12/28/2007	$ 636,250	$ 29,054,750	93%	70%	389
1/4/2008	$ 300,000	$ 29,354,750	94%	71%	393
1/11/2008	$ 180,000	$ 29,534,750	95%	71%	399
1/18/2008	$ 1,585,000	$ 31,119,750	99%	75%	421
					Needed to open
	Goal		$31,250,000	$41,562,500	**$130,250**

Bill

I include one final e-mail with regard to the capital raise. I think that it really rounds out the story of our efforts:

From: Bill Short
Sent: Monday, April 07, 2008 2:14 PM
Subject: Capital Update—Final

Touchmark Organizers, Officers, and Directors,

We have now closed out our Capital Offering with $34.7 million raised. When we net SAMCO's commission, our net capital raised is $34.5 million. This is $3.25 million above the minimum in our Offering Prospectus, and we have approximately 560 charter shareholders. 100% of our capital was raised from individual investors with no institutional money. This is truly a remarkable accomplishment in a very difficult environment for raising capital. Thanks to each of you for your efforts on our behalf.

As noted earlier, we will have our initial stockholders' meeting on Wednesday, May 21st, at 3:30 p.m. at the Atlanta Athletic Club. More details to follow, but please put on your calendars.

Thanks again to everyone for your support.

Bill

Bill Short

President & CEO
Touchmark National Bank
Touchmark Bancshares, Inc.

A Few Shout-Outs and Compliments Along The Organization Process

There was a bewildering number of partner and vendor decisions involved with our business start-up. In addition to the regulatory filings and organizational documents, there were facilities to rent, candidates to interview, logos and stationary and business cards to order, furniture, supplies, software, and security. The pace and variety were at times almost overwhelming. For those who are interested, following are the major partnerships needed for a bank start, along with why we chose them:

Attorneys: A complicated array of paperwork and sequential path of to-do's and deadlines face a banking organization both prior to and after opening. Like any sophisticated project, decisions made early on affect the later path and opportunities. Bank attorneys are a special breed; as Bill would say, *"They're expensive—but the good ones don't cost nearly what they're worth."* A shout-out here to Reese Porter, our primary contact first at Smith, Gambrell & Russell and later at Nelson, Mullins, Riley & Scarborough, where he moved to in early 2009. Reese, along with managing partner Bobby Schwartz at SGR, got us through the SEC, OCC, Federal Reserve, FDIC, and the Georgia State Department of Banking. Bill and I would come to refer to Reese Porter as our "filing cabinet." Reese was among the first people we met during the process—and I'm proud to call him my friend. Maybe I should have titled this section "All of My Friends Were Regulators, Auditors and Attorneys"!

Auditors: Just as there are banking-focused attorneys, there are also specialty-practice auditors. After interviewing seven qualified firms, Touchmark chose Ian Waller and William Sammons of Nichols, Cauley, LLP to serve as our internal auditors. The internal audit partners work as an adjunct to the bank's own staff until such time as it's economically feasible to hire internal staff accountants. Ian and William were enormously helpful with helping to craft securities language and in pulling together regulatory filings. If I hadn't mentioned it yet, no one in our organizing group—including me—had ever served as a principle executive in a publicly traded company...let alone a bank. More than anyone on our team, it fell to me to coordinate our SEC filings, and I couldn't have done it without Ian and one other professional: Richard Jones of Mauldin & Jenkins LLP. Whereas Nichols, Cauley LLP served as our hired internal audit team, M&J serve as external auditors on account of our SEC registration and Sarbanes-Oxley requirements (what a joy that was!). Auditors are protective of their reputations with the regulatory authorities, and they maintain their reputation by requiring good work product from their clients. As such, both internal and external auditors—but especially external—can be demanding of financial clarity before they'll sign off on a statement filing, because their name goes on it too–and each filing reflects on their reputation. Whenever you read about an auditor resigning from a client, the reason for the breakup may be related to confidence in the client management team (though of course, it could be their billing rates, too!). An auditor's reputation is reliant on the quality of their client's work. In Richard Jones, I'm pleased to write that I felt we had partnered with the best.

Core Processor: In reality, a commercial bank is more a purveyor of financial processes than it is a seller of financial products. Banks distribute funds via electronic systems like ATMs and debit cards, they clear checks and transfers by transmitting settlement instructions, and they validate credit decisions by means of trading information with credit reporting companies. The guts of all those systems are incredibly sophisticated—and prohibitively expensive for all but the largest of institutions to own outright. Probably more than in any other industry, outsourcing made possible the proliferation of community banks beginning in the early 1980s. Virtually all of a small bank's operations are not owned, but contracted. From everyday check cashing to the opening of a certificate of deposit, every electronic transaction in a small bank is most likely funneled through a contracted service bureau processor. Without getting too far into the details, core processors serve as the guts of a community bank's general ledger, transaction posting and check clearance.

Loan Administration: You'd think that loan underwriting is a fairly straightforward process: make the credit decision, fund the loan, book an amortization schedule and mail payment reminders, right? Well, knowing when interest counts as revenue, keeping track of interest earned, knowing what a payoff amount is, and all of the accounting entries that go with it is a very complicated process. Flexibility is key: the system has to be capable of almost every possible iteration of payment structure, fee schedule, and interest calculation. After all, community banking is all about customizing to meet the client's needs, right?

Security and Compliance: Banks are highly regulated, compliance-oriented businesses. The security and compliance are both critical and expensive.

Let's Get On With The Business of Banking!

I could go on (please!), but the point is this: selecting the right partnerships—with technology, consultants, professional organizations, and employees—are among the most important elements in launching a successful bank—or any other sophisticated enterprise, for that matter. And once you've selected the partnerships, *negotiating* the contracts is a must. One can do a great job with partner selection and yet lose the war with a poorly negotiated series of contracts.

In researching this book, I combed through an enormous amount of reference material about banking, bank start-ups, bank failures, and the astonishing range of analysis and opinion that has peppered the media—especially over the past five years. Prominent articles that launched phrases like "The Chernobyl of Banking" feel like landmarks along the evolutionary time line of the past few years. Looking back on it now from the so-called "recovery" of early 2013 makes me want to record certain parts for posterity...and permanently hit the delete key regarding certain others. One thing for sure: it was exhilarating to be a part of the process. It is *always* a privilege to be asked to become part of something significant; to be entrusted with the confidence of accomplished folks who judge you capable of getting the job done. I am grateful and proud that we did indeed get the job done.

Bill and I did a flying chest bump (much to the surprise of our Controller, Kellie Pressnall) on January 28, 2008—the day we opened Touchmark National Bank. We took photos of the ribbon cutting and invited the media. I remain undecided as to whether that chest bump would have made for a good photo...but it sure felt good!

Brian Schmidt, CEO of The Private Bank of Atlanta, once told me that "banking is a game played by piling up nickels and dimes. You've got to pile them awfully high in order to make money—and it takes a steady hand to keep them from falling over." It's an apt analogy. Banking is about scale; it's about leveraging money loaned against money borrowed. It's a balancing act of cost, effort, and opportunity, and it's a game of partnerships. We were one of the very last banks to open in the 1997–2007 cycle, and I'm more grateful for that moment now than I ever could have been at the time.

Our OCC charter and FDIC insurance certificates had been delivered. The regulators had "not opposed." We'd selected a host of vendors—as well as a team of fantastic employees. As improbable as it seems in hindsight, Team Touchmark had raised the money, approved the plan, assuaged the regulatory authorities and assembled the workforce.

It was time to open the bank.

Chapter 4

Running (Up) the Bank

"Nothing in the world can take the place of persistence. Talent will not; nothing is more common than unsuccessful men with talent. Genius will not; unrewarded genius is almost a proverb. Education will not; the world is full of educated derelicts. Persistence and determination alone are omnipotent."

Calvin Coolidge

"Alice laughed: 'There's no use trying,' she said; 'one can't believe impossible things.' 'I daresay you haven't had much practice,' said the Queen. 'When I was younger, I always did it for half an hour a day. Why, sometimes I've believed as many as six impossible things before breakfast.'"

Alice in Wonderland

UNITED STATES SECURITIES AND EXCHANGE COMMISSION

WASHINGTON, D.C. 20549

FORM 10-K
ANNUAL REPORT UNDER SECTION 13 OR 15(D) OF THE SECURITIES EXCHANGE ACT OF 1934

For the fiscal year ended December 31, 2007

TOUCHMARK BANCSHARES, INC.

(Exact name of registrant as specified in its charter)

Georgia	20-8746061
(State or other jurisdiction of incorporation or organization)	(I.R.S. Employer Identification No.)

3740 Davinci Court, Suite 150
Norcross, Georgia 30092
(Address of principal executive offices)

Commencement of Banking Operations. Touchmark National Bank, which began banking operations on January 28, 2008, will depend on net interest income for its primary source of earnings. Net interest income is the difference between the interest we charge on our loans and receive from our investments, our assets, and the interest we pay on deposits, our liabilities. Movements in interest rates will cause our earnings to fluctuate. To lessen the impact of these margin swings, we intend to structure our balance sheet so that we can reprice the rates applicable to our assets and liabilities in roughly equal amounts at approximately the same time. We will manage the bank's asset mix by regularly evaluating the yield, credit quality, funding sources, and liquidity of its assets. We will manage the bank's liability mix by expanding our deposit base and converting assets to cash as necessary. If there is an imbalance in our ability to reprice assets and liabilities at any point in time, our earnings may increase or decrease with changes in the interest rate, creating interest rate sensitivity. Interest rates have historically varied widely, and we cannot control or predict them. Despite the measures we plan to take to lessen the impact of interest rate fluctuations, large moves in interest rates may negatively impact our profitability.

Excerpt from the Touchmark Bancshares, Inc. 10-K report for the year ended December 31, 2007

As of March 20, 2010, there were 3,465,391 shares of common stock outstanding held by approximately 560 shareholders of record. All of our outstanding common stock was issued in connection with our initial public offering, which was completed on March 31, 2008. The price per share in our initial public offering was $10.

Excerpt from the Touchmark Bancshares, Inc. 10-Q report for the quarter ended March 31, 2010

The Original "Fiscal Cliff"

We cut a ribbon, we took some photos, opened accounts for employees and directors and set about the business of running our new banking company.

One more time: recall how banks generate revenue:

"Banking operations...will depend on net interest income for (its) primary source of earnings. Net interest income is the difference between the interest we charge on our loans and receive from our investments, our assets, and the interest we pay on deposits, our liabilities. Movements in interest rates will cause our earnings to fluctuate."

Below, courtesy of FedPrimeRate.com, is an insightful graph that displays primary interest rate trends between December 1999 and August 2012.

Chart 19

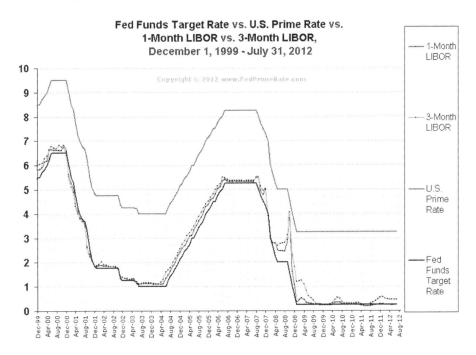

Alan Greenspan's Federal Reserve began raising interest rates in the fall of 2004 in order to dampen inflationary trends in the economy. Rising rates are generally good for bankers because, like gas stations, bankers are quick to bump up prices to stay ahead of rising costs. On the other hand, bankers try to lag price reductions when rates are falling to support their margins. Falling interest rates generally indicate a lower demand for lending, and smart bankers will prepare for softer business conditions. So by the fall of 2006 when the Fed had finished raising rates (represented by the plateau in the center of the graph), bankers were recording good margins as the economy adjusted to a higher rate landscape.

Had you been looking out over Atlanta in June 2006 from atop the majestic Prime Rate Plateau, you might have spotted the Formosa Rose organizers somewhere in Gwinnett County as they laid plans for a new banking enterprise. Were you to stroll through time across the level plain of 8.25% prime rate history into January 2007, you could have spotted Bill and I at the Houston's restaurant in Buckhead as we discussed working together in a new banking venture. Amble on further and you could watch as our management team labored over growth forecasts and hired employees ahead of launching our new bank. Finally, by peering over the September 2007 ledge of that 8.25% precipice, you could watch as the first of our 2,357 prospectuses was dropped into the US mail. Careful—don't take another step. The fall could kill you. You're standing on the *original* fiscal cliff.

During the course of our stock offering—between September 2007 and March 2008—the Open Market Committee of the Federal Reserve lowered the prime rate six times in rapid succession. *Six.* [1]

- Between the date that our prospecti first hit the mail and the date that we ultimately reached our minimum required raise, the prime rate was lowered three times, from 8.25 percent to 7.75 percent.
- From the date that we reached our minimum capital raise and the date that we opened for business, the OMC reduced the prime rate twice again, from 7.25 percent to 6.50 percent.
- Two days after we opened for business, the OMC lowered the rate one more time, from 6.50 percent to 6.00 percent.

And they didn't stop just because we'd opened our doors: by the end of December 2008, the prime rate came to rest at 3.25 percent—the same level it holds at the time this book was finalized for publication in 2013. For lending institutions, sliding down that precipice was nothing short of brutal. Here's the best analogy I can offer for the situation: cars can run on gasoline purchased at $3.99 per gallon just as well as they can on gas purchased at $2.50 per gallon. But when gas prices are falling, it's because there's less overall demand in the economy for fuel. The Federal Reserve lowers key borrowing rates to try and make funding cheaper when the demand for borrowing falls...which means that borrowers have less need for the fuel that the bankers are selling. Those familiar with the financial straits of 2008 will recall that the Fed released vast sums into the money supply and made extraordinary commitments during this time as worries over funding sources brought inter-bank lending to a standstill. It was a morbidly fascinating time to be a student of the markets.

That long flat line at the base of the December 2008 cliff is sadly symbolic of the ensuing cardiac arrest that befell the American economy. Oh, and those dotted graph lines below the prime rate? Those are Fed funds and LIBOR benchmarks also crashing to historic lows.

I see a hand waving in the back of the room. "I thought you just wrote that banks delay rate reductions in order to maintain margins? Then shouldn't these rate reductions have been good for banks? If the gas stations lower its prices and continue to sell gas, then why don't banks do the same?"

The answer, dear reader, is that when *movements in interest rates tend to fluctuate* downward, it means that economic activity is falling...and that *credit quality* is getting weaker as well:

> Weak business activity = lower income (or losses) = declining credit quality

When bankers face pressure to reduce loan rates (i.e., offer lower prices to their borrowing customers), banks in turn move to reduce the rates they're willing to pay for deposits (i.e., they seek price reductions from their suppliers). Depositors don't like that (i.e., they don't like that) and those depositors—who are *also* customers of the bank—begin to shop around for the best prices they can find on CDs, money markets, and checking accounts.

The result: when interest rates fall, depositors become harder to please...and borrowers get harder to qualify. Banks that were making loans or buying government bonds *before* interest rates went into free fall benefitted from higher revenue in comparison to banks that booked most of their assets when interest rates were lower...but both banks have to contend with customers who are less capable of paying them back! Such was the welcome that we received from the US economy when we opened for business in January 2008.

Here is the explanation I offered my directors in late 2009; email provided courtesy of a former Touchmark director:

From: Bob Koncerak
Sent: Monday, November 23, 2009 10:36 AM
Subject: ALCO follow-up: Touchmark 9-09 yield comparisons to Atlanta area peers

ALCO members,

Per discussion during our meeting last week, below are open dates of a few of our peer metro Atlanta institutions:

9/2012 Net Interest Income/ Average Earning Assets

Keyworth Bank – opened October 2007   3.36%

Touchmark – opened January 2008   3.02%

Resurgens Bank – opened June 2008   2.27%

In comparing the opening dates, remember that "timing is everything." One reason Touchmark asset yields don't compare favorably to peers is the dramatic decline in interest rates that began late in 2007 and continued through 2008 when we opened. The prime rate was at 8.25 percent between June 2006 and September 2007. The first of several drastic prime rate reductions began on September 17, 2007, when prime was reduced from 8.25 percent to 7.75 percent. As you know, prime is the most common index for our loan rates. Prime was at 6.00 percent when Touchmark opened in late January...and ended the year with a reduction to 3.25 percent in December 2008.

Oh, to have those 2007 loan and investment yields today!

Similarly, Fed Funds was at 6.25% from June 2006 until August 2007. Fed Funds relates to our cash and short-term investments. In September 2007, Fed Funds was reduced to 5.25%. The rate was at 3.50% when we opened, and it ended 2008 at 0.50%.

Chart 20

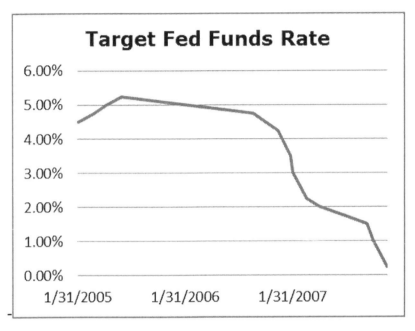

That being noted, it also seems reasonable that Touchmark should have a lower cost of funds than its combined peers…and indeed we do—even including peers that opened in 2008.

I am available to discuss further at your interest.

RDK

A Unique Path

If you were a brand-new banking company that opened for business in January 2008, at first you *wouldn't have* any customer deposits on your balance sheet. You would only have capital. In

Touchmark's case… $34,653,910 of capital. And in *that* case (as I recall), you would stand by and watch as the plans that you'd so carefully laid for deploying that capital became pretty much worthless.

One of the things that de novo bankers focus on ahead of opening day is building a "pipeline" of loan opportunities. The strategy is to line up borrowers (either new deals or poached relationships from competitors) and then fund them in the bank in order to kick-start earnings as soon as the bank receives its charter. As you might imagine…there wasn't much of a pipeline to be garnered in the months leading up to January 2008.

But if you were looking for a silver lining amongst all of those nasty storm clouds, there was this:

Chart 21

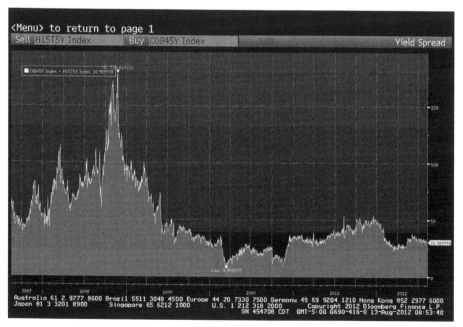

Source: Bloomberg

To the uninitiated, the Bloomberg chart above may look like a crazy blood pressure reading that spikes up and then settles back down. Well, in 2008, no doubt there *were* a lot of blood pressure readings that looked this was—so that wouldn't be a bad guess! To a bond trader, though, Chart 21 is an iconic pattern that both created and destroyed fortunes. For those in the bond business, the screen shot above elicits something between a tear of joy and a nauseating shudder. My respects in either case.

The graph displays the difference in yields (the spread) between US treasury and agency debt beginning in January 2007. Treasury debts are "full faith and credit" IOUs of the United States government. Agency debt—such as bonds issued by the Federal Housing Mortgage Corporation (Fannie Mae), Freddie Mac, and others—carry an *implicit* or *assumed* backing of Uncle Sam. That assumption of an *implicit* guarantee was being tested like never before in the spring of 2008.

The chart peaks on March 17, 2008. That's when the difference between the yields on treasury and agency debt reached its widest point. Global investors were flocking to purchase full faith and credit US instruments. An implied guarantee just wouldn't do. This pushed up the price on US treasury bonds and other explicitly guaranteed debt dramatically in relation to agency instruments. If you owned US government agency bonds in March 2008 and had to replace them with US treasuries because of fear, policy or liquidity tolerance (Bear Stearns was failing and the global markets were coming unglued), then you would have been forced to sell at as much as a 15% loss simply to swap to a "full faith and credit" government bond. That is a *big* principal hit in the bond world.

Bond prices and yields move in opposite directions: a 10-year Treasury bond purchased at par (full price) declines in price by 8.7% if interest rates rise by 1%. The bond loses 16.5% of its value if rates rise by 2% and by a whopping 23.6% if rates rise by 3%. Ouch! Of course…there is a similar price improvement when rates or spreads move in your favor ☺.

Here's another iconic screen shot from back in the day:

Chart 22

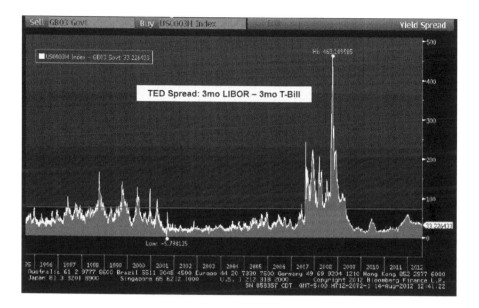

This chart displays a version of the much-followed TED spread, which measures the difference between ten-year and three-month US treasury debts. Those huge spikes beginning in 2007 display what happened to the rate that banks had to pay in order to borrow short-term ("overnight") funds to balance their books—if they could *find* an institution willing to lend them any money. It was a perilous time to be short on funds in the financial markets.

Impossible Things Before Breakfast

But here's the upshot: the panic that hit the US government debt markets in early 2008 had pretty much run its course by year's end. If you were a brand new bank looking for someplace to invest shareholder capital in early 2008, then so long as you had the stomach to invest in anything other than "full faith and credit" obligations, you were poised to earn a handsome return for your shareholders. As a former capital markets manager, for me it was as though the angels had come down from heaven and served up a $34.5 million opportunity on a plate. With the (edgy) backing of the bank's investment committee, Touchmark would become a significant buyer of investment-grade agency securities throughout the first several quarters of its history. Investment income and securities gains would subsequently provide more than half of Touchmark's gross revenue throughout its first two years of operation. Touchmark's bond portfolio as a percentage of assets was among the highest of any bank in the country at that time—and it is not an overstatement to contend that Touchmark is still in business because of it. The rich yield provided by the bond portfolio fed the bank through a terribly challenging period—with not a single dollar of defaulted loss. To this day, I am grateful for the trust and backing of Touchmark directors who supported me in acquiring the agency bonds, then corporate bonds, mortgage-backed securities and municipal issues that led ultimately to the bank's first profitable quarter in March 2010. My appreciation extends as well to our outside accountants and controller, Kellie Pressnall, who soldiered through all of the accounting and paperwork to keep track of my frequent buys and sells throughout this period. While we weren't "trading" bonds per se (which would be inappropriate for a new bank like Touchmark), we did have to change *strategy* often, which led to an extraordinary level of profitable turnover in the portfolio.

A bond, after all, is really a loan; it's a loan to a government or an agency or a company. Banks hold bonds for a variety of reasons. From 2008–2010, Touchmark held bonds because (in my opinion) that asset class was the single *best* use of our shareholders funds during the *worst* possible phase of the financial crisis. And the real kicker: *bonds don't require loss reserves the way that loans do.*

You see, before a bank makes a loan, that loan is given a risk grade. Depending upon the level of risk, a percentage of that loan is held in reserve against possible future losses. In that way, the bank establishes a cushion or an allowance for loan losses (ALLL) as it builds out a portfolio of loans. The lower the credit grade, the larger the provision expense for the loan. On a routine basis, the credit quality of the entire loan portfolio is evaluated, and the ALLL is adjusted accordingly. Because of this, funding a growing loan portfolio requires charges to the income statement to fund the loan loss reserve. However, *no such reserve is required when purchasing investment grade securities.*

Chart 23

Touchmark National Bank: Selected Annual Revenue Measures				
		2009		**2008**
Loan Interest Income		2,629,558		698,745
Gains on Sale of Loans		235,799		
Total Loan Revenue	$	**2,865,357**	$	**698,745**
Provision Expense		(2,243,898)		(401,890)
Loan Revenue less Provision	$	**621,459**	$	**296,855**
Securities Interest Income		1,844,648		1,344,249
Gains on Sale of Securities		1,217,825		96,979
Total Securities Revenue	$	**3,062,473**	$	**1,441,228**
Total Annual Revenue	$	**5,915,076**	$	**2,278,369**
Loan Revenue before Provision/Total Rev		48%		31%
Loan Revenue net of provision/Total Rev		11%		13%
Securities Revenue/Total Rev		52%		63%
Securities Revenue/Total Rev - Provision:		83%		77%

Source: Edgar/SEC

That's because bonds are transacted and valued at a "fair market price" between willing buyers and sellers. If a bond is purchased at less than 100 percent of face value, it is said to have been bought at a discount. At more than 100 percent, it's bought at a premium. Because the bond market is constantly evaluating (pricing) the credit quality of bond issuers, no allowance is needed in order to establish the risk level of that bond—the market does it for you by way of price. Market changes in the price of the bond are updated monthly on a bank's balance sheet. As noted in the table above, the securities portfolio provided 77 percent and 83 percent of Touchmark's 2008 and 2009 revenue after accounting for provision expense against the loan portfolio. I am both grateful and proud for those results.

2009 was a rough year for lenders—as well as for the credit quality of bond issuers. Touchmark incurred loan provision expense amounting $402 thousand in 2008 and $2.2 million in 2009 to cover losses and provide for loan growth on a $70 million portfolio (gross outstanding loans at December 2009). That's a lot of reserves. In contrast, the investment portfolio ended 2008 at $27.5 million and grew to $47.9 million by the end of 2009 with nary a nickel of provision expense. In ordinary times, banks expect to make much better returns on the loan portfolio than on the bond portfolio. But these were not ordinary times.

A Bond Junkie Illustration

With apologies to the non-junkie reader, allow me to relay a trade illustration for the bond enthusiasts among us:

Conditions in the fall of 2008 were so extraordinary that Touchmark was hitting home runs with single trades the likes of which aren't supposed to be possible in the markets. We managed to execute several transactions that *simultaneously*:

1. Provided a gain (we sold a bond at a higher price than we had bought it)

5. Increased yield (bought into a higher yield than we had sold)

6. Reduced risk (moved from a higher into a lower risk-weighted security), *and*

7. Reduced duration (a measure of volatility in the portfolio)

For example, in late 2008 we were holding longer maturity agency bonds (FNMA) and decided to shorten maturities. In doing so, we traded into full faith and credit GNMA bonds. The longer bonds had increased in price, and because we'd purchased them in March, spreads had "come in," so the comparative yields on the bonds we were buying were effectively higher than those we were selling, the risk weighting of exchange went from 20% to zero (FNMA to GNMA)...and shorter maturities provided a lower duration. *Ta da!* In spite of the remarkable profits, I'd prefer not to live through market conditions like that ever again.

Bond-junkie illustration complete.

An acknowledgement: the idea for the *Alice in Wonderland* quote at the top of this chapter comes from John Mauldin's 2010 book titled *End Game*. It was too good an idea not to repeat (read: steal). For those interested in reading more about the macro forces that led to the 2008 crisis—as well as some excellent thoughts on what lies ahead for the global economy, I highly recommend the read. Mauldin is an accomplished author and analyst.

Forecasting in the Storm

The forecasts I had built for Touchmark National Bank estimated that we could reach a profitable level of operations at around $150 million of earning assets. A 4 percent margin on $150 million amounts to $6 million of revenue, and that's what I figured would be required to show a sustainable profit with the three full-service branches and the twenty-five employees. Our estimated ramp-up time was twenty four months. Growing to a profitable size would require steady success in funding our loan and investment port-folios—with funds provided, of course, by our new depositors.[2]

As a bank builds its loan portfolio, the revenue covers salaries, tech-nology, and other expenses—until eventually the operation reaches a level of profitability (absent loan and investment losses!). That first month of sustainable profit is obviously a cause for celebration. At that point, the bank will have funded sufficient earning assets such that the revenue earned is greater than supporting expenses. Suc-cessive months of profitability enable the new bank to recoup its start-up expenses until the business becomes "cumulatively profit-able"—the point at which all start-up costs have been recovered. (For you accounting types, this is where "retained earnings" becomes a positive number.) Once a management team has opened for business and earned back all of its start-up expenses, it can *truly* brag that the enterprise has been a successful venture. Beyond that point, the book value of issued stock exceeds the initial price of the shares (at least on paper!)—and the ongoing profits increase shareholder value. As the bank grows beyond cumulative profitability, it can use its profits to pay dividends to shareholders, acquire new locations or begin other initiatives that suit its strategic interests. All of this activity is con-ducted in an atmosphere of regulatory monitoring and examination.

By the time it opened for business, Touchmark National Bank and its holding company, Touchmark Bancshares, Inc., were under the regulatory auspices of no fewer than five governing authorities: the Federal Reserve because we had a holding company, the Securities and Exchange Commission (SEC) because TMAK was a public reporting company, the Office of the Comptroller of the Currency (OCC) because we were a national bank, the Federal Deposit Insurance Commission (FDIC) because our deposits were insured, and the Georgia Department of Banking because we operated within the state's jurisdiction.

In the eyes of the SEC, the only difference between the stock of TMAK (our stock symbol) and that of the Bank of America was that BAC is traded on the New York Stock Exchange...and TMAK is not (it is traded Over The Counter—or OTC).

The Organized Versus the Disorganized
The FDIC Stops Returning Phone Calls

We had managed to open for business, deploy our capital, and—despite a rocky credit environment—began to generate returns for our shareholders. Our outcome was far better than the way things turned out for several of our de novo organizing brethren...

When Touchmark received its charter in January 2008, I recall that we didn't so much breathe a sigh of relief as we expressed irritation at the challenge it had been to reach our minimum capital goal. It was only much later that we came to appreciate just how lucky we'd been in the process. Our group had little grasp at the time for the gravity of the implosion that would, in short order, fell a historic number of Georgia banks, nor did we have reason to suspect that the country was on the verge of a historic recession. Surely the *Atlanta Business Chronicle* articles thus far provide helpful context for the disparity among bankers in understanding larger economic trends. The Touchmark management team could not have appreciated at the time that we had received our charter on the tail end of a remarkable cycle—especially in the metro Atlanta region—and that only a few more banks would actually open in Georgia and across the US before the door slammed and new charter issuance would fall to zero in coming years.

Despite the darkening economic picture in 2008—and the dramatic headlines of the previous year—the Touchmark organizers were not alone in pursuing a de novo banking charter in late 2007. In fact, there were more de novo applications on the Georgia Department of Banking's 2007 pipeline report than there had been in 2006. No fewer than twenty-six organizing groups appeared on the DOBF's October 2007 New Financial Institutions Report. Fifteen of those groups were headquartered in Atlanta metro counties. Because Touchmark pursued a national (OCC) charter, it wasn't listed among the state banking candidates below. Including Touchmark, the total October 2007 pipeline count was twenty-seven.

Chart 24

New Financial Institutions Applications Report*

APPLICANT NAME	CITY	COUNTY	RECEIVED	ACCEPTED	ACTION DATE	ACTION TYPE	BEGIN BUS	CAPITALIZATION
Milton Banking Company	Lakeland	Lanier	8/15/2007	9/28/2007	Pending			10,000,000
Resurgens Bank	Atlanta	KeKalb	7/27/2007	8/22/2007	Pending			12,250,000
Independence Bank of Georgia	Braselton	Barrow	7/16/2007	8/8/2007	Pending			18,000,000
Verity Bank	Winder	Barrow	6/1/2007	6/29/2007	10/3/2007	Approved		15,700,000
First Landmark Bank	Marietta	Cobb	5/24/2007	6/11/2007	8/23/2007	Approved		20,000,000
First Milton Bank	Milton	Fulton	5/11/2007	7/12/2007	Pending			16,250,000
LaGrange Banking Company	LaGrange	Troup	4/27/2007	5/14/2007	8/6/2007	Approved		12,500,000
Metro Bank	Douglasville	Douglas	4/5/2007	5/23/2007	9/18/2007	Approved		20,000,000
NOA Bank	Duluth	Gwinnett	3/29/2007	4/26/2007	Pending			15,000,000
Security Bank of the Coast	Brunswick	Glynn	3/7/2007	3/15/2007	5/18/2007	Approved		14,000,000
Community Business Bank	Cumming	Forsyth	2/22/2007	3/9/2007	6/5/2007	Approved		15,000,000
Keyworth Bank	Duluth	Fulton	2/13/2007	3/12/2007	5/22/2007	Approved	10/15/2007	36,000,000
Landmark Bank of Savannah	Savannah	Chatham	2/9/2007	5/3/2007	9/7/2007	Withdrawn		20,000,000
State Bank of Georgia	Fayetteville	Fayette	1/23/2007	2/12/2007	4/25/2007	Approved		12,500,000
Regional Bank of Middle Georgia	Macon	Bibb	1/17/2007	2/8/2007	Pending			8,000,000
American Pride Bank	Macon	Bibb	12/22/2006	1/23/2007	6/8/2007	Approved		12,500,000
First Choice Community Bank	Dallas	Paulding	10/17/2006	11/7/2007	1/11/2007	Approved	4/9/2007	18,000,000
Vinings Bank	Smyrna	Cobb	10/10/2006	10/24/2006	1/26/2007	Approved	7/9/2007	16,334,000
Georgia Primary Bank	Atlanta	Fulton	9/29/2006	11/15/2006	2/27/2007	Approved	10/22/2007	18,045,060
Atlantic Capital Bank	Atlanta	Fulton	8/11/2006	9/12/2006	1/2/2007	Approved	5/15/2007	119,314,004
Brookhaven Bank	Atlanta	DeKalb	7/3/2006	7/18/2006	12/11/2006	Approved	8/14/2007	23,407,958
Gold Hills Bank	Dahlonega	Lumpkin	6/15/2006	9/11/2006	10/27/2006	Withdrawn		10,000,000
First Citizens Bank of Georgia	Dawsonville	Dawson	5/22/2006	6/15/2006	9/15/2006	Approved	3/5/2007	12,400,000
Private Bank of Buckhead	Atlanta	Fulton	3/15/2006	3/30/2006	8/8/2006	Approved	12/11/2006	12,500,000
Republic Bank of Georgia	Suwannee	Gwinnett	2/27/2006	3/6/2006	7/28/2006	Approved	11/6/2006	24,000,000
Westside Bank	Hiram	Paulding	1/17/2006	2/8/2006	5/22/2006	Approved	8/8/2006	12,979,000

If you have questions about the information provided in this report, please send an e-mail to dbf@dbf.state.ga.us

*In descending order, using application receipt date (history back to 2006).

New Financial Institution Applications Received	
Applications Received	
FY 2006	11
YTD 2007	15

10/24/2007, page 1

Source: Georgia Department of Banking and Finance, October 2007

Several Atlanta-area groups that were still "in organization" reached out to Touchmark in various stages of desperation throughout the first half of 2008. Their management teams were in search of contacts and suggestions that might help them get final approval from the FDIC. In sensing the alarm in their voices, one could have believed that the FDIC had gone on vacation for the 2007 Christmas holiday...and never came back to the office. We met with several groups that were casting about for options to "get open" at the time—among them Monty Watson of The Piedmont Bank group, which ultimately invested in/acquired the troubled Republic Bank. Others, like Perimeter First, wanted urgently to partner with a de novo like Touchmark in order to avoid liquidation and reimbursement of organizing expenses to nervous investors. It was a tragic time for several groups that were caught between escrow and an FDIC approval.

January 19, 2009

FDIC turns down new Perimeter First Bank

Atlanta Business Chronicle by Joe Rauch, Staff Writer

Former NetBank CEO D.R. Grimes' latest bank venture has collapsed after bank regulators declined to approve the group for deposit insurance.

Alpharetta-based Perimeter First Bank, which has been organizing for more than a year, has shut its doors this month and begun returning $20.5 million from its initial stockholder offering to shareholders.

The bank had an internal deadline of Dec. 31 to conclude its initial stock offering and open for business, pending Federal Deposit Insurance Corp. approval to open.

Perimeter First is the first Georgia bank in years that failed to receive FDIC approval, according to industry consultants.

Perimeter First's failure to receive deposit insurance approval highlights the tougher standards, which some are calling an informal ban on new banks, enacted by the FDIC, amid the worst economic crisis since World War II.

As first reported in Atlanta Business Chronicle on Dec. 12, the FDIC has imposed strict provisions for approving deposit insurance to new banks, particularly those in the weakest U.S. banking markets, including metro Atlanta.

Under the bank chartering process, deposit insurance is required before any institution can open.

But it may also be shedding new light on the deposit insurers' approach during the ongoing downturn.

Grimes said in the last eight months of the organizing group's push to receive approval, it had no FDIC contact.

The group never received a formal denial from the FDIC, Grimes said.

"They never wrote to us after May 3, [2008]," Grimes said. "We never heard anything."

Instead, Grimes said he believes the FDIC did not want to approve the bank's application, but did not want to deny it either because it met all the outstanding criteria.

"The easiest decision is to not make one," Grimes said. "They asked if we had a manager or director with experience in the S&L Crisis. Our bank chairman is the former CEO of the Federal Home Bank of Atlanta. We did everything they asked of us."

David Barr, FDIC spokesman, declined to comment on Perimeter First's application, citing a standing policy that prohibits discussions about particular applicants.

Barr said the regulator communicates regularly with applicants, and any new bank must meet standard criteria.

Last year, proportionally fewer bank applicants received deposit insurance than the previous two years.

In 2008, the FDIC received 150 applications, approving 97 — a 64 percent approval rate. Those figures are lower than 2007, with 235 applicants and 186 approvals for a 79 percent rate, and 2006, when 180 were approved from 225 applicants, an 80 percent clip.

Grimes said, despite speculation, his bank's failure to receive deposit insurance approval did not stem from its headquarters being in the same Atlanta suburb some national media have dubbed the epicenter of U.S. bank failures, or Grimes' ties to one of those failed institutions.

Grimes' odyssey to start a new bank began two years ago, he said, meeting with FDIC examiners and other regulators to ensure the recent failure of his previous institution — Alpharetta-based NetBank in fall 2007 — would not influence their decision to approve his new venture.

Grimes said after the Alpha Bank & Trust and Integrity Bank failures last year, he offered to move the bank's headquarters to Roswell or Buckhead.

The bank organizing group will absorb roughly $2 million in startup costs as part of the failed venture.

April 27, 2009
Bank group shuts down after FDIC rejection
Atlanta Business Chronicle by Joe Rauch

Trident Bancshares has halted capital-raising efforts to open a new bank in Dunwoody after failing to receive deposit insurance approval from the Federal Deposit Insurance Corp.

The bank holding company is the latest in a series of local organizing groups to scuttle plans for new banks because the FDIC, according to bank organizers and industry insiders, is not approving new banks' deposit insurance.

***

The holding company's filing doesn't explicitly mention a failure to receive insurance approval, but a source familiar with the company said it could not get a green light from the FDIC.

Trident Bancshares received preliminary approval from the Office of the Comptroller of the Currency on Sept. 10, 2008.

At Trident Bancshares, the filing ends a yearlong pursuit of a charter to do business locally.

The bank would have been led by well-known Asian community bank executive Pin Pin Chau, and would have focused its business within a five-mile radius of its Dunwoody headquarters, according to the bank's last amendment to its initial offering filed Dec. 23, 2008, with the SEC.

Trident Bancshares' April 15 filing indicates the holding company had not sold any securities as part of the initial capital offering, but was attempting to raise at least $19 million from prospective investors to capitalize the institution.

***

The number of banks in the state shrunk from 352 to 334 from Dec. 31, 2007, to Dec. 31, 2008, according to FDIC data.

July 13, 2009
CAPITAL DEAL
Atlanta Business Chronicle by Joe Rauch, Staff Writer

The Piedmont Bank investor group has completed its capital injection and buyout of Republic Bank.

The group, led by former community bank CEO Monty Watson, added $16 million in capital to the two-branch bank in Suwanee and Lawrenceville after it failed to find deposit insurance approval for a new bank in the north metro.

Watson's most recent venture was Peachtree Bank, which sold to Alabama National Bancorp. in 2006.

Watson's investor team had previously attempted to buy the charter from Newnan-based First Choice Community Bank for $6 million last fall, but that deal fell through. Republic's name change became effective June 30.

I've come to know several organizing executives who were caught without a chair when the music stopped in the latter months of 2008. Some, like PinPin Chau, were involved with groups that were able to disband without having to reimburse investors. Monty Watson was able to switch strategies and garner support from his investors to take control of Republic Bank. Outcomes like that of D.R. Grimes, however, are brutal reminders that banking is ultimately a regulated industry. The experience of these groups certainly justifies the (reasonable) issuance of organizer warrants and the leverage that successful launches accomplish for those who put their fortunes at risk. Indeed in 2008, there seemed to be nearly as many risks associated with *not* getting a de novo chartered as there were in actually launching a banking business.

Footnotes:

Chart 25

[1] **Chart of Major Federal Reserve Policy Actions**

Table 2: Major Federal Reserve Policy Actions 9 August 2007 to 18 March 2008	
August 9	Increase in the level of temporary open market operations
August 10	FOMC statement
August 17	Cut in primary lending rate from 100 to 50 basis points above the federal funds rate target; an increase in the term of discount lending from overnight to a maximum of 30 days; and release of FOMC policy announcement
September 18	50 basis point cut in target federal funds rate at regular FOMC meeting

October 31	25 basis point cut in target federal funds rate at regular FOMC meeting
December 11	25 basis point cut in target federal funds rate at regular FOMC meeting
December 12	Announced creation of the Term Auction Facility (TAF) and the swap lines with the European Central Bank and the Swiss National Bank of $20 billion and $4 billion, respectively.
December 17	First TAF auction: $20 billion, 98 bidders
January 21	75 basis point cut in target federal funds rate at an unscheduled meeting, and cut in the discount rate
January 30	50 basis point cut in target federal funds rate at regular FOMC meeting, and cut in the discount rate
March 2	Announced intention to conduct 28-day repos cumulating to $100 billion
March 7	Announced an increase in the size of the TAF from $60 billion to $100 billion outstanding at any given time.
March 11	Announced creation of Term Securities Lending Facility and the intention to lend $200 billion worth of Treasury Securities to Primary Dealers. Increase in the swap lines with the European Central Bank and the Swiss National Bank to $30 billion and $6 billion, respectively.
March 14	Announced approval of loan to Bear Stearns through JPMorgan Chase
March 16	Announced creation of Primary Dealer Credit Facility (PDCF) 25 basis point cut in the discount rate to 3¼ percent; an increase in the maximum term of discount lending from 30 to 90 days; announced approval of $30 billion loan to JPMorgan Chase for the purposes of purchasing Bear Stearns.
March 18	75 basis point cut in target federal funds rate at regular FOMC meeting, and cut in the discount rate

Source: Board of Governors of the Federal Reserve System and Federal Reserve Bank of New York, various press releases.

Source: Monetary Policy and the Financial Crisis of 2007-2008
by Stephen G. Cecchetti

[2] Growth of the loan portfolio wasn't without its challenges. The goal of reaching $150 million of earning assets was compounded by several nonperforming loans and eventually significant write-offs by the fourth quarter of 2010. The bank accumulated several past due and nonperforming loans that became a drag on earnings in the latter half of 2009 and throughout 2010.

From Touchmark's 2010 10K filed on March 31, 2011:

The Bank has charged off loans amounting to $4,294,130 since commencing operations. Impaired loans at December 31, 2010 amounted to $8,176,314. This balance is comprised of 7 loans concentrated in 4 borrowing relationships. Impaired loans at December 31, 2009, amounted to $5,897,235. This balance was comprised of 4 loans concentrated in 2 borrowing relationships. In addition, we purchased several performing and non-performing loans at a significant discount during the fourth quarter of 2009 with intent to resell. The carrying value of these loans amounted to $518,995 and $1,832,412 at December 31, 2010 and 2009, respectively. Nonaccrual loans totaled $8,176,314 and $5,897,235 at December 31, 2010 and 2009, respectively. Accrued and unpaid interest on these loans represents $626,333 and $271,187 at December 31, 2010 and 2009, respectively. Other than the aforementioned non-accrual and non-performing loans, there were no loans contractually past due 90 days or more as to principal or interest payments, and no loans classified as troubled debt restructurings at either December 31, 2010 or 2009.

Chapter 5

Regulation, Controls and the 'Chernobyl' of Banking

I've had a perfectly wonderful evening. But this wasn't it.

Groucho Marx

Mortgage Crisis as Beer Party

An abiding theme of the 2007 downturn has been a hunt for the ruinous villain that started it all: a pathetic creature on whom we can roundly heap derision as the agent of our collective misfortune. After all, if we could identify a culprit, then perhaps we could isolate and fix the problem, right? Maybe at least bring a cad to justice?

As SpongeBob SquarePants, that sage of the obvious has oft been heard to say: "*good luck with that*".

The analogy of an underage drinking party offers a novel characterization of the 2008 mortgage banking crisis. While the comparison may seem a bit worn, certain specifics bear reciting. And I apologize in advance for disparaging the blessings of fermentation:

Some enterprising teenagers decide to play host when the parents depart one evening, and a select group of invitations are extended. A cover charge is imposed to recoup expenses, with an eye toward generating a profit in reward for an evening of fun and debauchery. Those invited partake and enjoy. Others along the way hear about the party and want to get in on the fun. They arrive at the door with dollars in their fists. The snacks soon disappear, but there is plenty to drink and the entertainment is grand. As it happens, if so many uninvited guests hadn't shown up, the party might never have gotten out of hand. The ones least welcome show up last, and their misbehavior inevitably causes the most damage. The parents return home and the party ends abruptly—certainly earlier than any of the off-list guests had anticipated. The late arrivers, who paid the same cover charge as A-list guests, understandably feel cheated—but the parents aren't offering a refund. The police show up just behind the parents—because the neighbors had gotten fed up with the noise. The neighbors are relieved that the cops are on the scene, but they are miffed that it took the cops so long to respond. While many of the underage guests get away unscathed, some are cornered and pressed into service to help clean up the mess. Those cornered are indignant and offer up the phone numbers of those who had managed to get away clean (rats!). The hosts (and their parents) are mad at the hoodlums that broke things during the evening—and they do their best to give information to the police in order to track down those who got away.

As it turns out, some of the guests who arrived early got in, had fun, and got out. The early "uninviteds" did OK as well. It was the *later* arrivers who either got caught by the police or managed to flee within an inch of their lives. The hosts have a vague recollection of how much money was collected in a shoe box. Remaining funds, however, aren't nearly enough to cover damages to the parents' home. Everyone who could be identified is eventually pulled back to the scene and pressed to help with the cleanup.

Now, did somebody tip off the hosts' parents about the increasingly raucous festivities...or were they just returning in the normal course of their evening? It doesn't really matter. Everybody at an underage drinking party understands what "over" means!

Will discipline be doled out equally across the offenders? *Well, that depends on who you consider to be an offender:*

- To the teenage hosts, it's the uninvited guests and the party crashers who were at fault.
- To the late arriving guests, the parents and the police were at fault.
- To the police, the parents *and* the teenagers share the blame.
- As far as the neighbors are concerned, the parents, the police, the teenagers and the guests are *all* at fault. They just want to get back to sleep!

And so who's the *victim* here?

- The teenage hosts feel like victims of the uninviteds and the party crashers.
- The guests feel like victims of the parents and the police— *and they want their money back!*
- The neighbors feel like victims of all the above—this subdivision is going to the dogs!

Do I even need to change the names and the story line to explain who feels like a victim in the mortgage crisis? I didn't think so...

Like searching for a villain in a hall of mirrors, the perception of the accuser is distorted by personal perspective. Is it the subprime borrowers who should have known better than to apply for mortgages beyond their means? How about otherwise responsible borrowers who thought they were "trading up" by means of building equity faster in hot markets? Is it the mortgage bankers who found buyers for all of those stilted mortgages? The investors who willingly bought the subprime mortgage bonds? The rating agencies who never anticipated that collateral values could fall on a national scale?

All we know for sure is that the process worked really, really well... until it didn't! "Over" meant *over*... and now regulatory authorities are reacting with a raft of controls in order to ward off such a thing from ever happening again. You can close that barn door now...

On Regularity and Relationships

Much has been written—both opinion and in fact—about the quality and direction of regulatory oversight since the onset of the 2008 financial crisis. The only point I would like to raise on this subject is that "regulators are people, too." While bank regulations are objective and defined, the regulators themselves have individual personalities and tendencies—surprise!—just like the bankers that they regulate. Bankers believe they have a pretty good idea of what success looks like in the banking business... and regulators do, too. Bankers think they have a pretty good understanding of what "risk" looks like...and regulators do, too. Bankers don't like having others point out their deficiencies, they don't like having their pride hurt, and they don't particularly like having their management abilities rated on a scale of one to five. Guess what? Regulators aren't fans of such things, either.

Was there lax regulatory oversight during the years when *success* was taken to *excess*? I think we can all agree that there was—but risks as they were *defined* in 2007 didn't fully incorporate the scope and scale of the 2007 slowdown. Were bankers in general willingly and intentionally reckless with shareholder capital? Of course not. Bone-headed exceptions, of course, can be found on both sides of banker/regulator choreography, but that doesn't mean banking is any more or less prone to bone-headedness than other professional pursuits.

Bankers love to make the case that it's *relationships* that banking work. Well, like it or not, regulatory authorities are *key relationships* in the operation of chartered companies. Regulators are charged to protect the interests of depositors and the integrity of the banking system itself. Regulators and bank examiners aren't paid to put up with insults, they aren't paid to behave like cops in a bad neighborhood and they aren't doing their jobs when give a questionable transaction the benefit of a doubt. Intelligent stakeholders recognize that financial institutions operate within an established regulatory framework. The purpose of regulation, then, is simply to maintain the framework.

As recited in Touchmark's 10-K:

All insured institutions must undergo regular on-site examinations by their appropriate banking agency. The cost of examinations of insured depository institutions and any affiliates may be assessed by the appropriate federal banking agency against each institution or affiliate as it deems necessary or appropriate. Insured institutions are required to submit annual reports to the FDIC, their federal regulatory agency, and state supervisor when applicable. The FDIC has developed a method for insured depository institutions to provide supplemental disclosure of the estimated fair market value of assets and liabilities, to the extent feasible and practicable, in any balance sheet, financial statement, report of condition or any other report of any insured depository institution. The federal banking regulatory agencies prescribe, by regulation, standards for all insured depository institutions and depository institution holding companies relating, among other things, to the following:

- internal controls;
- information systems and audit systems;
- loan documentation;
- credit underwriting;
- interest rate risk exposure; and
- asset quality.

My approach to banking management has always been to welcome regulatory reviews and to assure the examination team at the outset of their visit that my hope is to make their stay *"as boring and uneventful as possible."* Most items covered in the course of an exam are business practices that should already be in place in a well-run shop, anyway. To approach the process any differently only makes for awkward board discussions and uncomfortable exit interviews. In that regard, I respect banking regulators as auditors of the public's trust in my institution.

In the run-up to the 2008 banking crisis, I think it's fair to say that "relationship banking" suffered at the hands of "the next deal." Rather than focus on building lasting relationships one borrower at a time, it was the *next* relationship that became more important in order to maintain impressive growth on the balance sheet. That was not good business...and it is not good banking. That's part of the cycle that none of us bankers should repeat.

Touchmark had plenty of capital—and in the scheme of the banking industry we were a tiny de novo undertaking. Touchmark hadn't been around long enough to make aggressive loans during the real estate boom—so we were left to look on with bewilderment as credit markets deteriorated (though we did manage to take a few lumps of our own!). While regulatory reviews were important, we were always able to steer through them pretty easily because we had a capable system of internal controls.

Everything Is Under Control

Internal controls are the auditable checks that span every phase of a company's operations. Controls are *auditable* because they can be systematically tested to ensure that safeguards and standards are working and effective. The more critical or risky the function, the more controls one might expect to find in place. *The riskiest thing that a bank will ever do is to make a loan.* Because of that, it follows that a bank's credit policy, underwriting guidelines, loan documentation, and computer applications have among the longest lists of controls in the bank. Deposit operations and cash management controls are also critically important. Banks engage with audit firms to ensure that the full scope of controls is systematically tested throughout the course of a year. For public reporting companies, a second layer of audit checks came into being with enactment of Sarbanes-Oxley legislation in 2002. "Sarb-Ox" as it is called, requires public companies to engage separate outside firms to review and test a company's controls one step further...and bear the associated expense. More importantly to me, Sarb-Ox required that, once each quarter, the bank's executive officers (at the time, Bill and me) attest in an SEC filing that our controls were working and effective.

Consider what "effective" means for a moment, and you'll understand why Sarbanes-Oxley has come to be so controversial in the boardrooms of America's public companies: we started Touchmark as a start-up, legacy-free operation. I posted the first journal entries myself. Until we opened to the public, I printed our paychecks and managed the entire accounting functions on my laptop. Because I personally built the balance sheet from scratch, I *knew* where all of the money was going—and so I had no hesitation in attesting to the veracity of the company financial statements.

But imagine, for example, that I was *not* the first CFO of Touchmark National Bank. Imagine instead that I am the *fifth* CFO of Touchmark, and that I start as a newly minted chief financial officer in January 2017...fully ten years after the bank has opened its doors. In our example, Touchmark is now a $500 million bank with two hundred employees and ten branches. So I set about the process of finalizing the bank's 2016 financial performance and begin filling out reports for the Securities and Exchange Commission. As part of my preparation, I review the bank's report on internal controls. Millions of individual transactions have taken place over the past year. How on earth can I have confidence that my internal controls have been effective? The answer has two parts:

Part 1: I can require each department head to confirm that the controls assigned to his or her function in the bank are effective. If the department head doesn't know what I'm talking about, I send him his part of the list, I make a mental note about discussing controls at his next performance review, and I go on to part 2:

Part 2: I dial up my external auditor, who is responsible for attesting to the *sufficiency* of my span of controls. Since the external auditor's job is to inform me if he's uncovered any weaknesses, we review areas of concern that we might want to tighten up in the course of the coming year. Then I sign my final attestation letter, and the reports get filed.

Upon filing my annual report and 10-K, I ask my external auditor for his 2017 engagement proposal. He tells me his work will cost about $250,000. That's separate from the work of my internal auditor, who will be testing all the controls to begin with. I balk, I fuss and I negotiate a little...but ultimately I sign the agreement. Why? *Because I am entirely reliant on my external auditor's opinion of my bank's controls in order to attest my confidence to the SEC*—and in due course to the shareholders of my company. I had no personal involvement with the compilation of those financial statements—so I *have* to rely on outside professionals. *Without external testing and validation of my internal auditor's work, the SEC won't accept my attestation.* Can you understand now why Sarbanes-Oxley has been such a boon to the auditing industry? For larger companies, the costs are *even more* expensive because the external auditor is required to re-test the controls that were completed internally. And therein resides the controversy.

SEC reporting and Sarbanes-Oxley compliance cost Touchmark Bancshares, Inc. roughly $200,000 for each year between 2008 and 2011 (the bank filed to delist in July 2012). My hope is that Touchmark maintains the lessons of good controls as a de-listed company while avoiding the duplicity of the expense.

Beautiful Mausoleums

The Georgia landscape is adorned with beautiful bank buildings. Some are embellished with majestic white columns that convey a sense of prosperous permanence. All of them were expensive to build. Bill Short liked to say that a stately bank headquarters positioned at a busy intersection is really just a very expensive billboard.

It has long been a tradition in the banking industry to build structures that inspire confidence, permanence and significance. With the benefit of hindsight, it would also have been convenient had the marquees of those buildings been designed to allow for quick institutional name changes: between January 2008 and December 2012, the FDIC has either replaced or covered over the signage on 468 separate bank headquarters buildings—85 of them in Georgia. Many are now occupied by new groups of bankers. As of this writing, a lot of them also sit empty.

As a chief financial officer, it is my job to ensure that the assets of my company are put to productive use. For example, our management team planned to lease all of Touchmark's branches rather than own them. The way to make money in banking, after all, is to maximize *earning* assets on the balance sheet. No matter how impressive bank buildings may appear, they don't *earn* anything...they only depreciate. Touchmark's strategy was to maximize earning assets rather than sink significant sums into non-earning property...like draperies. We leased our initial office space and also our two subsequent branches (the ten acres that Touchmark's holding company owns along Satellite and Old Peachtree in Gwinnett County I'll neither discuss nor defend in these pages).

Touchmark's eventual headquarters location, though, turned out to be another matter altogether—and I was delighted with this one exception that we made to our lease holding strategy.

From Alpha to Omega

In May 2006, the capable organizers of Alpha Bank and Trust had just completed the largest capital raise in Georgia de novo banking history. They celebrated in part by constructing an 8,600 square foot craftsman-style headquarters in the commercial epicenter of Alpharetta, Georgia.

In October 2008, the unfortunate *directors* of Alpha Bank and Trust went on to distinguish themselves again as perhaps the shortest-lived banking entrepreneurs in Georgia history. Alpha Bank was shuttered by the FDIC a mere twenty-eight months after it opened [1]. The de novo phailed ten months after celebrating the grand opening of its headquarters. On Alpha's December 2006 balance sheet, the property and associated assets were valued at $5,455,000.

As the building sat empty through the winter of 2008, Bill Butler, a Touchmark director and an astute commercial realtor, took note of the property with other Touchmark directors and watched for an opportunity to bid. The bank's real estate committee had considered several similar buildings, but nothing fit better within Touchmark's strategic service area than a headquarters in one of the most robust commercial zip codes in the South.

The moment came in June 2009 when a regulatory lockout period expired, and Butler stood ready at the FDIC's offices with a cash offer. With no competing bids, Touchmark acquired the building and two acres of surrounding property at the rock-bottom price of $1.6 million. For those without fast fingers, that works out to a mere 29 percent of construction cost for a complete headquarters building with curbed and landscaped parking. As if that weren't enough, we subsequently acquired the entire *contents* of the building—everything from limited edition artwork to the safe deposit boxes and teller stations—for the tidy sum of $75,000. The building was beautifully furnished and stocked with laptops (hard drives removed), operational equipment and office supplies. While we celebrated *our* success, I couldn't help but feel conflicted over the devastating loss suffered by Alpha's shareholders. Our good fortune on the heels of their closure felt more like "spoils of war" than an outright purchase.

Beyond the good fortune of a discounted purchase, I felt that we had accomplished something equally as valuable: the "instant headquarters" enabled our team to stay focused on the business of banking rather than the distraction brought on by a major construction project. Selecting a property, hiring an architect, building designers, interiors, vendors and technology providers all encompass a project that amounts to a two-year business interruption for a management team—and does *nothing* to attract a client base. I recall listening sympathetically as my counterparts at Vinings Bank, First Landmark and Keyworth recounted stories of effort and frustration attributed to their considerable building projects...and I'd heave a sigh of relief as I turned toward my own set of challenges. Butler supervised a few enhancements on site and then handed Bill Short the keys to our new headquarters in mid-August 2009. The total capitalized sum amounted to $1.8 million. To this day, the building at 3651 Old Milton Parkway stands as the single largest gift yet to the shareholders of Touchmark National Bank—and we have Bill Butler to thank for his agility and resourcefulness.

Butler also oversaw the design of our branch locations: we opened the Duluth branch with Debbie Ganns as manager in April 2008, and Doraville with Vitra Darden as manager in October of that year. Because we didn't bear the overhead of an expensive headquarters, Touchmark allocated funds into a novel marketing campaign with billboards, targeted television commercials and business magazine ads. It was a pragmatic approach to attracting clients in a deteriorating business environment...and deteriorate it did.

June 10, 2009

Failed Banks Dot Georgia's Vista
The Wall Street Journal

How a Risk-Regulation Imbalance Drove Many Insolvencies – With More Likely
By DAMIAN PALETTA and DAN FITZPATRICK

The U.S. government's decision to let 10 big financial companies repay their taxpayer-funded investments is a break in the clouds for the banking system. In Georgia, though, the storm is raging unabated.

The state is home to just 4% of all U.S. banks, but 20% of the nation's bank failures since August. More banks have collapsed in Georgia than in any other U.S. state, even foreclosure-racked California and Florida. Six Georgia banks have been seized by regulators this year, burned by too much expansion in the past decade and bad real-estate bets. Given the high level of delinquent loans haunting the remaining Georgia-based banks, more failures are expected.

About 30 banks in the state are at risk of failing, according to bankers and lawmakers.

"Georgia is basically the Chernobyl of banking right now; it's radioactive down there," said Camden Fine, head of the Independent Community Bankers of America, a trade group.

Even after the recession ends, the problems dragging down Georgia banks could resurface in the next downturn, because the regulatory revamp being drawn up by the Obama administration likely won't tackle one cause of the problem: the division of power between state and federal regulators.

Georgia had 334 banks at the end of 2008, not counting branches of banks based elsewhere, such as Bank of America Corp., of Charlotte, N.C., and Wells Fargo & Co., of San Francisco. Since 2000, 112 banks and thrifts were started in Georgia, the third-highest total in the U.S., after California and Florida.

Rob Braswell, commissioner of the Georgia Department of Banking and Finance, the top regulator of banks that have Georgia charters rather than federal ones, said that if most people with banking experience applied for permission to open a new bank, "it was hard to say no when they had such an abundance of capital." Mr. Braswell has 62 examiners to monitor more than 150 state-chartered banks.

During a recent meeting with Georgia bankers, Federal Deposit Insurance Corp. Chairman Sheila Bair asked Christopher Maddox, head of Peoples Bank in Winder, Ga., why Georgia had so many banks. "Ma'am, may I respectfully submit that the FDIC approved every one of the applications," he recalls replying.

Georgia's predicament also is the result of a rapid expansion of the banking industry. Many of the new banks were small, and as they jostled for slivers of the market, they often made risky loans in speculative markets such as commercial real estate.

That was exacerbated by Atlanta's housing expansion and a decentralized government structure of 159 counties, where tradition holds that "every county has its own bank," said Christopher Marinac, managing principal at FIG Partners, a bank-research firm in Atlanta.

. . . .

Its now infamous designation as the "Chernobyl of Banking" has haunted Georgia since publication of that 2009 WSJ article. As you might imagine, Georgia bankers weren't pleased with the distinction.

In defense of Georgia's predicament—and with acknowledgements to Camden Fine, President of the Independent Community Bankers Association, following is an exchange that took place in June 2009 between Touchmark's board chair and the ICBA:

June 11, 2009
Mr. Camden R. Fine
President & CEO
Independent Community Bankers Association
1615 L Street NW
Washington, DC 20036

Dear Mr. Fine:

We have not met, but I am Chairman of the Touchmark National Bank a new De Novo Bank in Atlanta, Georgia. I think our dues help pay your salary, as well as some of the others at the ICBA. With the banking industry in the mess we are in the last thing I would expect to hear coming from the leader of one of our industry associations is a destructive comment about "Georgia being the Chernobyl of banking, it's radioactive down there." Neither our bankers nor our state needs this kind of help from you, we certainly expect more for someone with your skills, knowledge and experience in dealing with the media.

While I have admired much of what you have done regarding TARP and your leadership in other areas of our industry in Washington, I must tell you I was deeply offended by your comments regarding Georgia banks. I am confident that I am not alone in my way of thinking.

For your information there are 100's of banks in Georgia that are doing very well. They have strong leadership and boards of directors that have made sure that their banks are sound and profitable for our depositors and that our shareholders are protected and will weather this storm. Perhaps you need to visit with some Georgia bankers so we can share our thoughts about the industry here in Georgia, as well as, the south.

I strongly recommend that you apologize to all the bankers in Georgia and to all community bankers everywhere. Your comments could easily be about any state in America right now. Your job is to represent our industry in positive manner and not to make cute comments that will get you in print. Our industry has had enough negative ink without you adding your untimely comments.

Your statement sent a chill down my back and certainly would cause any of the thousands of investors in small community banks around our country and especially here in Georgia to "Ask should I ever in invest in a bank in Georgia," what were you thinking?

I have instructed our CEO to review our membership and our dues and to strongly consider dropping our membership in Independent Community Bankers Association. "You May Have Awakened a Sleeping Giant" as a matter of fact I think all Georgia bankers have their eyes open wide.

Respectfully,

Thomas E. Persons, Sr.

A response from Mr. Fine—including a worthwhile explanation of the interview, was fast in coming:

From: Cam Fine
Sent: Friday, June 12, 2009 1:24 PM
To: Tom Persons sctech.org
Subject: WSJ Article and your letter to me
Importance: High

Dear Mr. Persons,

I deeply appreciate your letter and fully understand how you feel. I would feel the same way if I sat where you are now. You are correct, I don't believe we have had the pleasure of meeting in person, I hope we can do so someday. First, let me say that I meant no offense to you or your bank and regret if offense was taken. I guess an out of context phrase together with a poor choice of words was bound to happen sooner or later given the non-stop press inquiries and interviews these days. As you know, sometimes papers can be very selective in what they print. If they had put my statement in context you would have read that I was not referring to the banks, but to the general economy, especially real estate, in certain areas of the southeast.

I was interviewed for about 40 minutes by the reporter. The central theme of my message was that the vast majority of community banks in Georgia were coping fairly well with the harsh economic conditions in parts of the state, but that the regulators were totally overreacting and were being unreasonably severe on the banks. My focus in the interview was to draw attention to the plight of many institutions in Georgia and the fact that there is severe regulatory overreaction falling on to the banks in Georgia. I am working hard to convince the bank regulatory agencies that they need to give banks in states like Georgia, California, Michigan and Florida more time to work out of their challenges. Many of the regulatory personnel in Washington consider states like Georgia as toxic and are not treating banks in your state and some others fairly in relation to states that have not been as hard hit. I have spoken out in public on this matter many times and will continue to do so.

I am not sure you know my background. Until just five years ago I was a career community banker in Missouri. My wife and I owned a bank

(MainStreet Bank of Ashland, MO) and I started and ran the Missouri Independent Bank, a banker's bank, in Jefferson City, MO. I have a passion for community banking and am a survivor of the 1980's Ag crisis in Missouri when our state lost 11 banks to failure. I lived through a very harsh regulatory period in the same way banker are living through it now.

I am terribly distressed that the WSJ lifted one phrase (that was itself pieced together) without reporting the meat of what I said about community banks. I readily admit that it was a poor choice of words made more so by the lack of context. As I said, after hundreds and hundreds of these interviews over the last 18 months, it was bound to happen sometime.

Let me again say how much I regret any offense I may have caused, and that I assure you that none was intended. I hope you can forgive my error. You may reach me directly by emailing xxx.xxx@icba.org and you can call me at xxx-xxx-xxxx.

Please visit me if you find yourself in Washington.

Best personal regards,

Cam

Pride And Prejudice

By December 2008, Touchmark's loan portfolio had grown to $31.5 million. Securities amounted to $25 million, and the bank's total assets were a little over $71 million. By June 2009, total assets were approaching $95 million. In August 2009, the bank reached $100 million in total assets, and Bill and I were thinking seriously about a strategy to motivate our leadership team for a final push to sustainable profitability.

As evidenced throughout its 2010 SEC filings, Touchmark's board had for some time been wrestling with a significant divergence of opinion in matters related to strategic direction and internal control (how's that for diplomatic parlance?). Board actions regarding these matters led ultimately to the resignation of chairman Persons and other directors in the early months of 2010.

As a practical matter, getting the bank open and negotiating the hurdles of a business launch provided few occasions for board conflict. There just wasn't much to argue about. It was only as the business began to gain momentum and show progress that "who was driving" began to advance as an issue.

The final chapter of my Touchmark story relays some of the implications and the ultimate consequences of these differences. In advance of my last Touchmark chapter, titled "Dead Indians", it's worth bearing in mind that *reasonable minds can differ* when it comes to shepherding a consensus. However, the ultimate test of a board of directors lies in their ability to establish a course, and maximize shareholder value in a manner consistent with adopted values and objectives.

Prior to concluding my part in the story of Touchmark National Bank, the next chapter—a speech by financial author John Mauldin—is included to provide some context for the broader picture of what was happening in the economy in the years leading up to 2007. You'll find John to be both an entertaining and insightful writer.

Footnote
[1] The *Atlanta Journal Constitution* published a well-researched article on the history of Alpha Bank on September 19, 2009, titled "Risky Loans Fuel Bank's Fast Fall."

Chapter 6

The Trend Is Not Your Friend

I've been a fan, if not a student, of John Mauldin's work for more than 10 years. In my opinion, John has proven himself as one of the more astute and prolific financial writers of our time. In searching for a national "backdrop piece" against which to frame the Georgia banking narrative, I wanted a relatively short article that could summarize the dynamic financial growth that led to such a dramatic downturn. I first read this article more than three years ago, and I'm not surprised that it remains relevant for inclusion here. It is an outtake, included by permission, from John's April 17th 2009 "Thoughts From the Frontline" (www.investorinsight.com). The section reprinted is actually from a speech that John delivered at one of his Altregis investment conferences. In the eloquence of about 2,500 words, John will summarize US Banking history, the run-up to our most recent crisis, the human tendencies and financial alchemy that enabled the boom that preceded it—and throw in some remarkably accurate predictions as a bonus. It's quite worth the read, and I'm confident you'll understand why I included it after you've turned through the next few pages.

The Trend May Not Be Your Friend
John Mauldin, *Thoughts from the Frontline*, 4/18/2009.

In the beginning there were banks, and the banks were without form or regulation. That lack of regulation begat panics. You had the panic of 1807, then the 1827 panic and Andrew Jackson got rid of the Bank of the US. Then you had the panic of 1873 and the panic of 1907 And over time, the powers that be, not wanting to have any more panics, created first the Federal Reserve and then the FDIC. After World War II, there were basically no more worries about bank deposits. The FDIC covered them, and we entered a new era of "stability." This did not repeal the business cycle and prevent recessions, but it did stop major bank runs and banking panics. We can clearly have financial crises, but they will be different than those of the Depression.

Stability, though, as we were taught by Hyman Minsky, leads to instability. The more stable things become and the longer things are stable, the more unstable they will be when the crisis hits, because we human beings learned to trade and invest by dodging lions and chasing antelopes on the African savannah. We now chase momentum and dodge bear markets. We are hard-wired to look around at our circumstances and predict trends far into the future.

We take the current trend and we project it forever. But the one thing we know about trends is that they are eventually going to end. The trend is only your friend until it ends. Trends are notoriously fickle. That stability breeds instability. Calvin Coolidge said in early 1929 that "In the domestic field, there is tranquility and contentment and the highest record of prosperity in years." The trend ended. "Apres moi, le deluge."

Now, so what happened in 1929, after this era of stability? The bubble burst and the stock market crashed.

By the way, I thought one of the great headlines in the papers from those days was, *"The Deluge of Panic Selling Overwhelms The Market. 19 Million Shares Change Hands."* 19 million shares changing hands caused the crash in 1929! That's about a minute worth of trading today. Okay, before the Great Depression, Coolidge was telling us, at the end of his presidency, that everything was cool, and then we got Hoovered. They tried to balance the budget, and they didn't really provide any stimulus. We got

Smoot-Hawley. Given the massive implosion of capital and the closing of banks, there clearly was not enough growth in the money supply. Government and the Fed just did a lot of wrong things.

So at the height of the Depression, in 1933, as Roosevelt was coming into his first term, we had 25% total unemployment; 37% (!) of non-farm workers were unemployed; 4004 banks had failed; $3.6 billion in deposits was lost. That's like trillions in dog years, okay? At least in 2009 dog years. You end up with bread lines, and the stock market just keeps going down, down, down (with a few marvelous bear-market rallies – maybe like what we are seeing today?).

Roosevelt comes along and we get the New Deal. He applied massive stimulus. By the way, his stimulus hired people. He put them to work building parks and the Tennessee Valley Authority. They were building a lot of infrastructure. He didn't put it into Democratic wish lists and permanent wealth transfers and welfare and special-interest agendas to increase the overall budget beyond what we could ever hope to actually pay for (without even more radical tax increases), which the Obama Administration is clearly doing. We'll get to the effectiveness of current policies in a moment.

Then let's look at what he did in 1937. With the economy somewhat on the mend, he tried to balance the budget, raise taxes, reduce deficit spending. And what happened? We had another deep recession and unemployment jumped back up to 20%. It was hard to pull that stimulus back out. And it's particularly dangerous to raise taxes in a weak economy.

Most of the people in this room are old enough to remember the Blue Screen of Death. Remember, you would be typing along on your computer and all of a sudden you would get this screen, saying, "You have an impossible error." (Okay, what's an "impossible" error? Clearly something happened that was possible.)

And the only thing you could do was just unplug the thing. You couldn't even turn it off – you just had to unplug the computer. It was the Blue Screen of Death. Well, that is kind of what World War II was for the world. We unplugged the world economy, and then we started from a new base. We hit the reset button. We were at lows everywhere in the world; places were in a mess. So we began to grow from there. The debt super-cycle started. For all the recessions and bear markets, a new stability ensued, and debt and leverage began to grow.

We'll revisit that point in a moment. We are doing just what I do in my regular e-letter: I'm going to take three or four ideas, and at the end I'm going to try and tie them all together. Let's see how successful I am.

What Is Money?

Let's talk about what money is. For some people it's M-1 or M-2, and they worry that the money supply is growing too much. For some people it's gold; gold is the only real currency. I think those ideas each have their place, and there's some truths to them, but they focus us on the wrong thing.

It's a bit misleading to talk about money supply, because what money really is is roughly $2 trillion of cash and then $50 trillion in credit. Because what do the banks do? They take deposits in and then they borrow money to leverage them up. I take my credit card and I spend with it. I borrow against a house. I have an asset that rises, and I borrow against it.

We have two trillion dollars of actual cash propping up $50 trillion in credit. If we all decided to settle and pay off everything, we couldn't do it because there is not enough cash. There would be massive asset deflation. We, as a nation, are levered 25 to 1, or we were. Now, that $50 trillion is in a real sense the money supply because that is what we are all pretending is real money. I lend you money and you pretend you are going to pay me back. Then you pretend he [pointing at another attendee] is not going to call your debt for cash, and we are all going to keep the system going. Because if we all try to pay each other back at once, we are all collectively – and this is a technical economic term – screwed.

So we keep the system going. Now, where are we today? We are at the Great Deleveraging. We are seeing massive losses and destruction of assets, on a scale that is unprecedented. There was massive destruction of assets during the Great Depression, which caused a lot of problems, and we are seeing the same thing today. We are watching trillions simply being poofed (another technical economics term – which will drive my poor Chinese translator crazy!). We are watching people pay down their credit lines, which is one way of saying the supply of money and credit is shrinking.

This is not just in the US, but all over the world. Because when you start adding European cash-to-credit, and Japanese cash-to-credit, and Indonesian and Chinese cash-to-credit, it becomes multiple tens of trillions, and we are watching a goodly portion of that credit be vaporized. So we – individuals and businesses – are trying to find that $2 trillion in real cash and get some of it to pay down our debts. We are reducing that massive leveraged money supply down to some smaller number. We are hitting the Blue Screen of Death. We don't know what it is going to reset to, but we have permanently seared the psyche of the American consumer, and it is going to get reset to some lower number, about which I will speculate in a minute.

Now to give you some idea of how important credit was in our recent period of economic growth – and I keep using this slide, but it is an important slide because it shows you what would have happened in the economy without mortgage equity withdrawals. The red lines (RDK comment: the lighter grey is 'red') are what GDP would have been without MEWs. Notice that in 2001 and 2002 we would have had negative GDP for two years, that's 24 months. It would have been as long as or longer than the current recession. Not quite as deep, because we had the Bush stimulus and Bush tax cuts at the time. The Bush tax cuts were very important in keeping the economy rolling over in 2001 and 2002.

Chart 26

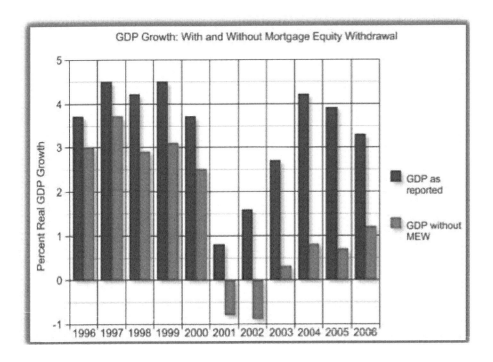

GDP Growth: With and Without Mortgage Equity Withdrawal

But notice that the recovery for the next four years would have been under 1%. We would have had under 1% GDP for four years running, without mortgage equity withdrawals, without people being able to spend more. That doesn't even count the leverage we increased on our auto loans, on credit cards – you saw the two charts that Louie [Gave] and Martin [Barnes] used yesterday about the growth of credit, and we are now seeing it in reverse. Do you think George Bush would have stood even a small chance of being reelected without mortgage equity withdrawals?

Quarter 1-2006 we had $223 billion in mortgage equity withdrawals. Quarter 2-2008 it was $9.5 billion. Is it any wonder we were in recession by 2008? By the third and fourth quarters there was no money to keep the treadmill going That $50 trillion in credit was shrinking fast. We were imploding it. Further – just as a little throwaway slide – if you look at 2010 and 2011, we are getting ready for another huge wave of mortgage resets.

Now, we've gone through the last wave and we saw what happened; it created a lot of foreclosures. We are not out of the woods yet. It is going to be 2012 before we sell enough houses to really get back to reasonable levels, because we had 3.5 million excess homes at the top. We absorb about a million a year, it takes 3 years, that's kind of the math.

By the way, this AIG thing and the bonuses, that's so bogus. I mean, the 40 people that created the problem were gone, they go to 40 other people and say, stick around because we've got to have somebody who actually knows what these things are to try and unwind it, and we'll give you a bonus. Some of them worked for a dollar against getting that bonus, and now we've told the world that a contract isn't a contract in the US of A, for a lousy 160 million dollars. No bank is going to want to play with the US again, because you don't want to be hauled up in front of Barney Frank.

MV=PQ

Okay, when you become a central banker, you are taken into a back room and they do a DNA change on you. You are henceforth and forever physically incapable of allowing deflation on your watch. It becomes the first and foremost thought on your mind: "Deflation, we can't have it." So let's move along to the next point, and then I'm going to tie them all together.

MV=PQ. This is an important equation; this is right up there with $E=MC^2$. M (money or the supply of money) times V (velocity, which is how fast the money goes through the system – if you have seven kids it goes faster than if you have one) is equal to P (the price of money in terms of inflation or deflation) times Q (which roughly stands for the quantity of production, or GDP)

So what happens is, if we increase the supply of money and velocity stays the same, if GDP does not grow, it means we'll have inflation, because this equation must balance. But if you reduce velocity (which is happening today), and if you don't increase the supply of money, you are going to see deflation. Now, we are watching, for reasons we'll get into in a minute, the velocity of money slow. People are getting nervous, they are not borrowing as much, either because they can't or because the "animal spirits" that Keynes talked about are not quite there.

To fight that deflation (which we saw in this week's Producer and Consumer Price Indexes) the Fed is going to print money. A few thoughts. The Fed has announced they intend to print $300 billion. That is different from buying mortgages and securitized credit card debt – that money (credit) already exists.

When they just print the money and buy Treasuries, like the $300 billion announced, they can sop that up pretty easily if they find themselves facing inflation down the road. But that problem is a long way off.

But sports fans, $300 billion is just a down payment on the "quantitative easing" they will eventually need to do. They can't announce what they are really going to do or the market would throw up. But we are going to get quarterly or semi-annual announcements, saying, we are going to do another $300 billion, another $500 billion.

When we first started out with TALF and everything, it was a couple hundred billion here and there, and now we throw the word *trillions* around and it just drips off of our tongues and we don't even think about it. A trillion is a lot. It's a big number. And the total guarantees and back-ups and all this stuff we are into – I saw an estimate of $10-12 trillion. That's a lot of money.

Understand, the Fed is going to keep pumping money until we get inflation. You can count on it. I don't know what that number is, I'm guessing $2 trillion. I've seen some studies. Ray Dalio of Bridgewater thinks it's about $1.5 trillion. It's some big number, some number way beyond $300 billion, and they are going to keep at it until we get inflation.

Side point: what happens if the $300 billion they put in the system comes back to the Fed's books because banks don't put it into the LIBOR market because they are worried about credit risks? If that happens, it does absolutely nothing for the money supply. Okay? It's like, goes here, goes back there – it doesn't help us. If the Fed creates money which is simply deposited back with the Fed, then there is effectively no money creation. We are still faced with deflation. The Fed has got to somehow get it into the financial system. They've got to figure out how to create some movement.

Will it create an asset bubble in stocks again? I don't know, it could. Dennis Gartman talked about being nervous yesterday. I would be nervous about stock markets, both on the long side, as I think we are in a bear market rally, but also there is real risk in being short. Bill Fleckenstein will be here tonight. He is a very famous short trader. He closed a short fund a couple of months ago. He says he doesn't have as many good opportunities, and basically he's scared of being short with so much stimulus coming in. So it's going to work, at least in terms of reflation, but the question is when. A year? Two years?

RDK comment: Well, it took more than three years, but as of May 2013 the "asset bubble" in stocks has certainly arrived. The Dow is closing in on 15,000—new record territory. Thanks, John, for allowing me to reprint a bit of your colloquial expertise.

Chapter 7

Strategic Plans and Avoiding the Exploding Hippo

"People are like tea bags. You find out how strong they are when you put them in hot water."

Eleanor Roosevelt

A company is a group of people who have come together to fulfill a common purpose. That purpose typically involves a product or a service—and a plan for selling it with funds left over that can be accounted for as profit. Unless there is a strategic common *purpose*—and agreement as to what's important to fulfilling that purpose, frustration and conflict will ensue.

A rowing crew provides a ready comparison: the keys to racing gracefully across the water are staying organized, maintaining rhythm and building coordinated endurance as a team. It is impossible to mark competitive time if a teammate begins calling his own pace...or if someone starts whacking you over the head with a paddle.

In my experience, a lack of consensus in strategic planning leads to one of three ultimate outcomes:

1. Stagnation and atrophy

2. Dissolution of the company

3. Resolution of disagreement by means of negotiation, resignation or the vanquishment of opposing views

Because the first two options are generally unacceptable to a company's owners, it is option 3—despite its unpleasantness—that is the path most often taken in organizations. Unfortunately, there is no certainty that those who "win" by means of negotiation or vanquishment will better the odds for success in the venture...it merely means that the weight of their vote carried the day. It is a hard fact that "winning" in the boardroom is only of value to shareholders when those who muster a majority can demonstrate better performance than the new minority. To that that end, those who lead a boardroom coup obligate themselves to a burden of proof for having forced a change.

As conveyed in the SEC filings incorporated later this chapter, it was apparent by late 2009 that the board of Touchmark Bancshares, Inc. was internally at odds over its strategy and priorities. As a practical matter, the problem of diverging agendas among the board members was no more or less unique than could be imagined across a thousand other companies and their management teams. Whether spawned by ego or philosophy or culture or greed, life eventually proves to us all that there is no shortage of ways that individual opinions can adapt and evolve. Add in the challenge of balancing business and personal affairs in the midst of a global financial crisis, and it becomes easy to imagine how agendas can diverge. *Reasonable minds can differ.* Unreasonable minds can, too. So when leadership is unable to maintain authoritative uniformity around the strategic plans of a company, vanquishment (option 3) takes over and is accomplished by a majority faction—or ultimately by shareholder vote.

Why Strategy Matters

Like most forays in life, success in business is part art (ability), part science (experience), and part divine intervention (or "luck" if you're agnostic). Building a profitable banking franchise requires informed and disciplined choices about how to loan money, how to build a deposit base and how to champion a business model that fosters relationships by way of those loans and deposits.

The type of lending that a bank pursues provides a good example of the mix of that art and science. A successful banking business model depends as much on the makeup of the communities that the bank serves as it does on the expertise of the management team. For example, if a bank is located in farming country, then lending and repayment schedules will need to follow the calendar and cash cycles of the planting and harvest seasons. Alternately, a bank serving residential neighborhoods had better offer an array of consumer loans and home financing options. The business expertise for underwriting crop cycles bears little resemblance to the subtleties of qualifying a car loan. The risk and the profitability of lending decisions vary greatly by industry—which means that banking, while a homogenous industry, carries within it a broad range of business models and disciplines depending on the type of markets that the bank has need to serve.

The folks at Bank Intelligence/Fiserv identify nine distinct lending classifications—coinciding with bank regulatory reporting—that help to differentiate among varied risk types and lending concentrations:

- **Commercial and Industrial (C&I):** lending on the value of inventory, receivables, and other business assets

- **Commercial Real Estate (CRE)**: lending to developers to finance the construction of buildings and land development

- **Small Business (SBU):** financing the growth and liquidity needs of businesses generally under $5 million in revenue

- **Agricultural Related (AGR):** crop and farm-equipment related

- **Personal Loans (PER):** consumer purpose loans—auto, personal, etc.

- **Residential Real Estate (RRE):** home mortgages

- **High Residential (HRR):** high-end residential and "jumbo" mortgages

- **Diversified (DIV):** balanced exposure to an array of the above with no particular concentration in lending specialization

Each of these sectors is cyclical, based on a range of market factors. To demonstrate the variability of returns in these models, below is the graph that BI uses to compare returns based on lending type. The chart below displays return on equity (ROE) across the various lending categories for the quarter ended December 31, 2012:

Chart 27

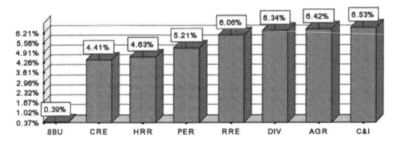

Return on Equity
By Lending Strategy as of December 2012

Lending Strategy

Placement within a Lending Classification requires that the category be the largest category for the bank and meet the minimum amount threshold. Designations as a Small Business lender requires that Commercial & Industrial or Commercial Real Estate lending is the maximum category and that 75% of those loans are classified as small business or the bank identifies itself as a significant small business lender.

Return on Equity

Perhaps the most frequently cited macro-profitability measure, return on equity (ROE) depicts the annualized level of net income generated as a percent of average total equity. As a measure of return on investment, ROE reflects not only the profitability (return on assets), but also the extent to which equity capital has been fully deployed (equity multiplier).

Source: Bank Intelligence   www.bankintelligence.com
       Solutions Fiserv

Note that for the fourth quarter of 2012, C&I focused institutions garnered a 6.53% ROE, compared to CRE-focused institutions, which performed at an industry wide ROE of 4.41%. In the same way, the type of deposits that a bank attracts is critical to both funding a loan portfolio and generating stable profits. A bank funded primarily by certificates of deposit (CDs) can't generate the level of service charges associated with checking accounts because there are fewer transactions to generate those fees. Similarly, a bank that caters to large-business depositors won't need as many employees as one that focuses on mass-market consumer checking. It's a fact that strategy matters, as does diligent market planning, in order to deploy a successful strategy. Without top-down consensus and buy-in around strategy, it is difficult to execute in the marketplace...especially during a banking crisis.

Touchmark's initial board was composed of a diverse group of business-minded risk-takers with an assortment of cultural values, experience, and worldviews. Membership had not been vetted by any one individual—or to any particular standard. Instead, recall that the group had come together by way of introductions and personal associations. As such, membership on the board was not beholden to any one individual—such as an organizing chairman or the CEO. While directors had credentialed success across a variety of professional endeavors, uniformity—and bank board experience—was not a prevailing strong suit across the group. Diversity, in fact, had been trumpeted as one of Touchmark's greatest strengths, and the group heralded that distinction as a differentiator within the ranks of Atlanta's de novo institutions. That diversity, however, bred a variety of opinions as to what "success" actually looked like.

Call of Duty

The responsibility of serving as a bank director is best viewed from two distinct perspectives: that of the regulator and that of the shareholder.

The OCC's *Director's Handbook* lists six qualifications for a national bank director. The list includes a "basic knowledge of the banking industry," "a willingness to put the interests of the bank ahead of personal interests," "a willingness to avoid conflicts of interest," "knowledge of the communities" that the bank serves, and "a willingness to...commit the time." The sixth qualification is simply "background, knowledge, and experience in business or another discipline to oversee the bank."

In the eyes of a banking regulator, if an ambitious, honest person has the time and inclination, he or she is qualified to serve as the director of a US bank.

Alternately, a board of directors has three responsibilities to shareholders: a *duty of care, a duty of loyalty,* and *a duty of obedience.* While a cacophony of consultants, auditors, and law firms counsel directing boards across all manner of governance issues, the foundational requirement is that members comprehend—and affirm—the scope and the limitations of these three roles.

Duty of Care

The *duty of care* addresses the level of competence expected of a board member, commonly defined in governance policies as "care that an objective and prudent person would exercise in a like position and under similar circumstances." This means that board members have a duty to exercise reasonable judgment when casting votes as stewards of the company they serve. *Independence* matters often fall into this category; when a director uses the force of personality or belligerence to impair the independence of others, the boardroom becomes a perilous place. Further, board members have a responsibility to understand and keep up with industry trends and practices. Members of an audit committee, for example, should clearly have expertise in dealing with matters of accounting and internal controls.

Duty of Loyalty

The duty of loyalty is a standard of faithfulness and, in some companies, of fiduciary responsibility. Board members are expected to put shareholders first in all matters affecting the company and to avoid conflicts of interest at all cost. This means that a board member should never use restricted information for personal gain or promote an idea that will derive personal benefit ahead of other shareholders. While business interests often intersect across companies, conflicts of interest should be clearly disclosed and documented in board meeting minutes to prevent even the appearance of preferential treatment.

Duty of Obedience

The duty of obedience holds that board members must be faithful to the company's mission and to its strategic agenda. Board members should avoid acting in ways that impede the strategic plan or the stated goals of the organization. In regulated industries, this duty extends to issues of compliance with state and federal authorities. The monitoring of internal controls and reporting have become hot topics with contemporary boards. A veritable industry of seminars and consulting expertise has grown up to assist directors with an understanding and application of internal controls.

The role of a director versus that of management needs to be clearly established and respectfully enforced. In healthy organizations, the role of a director is centered on issues involving policy, strategy, and networking referrals. A director who exceeds these boundaries is often times pressing for influence in the operation of the business. In doing so, he or she is intruding on the role and responsibilities of management. A board of directors is best positioned to *champion* a management team and *enable* management to make the company successful. To exceed the role of "director-champion" is to invite conflict and to diminish management's role. "Too many cooks in the kitchen" is a recipe for conflict. The battle for business success needs to be fought with the competition—not across the board table.

"O" Oh...

The OCC's Regulation O pertains to guidelines for loans made to officers and directors—the so-called insiders of a regulated institution. "Reg O" has proven to be one of the more contentious facets of bank administration. The key question is this: *In addition to being in business with these people, will you also lend them your money?* Driven by a variety of compliance and philosophical opinions, banks take a diverse approach to the question of whether or not directors and officers should transact business with their own bank. While it might seem obvious that a bank should expect its directors, officers, and employees to have accounts and transact business at the institution they control, that is not always the case—and for some good reasons.

Directors and officers are likely to already have established banking relationships at the time they become involved with a start-up. Those relationships can be hard to break because of collateral documentation, business partnerships or just the plain hassle associated with moving accounts from one bank to another. But there are also confidentiality and disclosure concerns: loan applications require a significant degree of financial disclosure, and it can be awkward for a director to open up his or her private affairs to the rest of the board and to management in order to pursue a loan from his or her own institution.

Then there's the matter of risk management: how does the bank respond when a key officer or director encounters financial hardship? What happens when asset values decline and loan covenants call for additional collateral...but the insider doesn't want to pony up? Do you sue or foreclose? Ouch. See the problem?

In the fallout of the banking crisis—in Georgia and elsewhere, one can only *imagine* the number of times this issue became a matter of awkward and incendiary discussion. After all, insiders—and a board of directors in particular—are *obligated* to look after the best interests of the bank that they serve...but what is the "right thing" to do when an insider becomes a part of the problem? There are no easy answers to such a predicament. See now why some banks don't make loans to insiders?

A Few More Thoughts on Leadership and Planning

Differences of opinion make the world go around. The market-place of ideas creates, destroys, refines and winnows all manner of concepts and strategy. In a healthy business, strategies are aired and debated in an environment of candor and respect, with decision makers acting in the best interests of the business as a whole. One of my favorite quotes from Andrew Carnegie fits the bill in this sense: *"While the law [of competition] may be sometimes hard for the individual, it is best for the race, because it ensures the survival of the fittest in every department."*

That means decision makers must be in general agreement as to what constitutes "the best interests" of the business. That is why the process of strategic planning—and the board retreats, training and conferences that go with it—are so vital to the success of organizations. The goal of strategic planning is for leadership to coalesce around common goals and to provide management with a clear understanding of what success looks like. In a productive planning environment, both the annual budget (balance sheet growth, revenue, expense, and profit) as well as the capital plan (risk metrics) are outgrowths of the strategic plan. Without a common definition of success, differences of opinion lead to frustration, lack of progress, and, ultimately, to alternate agendas. Conflicting agendas in the boardroom undermine the foundations of shareholder value.

Just as it happened earlier in my career, I learned as much about people during my tenure at Touchmark as I did about the profession of community banking—and I've learned a *lot* about community banking over the past few years!

The advice that Paul Dimmick offered up in 2001 served me just as well in 2010: "Pay attention and keep good notes. Help good people when you can. And above all else, *conduct yourself so that you'll be proud of your work and your reputation regardless of whether you stay or you leave.*" That last sentence is as much an admonition as it is solid advice.

Service with a Smile

One of my personal mantras is that I refuse to be a negative contributor to any organization in which I hold a position of responsibility. If I don't agree with the organization's mission, or if I can't find a way to help and encourage, then it's best that I back away and leave the group to its own devices. No paddle-whacking. Leading organizations is just too hard to do otherwise. Unless it's a question of legality or a matter of significant personal risk, if you can't support the team, then go find someplace where you *can* contribute constructively. Heaven knows there are plenty of opportunities where a *positive* influence is appreciated.

From the standpoint of leadership and organizational involvement, here are three suggestions to consider before accepting an executive position or a directorship:

1. What is the vetting process for selecting the leadership team, and on what credentials is your involvement being solicited? Are you satisfied with the standards for admission?

2. Are you satisfied that the leadership team is unified around a common mission and business plan?

3. Do you believe that you can champion the plan?

Alas, No Exploding Hippo

I'm finishing this chapter on the flight back from a bank valuation conference in New York. During my early morning reading time, I came across the perfect metaphor for my ex-insider status in a *Times* article. I decided on first read that I had to fit it somewhere in this book. In the article, Neil Genzlinger is reviewing an *Animal Planet* TV special (NYT Sunday 9/15/12) in which the leading role is played...by a dead hippo. The documentary, which aired later the following week (I didn't bother to watch), examined the consumption process of an animal carcass on the African plain. Stay with me here...

"For a time, it looks as though it (the hippo) *won't be distributed at all. Not many animals can bite through a two-inch thick hippopotamus hide. A lion tries to nibble, and vultures poke, but for a long stretch, the carcass remains basically intact*, which makes possible this enticing bit of narration (at a pointed moment during the documentary): *'Bloated by decomposition gases, it could explode if nothing punctures its skin.'* But alas, we get no exploding hippo."

In delectably descriptive prose, Genzlinger explains that the *reason* the poor hippo doesn't explode all over the savannah is because a crocodile manages to rip off his...well, you'll just have to look up the article if you really need to know. As far as I'm concerned, Genzlinger's review provided a great public service in warning against watching the documentary itself...but enough of that. *The fact is that the hippo doesn't explode.* An alternate event provides for dismemberment and eventual decomposition of the carcass. An exploding hippo, after all, would create a terrible mess across some untold perimeter. It's a situation best to be avoided.

The point of all this: to my way of thinking, that swollen, dead hippo offers a perfect metaphor for inappropriate disclosure and disparagement. Everything necessary to describe the hippo's state of affairs can be readily observed at a distance. *Getting too close can be messy.* As an SEC reporting company, Touchmark Bancshares was obligated to submit filings of any material change in its condition or manner of operations. Because of this, the inclusion of what is publicly available enables me to respect the conditions of my non-disclosure agreement, while at the same time illuminating board differences that arose during the period covered in this book. With two years' hindsight, I can attest that the intensity of those times taught all of us a number of important lessons—and experience can be a hard teacher. The public filings that follow relay just enough information to "puncture the hide" and enable an interested reader to contemplate how differences amongst the board led to a vanquishment (our option 3)—without my taking sides in the matter. Time has moved on, and "sides" are no longer an issue. The history, though, holds lessons that are instructional.

From an SEC filing dated January 22, 2010:

UNITED STATES
SECURITIES AND EXCHANGE COMMISSION
WASHINGTON, D.C. 20549

FORM 8-K
CURRENT REPORT

Pursuant to Section 13 or 15(d) of the Securities and Exchange Act of 1934

Date of Report (Date of earliest event reported) January 19, 2010

Item 5.02   Departure of Directors or Certain Officers; Election of Directors; Appointment of Certain Officers; Compensatory Arrangements of Certain Officers.

(b) Effective January 19, 2010, Mr. C. Hiluard Kitchens, Jr., a director of Touchmark Bancshares, Inc. (the "Company") and the Company's national bank subsidiary, Touchmark National Bank (the "Bank"), resigned from his position as director of the Company and the Bank.

Date of Report (Date of earliest event reported) March 9, 2010

Item 5.02 Departure of Directors or Certain Officers; Election of Directors; Appointment of Certain Officers; Compensatory Arrangements of Certain Officers.

(a) On March 3, 2010, Mr. Thomas E. Persons, Sr., age 65, a director of Touchmark Bancshares, Inc. (the "Company") and the Company's national bank subsidiary, Touchmark National Bank (the "Bank"), announced his retirement from his position as chairman of the board and director of the Company and the Bank. Mr. Persons was a member of the Company's audit committee and executive committee. Mr. Persons informed the board that he was retiring in order to allow for a new chairman who could promote more cohesive board action at the Company and the Bank. Mr. Persons' letter, which is attached hereto as Exhibit 17.1 and incorporated herein by reference, includes a description of the circumstances related to his retirement. The Company has provided Mr. Persons with a copy of the disclosure set forth herein.

Exhibit 17.1

March 3, 2010

Dear Members of the Touchmark Board of Directors and Senior Management Team:

It has been my honor to serve as your chairman during our formative years and for the last two years of our operation. I am extremely proud of our results and the growth that our bank has reached since our opening. We have grown to more than $130 million in assets during the most challenging time for the bank industry in our lifetimes. Our capital level is strong and our pipeline is robust. With focused attention the bank should begin to breakeven later next quarter.

I am extremely proud of our senior leadership team and each member of our Touchmark Family for the professional manner in which each of you have grown our bank. Our recent review by the OCC strongly confirms that our bank is doing well and that we have made great progress during the past two years.

I am proud of our board and the many contributions each of you have made during our time together. We have made many decisions around the board table and together we have always worked to do what was best for our shareholders.

I have worked hundreds of hours to help lead our bank in a positive manner. I have always been a leader who "takes the high road" and "the glass is always half full" while finding the good in everything people do. I have been proud of our diverse board of directors. It is because of some of our cultural differences; a group of our board members see things through their lenses and are extraordinarily different for others on our board in their perspectives. I cannot support many of the recent actions and will not allow our bank to go through an expensive and nasty proxy fight under my leadership. I am exhausted with the split in our board. Our legal cost for the management review that is being conducted has already cost our bank much more than was ever necessary.

I have searched my soul and used all my managerial skills to lead our board to a resolution that could bring us back together again. I have come to the conclusion and what I feel is the right decision for our shareholders and our bank. I cannot get us there and something must change. Our board and our shareholders need a Chairman that can be in the bank and in the community on a daily basis. A community bank should require that all member of the board live and work in the market area of the bank.

I am hopeful that my decision will also encourage our other board members who are not members of our banking community to also consider this the same way.

Thank you for the past five years. The progress and growth of our bank is more important than any of you will ever know.

I am therefore announcing my retirement from the board of directors effective today. I am most hopeful my decision is the best one for our bank and shareholders. I strongly encourage our board to consider appointing Dr. Kaufman or Bill Butler to the lead our bank during the interim. At the present time there is no way that either of the Vice Chairmen can lead our board under the current circumstances.

I wish you Godspeed and great success for the future.

Best regards,

Thomas E. Persons, Sr.

Date of Report (Date of earliest event reported) March 9, 2010

Item 5.02 Departure of Directors or Certain Officers; Election of Directors; Appointment of Certain Officers; Compensatory Arrangements of Certain Officers.

(b) On March 8, 2010, Daniel B. Cowart resigned from his position as a director of the Company and the Bank.

With Dan Cowart's departure, a prevailing faction moved quickly to press for control. Bill Butler and John Johnson followed Tom Persons' lead in attaching candid resignation letters to the SEC filings that accompanied their departures. The purpose of attaching such a letter is to communicate motives and sentiment to the shareholder base.

And so it was that on the eve of the bank's earliest financial success—a first profitable quarter in the midst of a worldwide financial panic—outcome 3 began to unfold for Touchmark Bancshares, Inc.

UNITED STATES
SECURITIES AND EXCHANGE COMMISSION

WASHINGTON, D.C. 20549

FORM 8-K
CURRENT REPORT

Pursuant to Section 13 or 15(d) of the Securities and Exchange Act of 1934

Date of Report (Date of earliest event reported)
March 17, 2010
Touchmark Bancshares, Inc.
(Exact name of registrant as specified in its charter)

Item 5.02 Departure of Directors or Certain Officers; Election of Directors; Appointment of Certain Officers; Compensatory Arrangements of Certain Officers.

(d) On March 17, 2010, the board of directors of Touchmark Bancshares, Inc. (the "Company") elected William Crosby to serve as a Class II director to fill the unexpired portion of the term of C. Hiluard Kitchens, Jr., resulting from the vacancy left by Mr. Kitchen's resignation.

Mr. Crosby will serve until the Company's 2010 annual meeting of shareholders and until such time as his successor is duly elected and qualified.

In addition, on March 17, 2010, the board of directors of the Company elected Jayendrakuma J. ("J.J.") Shah to serve as Chairman of the board of directors of the Company.

On March 19, 2010, Daniel J. Kaufman resigned from his position as a director of the company and the company's national bank subsidiary, Touchmark National Bank.

April 13, 2010

Item 5.02 Departure of Directors or Certain Officers; Election of Directors; Appointment of Certain Officers; Compensatory Arrangements of Certain Officers.

(a) On April 13, 2010, Touchmark Bancshares, Inc. (the "Company") received notice of the resignation of J. William Butler from his position as a director of the Company and the Company's national bank subsidiary, Touchmark National Bank. Mr. Butler informed the Company that he was resigning due to certain practices of the boards relating to the discussion of business matters. Mr. Butler's letter, which is attached hereto as Exhibit 17.1 and incorporated herein by reference, includes a description of the circumstances related to his resignation. The Company has provided Mr. Butler with a copy of the disclosure set forth herein.

April 23, 2010

Item 5.02 Departure of Directors or Certain Officers; Election of Directors; Appointment of Certain Officers; Compensatory Arrangements of Certain Officers.

(a) On April 21, 2010, Touchmark Bancshares, Inc. (the "Company") received notice of the resignation of John L. Johnson from his position as a director of the Company and the Company's national bank subsidiary, Touchmark National Bank. Mr. Johnson informed the Company that he was resigning due to his perception of certain practices of the leadership of the boards related to board discussions of business matters. Mr. Johnson's letter, which is attached hereto as Exhibit 17.1 and incorporated herein by reference, includes a description of the circumstances related to his resignation. The Company has provided Mr. Johnson with a copy of the disclosure set forth herein.

Item 7.01 Regulation FD Disclosure.

On April 23, 2010, the Company mailed a letter to its shareholders. A copy of the letter is attached hereto as Exhibit 99.1 and incorporated herein by reference.

We took the opportunity to notify shareholders in a carefully, but tastefully, constructed letter:

April 22, 2010

Dear Shareholder,

Touchmark completed its second year of operation in what can readily be described as a challenging business environment. Our well-capitalized status has enabled us to grow our assets and customer base in spite of considerable headwinds, and we believe that we are favorably positioned to benefit from the coming economic turnaround. Banks fortunate enough to have a strong capital position, a diverse funding mix, and a healthy portfolio of earning assets should thrive as recovery builds across metropolitan Atlanta.

Touchmark's strategic planning process has helped us to remain focused on our priorities of *soundness, profitability, and growth.* We continue to build net interest margin and pursue fee income opportunities while strategically managing our expenses. We are diligent in our credit underwriting process and move swiftly to manage out weakened credit situations. We continue to evaluate services and market opportunities that will allow us to grow and benefit from economies of scale. Our entry into the SBA market has shown rapid success and provides us with timely resources to meet our clients' needs and to diversify our revenues in a difficult credit market.

Enclosed you will find our 2009 audited financial statements. We ended 2009 with $129.2 million in assets, an 81% increase over 2008. Loans net of allowance grew by $36.9 million or 217% while deposits grew by $48.3 million or 274%. Touchmark recorded a loss of $2.9 million or $0.84 per share as we increased our provision against loan losses by $1.04 million to $1.45 million. This resulted in an allowance for loan loss amounting to 2.12% at year-end.

We are very pleased to report that the first quarter of 2010 has gotten off to a good start as we produced a small profit for the first three months of this year—our first profitable quarter since opening for business in January 2008. Our earning asset growth has been steady, and we are working diligently to continue our success and enhance shareholder value.

In mid-March 2010, Dr. JJ Shah was elected Chairman of both Touchmark National Bank and Touchmark Bancshares, Inc. upon the retirement of Thomas E. Persons, Sr. Dr. Shah was a founding Organizer of the bank and has been an active director since our inception. We congratulate Dr. Shah on his leadership position with Touchmark, and we sincerely thank Tom for his time and service that has enabled us to accomplish our considerable success thus far.

Thank you for your continued support and investment in Touchmark.

William R. Short

William R. Short

President & CEO

Chapter 8

Dead Indians

"Don't cry because it's over; smile because it happened."

Dr. Seuss

By this point, gentle reader, you've realized that the tone reflected in the disclosures in the previous chapter suggest a deeper frustration than I've chosen to relay in this story. While the particulars that culminated in a board split might make for titillating reading, there's enough here already to get the point across. Both Johnson and Butler attached letters with their resignation notices that I chose not to include in this chapter—they're on the web for any who wish to view them. Hindsight and reflection have enabled me to appreciate that accomplished individuals don't necessarily make for an accomplished team. In such cases the team is inevitably restructured.

All-Star baseball games are fun to watch. Each player has been chosen for the team by distinguishing himself individually on the field of professional play. As such, All-Star games are more about showcasing the prowess of individuals than they are about the coordinated accomplishments of a team. "Team" requires leadership, discipline and a willing spirit. Team requires that a unified strategy be developed for the field of play. Team recognizes that a corporation is not a democracy and that leadership must ultimately choose the path to success.

Team Touchmark took the field at the outset of stormy conditions—and the rules of the game offered no quarter on account of rain.

Dead Indians

While driving to work one morning in April 2010, I listened to a radio story about the Cherokee Indians who once populated the hills that now are the northern reaches of metro Atlanta. The report was about a ceremonial site that had been uncovered during renovation of a strip shopping center. It was a story about fate, cursed land and native remains. Conventional wisdom holds that it's bad luck to build over Indian graves.

I mentioned the story to Bill when I got to the office...and wondered aloud about what might lie under the headquarters of Touchmark National Bank. It had been a rough couple of months for us both. Bill chuckled. He agreed that there might be something to it. After all, the pavement in front of our building had been buckling for the past several weeks.

Later that summer I had lunch with Joe Briner, the former president of Alpha Bank & Trust. I mentioned the Dead Indian hypothesis and the buckling pavement to him as well. He agreed that it seemed mighty suspicious.

Hello, I Must Be Going

Ask anyone who's done it, and they'll tell you that starting a regulated business is a formidable challenge. From planning to funding to hiring people—and dealing with regulators to boot—success in the process is a proud accomplishment. As I came to phrase it: *It's the most fun that I never want to have again.* From securities registration to banking regulation, the process must rank among the most meticulous and demanding of business starts. I wouldn't recommend it...but I don't regret a minute of it, either.

By June 2010, the divergence of interests among Touchmark board members had reduced their numbers from seventeen directors to ten. Of the nine non-employee directors, three lived in South Carolina and as such were largely removed from the daily affairs of bank politics. The new board leadership was pursuing an agenda markedly different from the previous regime. The situation was ripe for management change.

Bill Short and I were employees #1 and #2 for Team Touchmark. We'd joined the team together, and it didn't take long after the change in chairmanship to realize that the new board leadership would best be served by managers who were disposed to follow their lead. It was also apparent that we'd done as much as we could to advance the success of the company as it was. New leadership—with markedly different expectations for authority and control—would need to be handed the reins. In due course, Bill was offered a modest severance package in return for his resignation. Gracious and professional as ever, Bill accepted after appropriate consideration. Bill Short's last day of service would be July 2, 2010.

On June 11, 2010, I was attending a Federal Home Loan Bank conference at the toney Ritz Carlton Resort on Amelia Island. Two years and four months had passed since I'd started my community banking adventure at the sumptuous Ritz Carlton in Atlanta (sweet irony!). After a day of networking and seminars, I was recovering poolside with a drink in my hand, basking in this uncommon perk of leadership. My cell phone rang. It was Bill. The board had met earlier that afternoon and had determined that further changes in executive management were necessary. The board had voted to ask for my resignation, and Bill had been given the task of calling me to relay their request. Fortuitously, the drink in my hand had not been my first of the evening. Within the coming week, my own severance package would be arranged, and my separation was finalized for July 9. Bill and I both met with our successors, and announcement our departures was arranged.

UNITED STATES SECURITIES AND EXCHANGE COMMISSION

WASHINGTON, D.C. 20549

FORM 8-K
CURRENT REPORT

Pursuant to Section 13 or 15(d) of the Securities and Exchange Act of 1934

Date of Report (Date of earliest event reported) July 2, 2010

TOUCHMARK BANCSHARES, INC.

Item 5.02 Departure of Directors or Certain Officers; Election of Directors; Appointment of Certain Officers; Compensatory Arrangements of Certain Officers.

(a) On July 2, 2010, William R. Short resigned from his position as a director of Touchmark Bancshares, Inc. (the "Company") and the Company's national bank subsidiary, Touchmark National Bank (the "Bank"). Mr. Short was a member of the executive committee of the board of directors.

(b) 1. On July 2, 2010, William R. Short resigned from his position as President and Chief Executive Officer of the Company and the Bank.

2. Effective as of July 9, 2010, Robert D. Koncerak resigned from his position as Chief Financial Officer of the Company and the Bank.

(c) 1. On July 2, 2010, the Company and the Bank entered into an Employment Agreement with Ms. Pin Pin Chau to become the President and Chief Executive Officer of the Company and the Bank. Ms. Chau's appointment as President and Chief Executive Officer of the Company and the Bank became effective on July 2, 2010.

Ms. Chau, age 69, has over 30 years of experience in the banking industry. She previously served as the President and Chief Executive

Officer of The Summit National Bank from February 1993 until it was acquired by UCBH Holdings, Inc. in 2006. She was elected as a director of UCBH Holdings in 2007 and served on its board until her resignation in 2008. Most recently, she was involved in an organizing effort for a national bank in north Georgia. Before joining The Summit National Bank in 1993, Ms. Chau was President and Chief Executive Officer of United Orient Bank in New York. Prior to that, she was with National Westminster Bank USA in domestic and international posts. She has served on numerous public and educational boards, including gubernatorial appointments to economic and finance boards for the State of Georgia. She graduated magna cum laude, Phi Beta Kappa, and Phi Kappa Phi from Coe College. Ms. Chau received her M.A. degree from Yale University and is a graduate of Stonier Graduate School of Banking.

Ms. Chau's Employment Agreement with the Company and the Bank is for a thirty-six (36) month term. During this term, Ms. Chau is entitled to an initial base salary of $250,000 per year. Ms. Chau is also entitled to or eligible for an annual performance bonus, options to purchase 50,000 shares of the Company's common stock at a price of $8.39 per share, participate in our benefits programs, and receive certain other perquisites and reimbursements.

Pursuant to the terms of her employment agreement, Ms. Chau is prohibited from disclosing our confidential information. The employment agreement also contains certain restrictions on competition and solicitation of customers or employees. The employment agreement also contains provisions related to payments upon termination or a change of control.

2. On July 7, 2010, the Company and the Bank hired Mr. Jorge L. Forment to become the Chief Financial Officer of the Company and the Bank. Mr. Forment's appointment as Chief Financial Officer of the Company and the Bank became effective on July 9, 2010.

Mr. Forment, age 52, has over 30 years of experience in the banking industry. He previously served as the President and Chief Executive Officer of United Americas Bank, based in Atlanta, Georgia, from April, 1999 to April, 2010. Prior to that, he served as the Chief Financial Officer and a Senior Vice President with Etowah Bank in Canton, Georgia. Mr. Forment attended the College of Business at Florida State University, where he received his B.S. in Finance and Economics.

Mr. Forment's Employment Agreement with the Company and the Bank is for a twenty-four (24) month term. During this term, Mr. Forment is entitled to an initial base salary of $150,000 per year. Mr. Forment is also entitled to or eligible for options to immediately purchase 5,000 shares of common stock for $8.39 per share and options to purchase an additional 5,000 shares of common stock at a future date, participate in our benefits programs, and receive certain other perquisites and reimbursements.

Pursuant to the terms of his employment agreement, Mr. Forment is prohibited from disclosing our confidential information. The employment agreement also contains certain restrictions on competition and solicitation of customers or employees. The employment agreement also contains provisions related to payments upon termination or a change of control.

(d) On July 7, 2010, the boards of directors of the Company and the Bank elected Ms. Pin Pin Chau as a director. Ms. Chau is expected to serve on the executive committee of the board of directors.

I spent my final week working with the new CEO. There was no alcohol on the premises from the moment of Ms. Chau's arrival. The manner in which I disposed of it will be left entirely to reader imagination.

From an initial start-up fund of $220,000 and a $2.5 million line of credit in February 2007, here is the balance sheet that was filed with the SEC for Touchmark Bancshares, Inc. for the quarter ending June 30, 2010:

Chart 28

TOUCHMARK BANCSHARES, INC.
AND SUBSIDIARY
Condensed Consolidated Balance Sheets
June 30, 2010, and December 31, 2009

		unaudited June 30, 2010		December 31, 2009
ASSETS				
Cash and due from banks	$	2,406,709	$	1,695,884
Federal funds sold		1,100,000		—
Interest-bearing accounts with other banks		1,492,943		3,073,627
Investment securities:				
Securities available for sale		52,438,697		43,230,785
Securities held to maturity		10,638,051		4,619,299
Restricted stock		1,505,700		1,365,750
Loans held for sale		792,797		1,832,412
Loans, less allowance for loan losses of $2,083,603 and $1,445,522, respectively		79,552,923		66,609,313
Accrued interest receivable		856,840		543,334
Premises and equipment		2,901,271		3,043,646
Foreclosed real estate		291,377		—
Land held for sale		2,409,023		2,409,023
Other assets		621,480		839,402
Total assets	$	**157,007,811**	$	**129,262,475**
LIABILITIES AND SHAREHOLDERS' EQUITY				
Liabilities:				
Deposits:				
Non-interest bearing demand	$	5,044,722	$	3,489,983
Interest-bearing		108,892,924		72,553,691
Total deposits		113,937,646		76,043,674
Accrued interest payable		74,991		60,624
Federal Home Loan Bank advances		11,400,000		11,400,000
Secured borrowings		2,839,497		—
Other borrowings		—		12,525,000
Other liabilities		161,931		599,935
Total liabilities		**128,414,065**		**100,629,233**
Shareholders' Equity				
Preferred stock, no par value,, none issued		—		—
Common stock, $.01 par value, 50,000,000 shares authorized, 3,465,391 issued and outstanding		34,654		34,654
Paid in capital		35,948,215		35,827,141
Accumulated deficit		(7,663,297)		(7,471,431)
Accumulated other comprehensive income		274,174		242,878
Total shareholders' equity		**28,593,746**		**28,633,242**
Total liabilities and shareholders' equity	$	**157,007,811**	$	**129,262,475**

Not bad...not bad at all.

The employees gave me a very nice send-off on the day of my appointed departure, complete with a memento and a card filled with well wishes. There were no directors in attendance other than Pin Pin herself. As Touchmark's new CEO, she was most gracious.

July 7ᵗʰ, 2010

To the employees of Touchmark National Bank

Friday, July 9, will be my last day of service with Touchmark National Bank. While I regret that this announcement is sudden, my departure has been "in the works" for some time and the process of negotiating my exit and securing my replacement has been confidential by necessity. I've found community banking to be a rewarding experience. The opportunity to have started with an organizing group in 2007, successfully complete one of Georgia's largest-ever community bank capital raises, and help lead the organization to $150MM in assets and through to its first profitable quarter has been humbling, exhilarating, sometimes astonishing—and always rewarding. That we accomplished so much during such a formidable period of financial history has made it all that much more of an adventure. I'm grateful for the relationships I've made, and I hope to maintain them into my next venture.

Serving as a de novo SEC-reporting community bank CFO from February 2007 to July 2010 has been quite a ride. Touchmark has grown from an initial organizing group to 3 full-service branches with 25 fantastic employees and an impressive array of innovative products and services. Key to it all have been the partnerships and relationships that have enabled me to select vendors, hire talent, manage investments, coordinate operations, handle marketing, navigate compliance, make payroll, accomplish OCC, SEC and Federal Reserve Reporting...and keep the headquarters kitchen clean on Friday afternoons! Such is the life of a community banker!

Jorge Forment is Touchmark's incoming CFO. His e-mail is <u>xxxx</u>. I hope that you will welcome him and demonstrate both your experience and expertise for his benefit in the coming days. After today, I can best be reached at <u>xxxx</u>. I plan to take a couple of weeks off to enjoy my family. My daughters are all at home this summer and we've got several trips lined up to enjoy some personal time before the older two head back to school.

Thanks again for your friendship, partnership and professional support. I hope our paths will cross again soon.

God Bless and All The Best to You,

RDK

At Present

Touchmark National Bank began its fifth year of operation in January 2013 and has posted modest profits in recent quarters. As of March 31, 2013 total assets amounted to $121 million, first quarter income was $189,000 and retained earnings stood at -$5.3 million, which represents the amount the bank still must earn in order to become cumulatively profitable. Touchmark Bancshares, Inc. deregistered from the SEC in August 2012 with the filing of its June 2012 financial statements. Quarterly financial reports remain available on the FDIC's website, and holding company updates are filed with the Federal Reserve.

As a shareholder, I choose to remain optimistic—and I wish team Touchmark every success.

List 2

Georgia Bank Failures 1997-2012

	Close Date	Bank Name	City	Acquiring Institution
1	28-Sep-07	NetBank	Alpharetta	ING DIRECT
2	29-Aug-08	Integrity Bank	Alpharetta	Regions Bank
3	24-Oct-08	Alpha Bank & Trust	Alpharetta	Steams Bank, N.A.
4	21-Nov-08	Community Bank	Loganville	Bank of Essex
5	5-Dec-08	First Georgia Community Bank	Jackson	United Bank
6	12-Dec-08	Haven Trust Bank	Duluth	Branch Banking & Trust Company
7	6-Feb-09	FirstBank Financial Services	McDonough	Regions Bank
8	6-Mar-09	Freedom Bank of Georgia	Commerce	Northeast Georgia Bank
9	20-Mar-09	FirstCity Bank	Stockbridge	No Acquirer
10	27-Mar-09	Omni National Bank	Atlanta	No Acquirer
11	24-Apr-09	American Southern Bank	Kennesaw	Bank of North Georgia
12	1-May-09	Silverton Bank, NA	Atlanta	No Acquirer
13	19-Jun-09	Southern Community Bank	Fayetteville	United Community Bank
14	26-Jun-09	Neighborhood Community Bank	Newnan	CharterBank
15	26-Jun-09	Community Bank of West Georgia	Villa Rica	No Acquirer
16	17-Jul-09	First Piedmont Bank	Winder	First American Bank and Trust Co
17	24-Jul-09	Security Bank of Jones County	Gray	State Bank and Trust Company
18	24-Jul-09	Security Bank of Houston County	Perry	State Bank and Trust Company
19	24-Jul-09	Security Bank of Bibb County	Macon	State Bank and Trust Company
20	24-Jul-09	Security Bank of North Metro	Woodstock	State Bank and Trust Company
21	24-Jul-09	Security Bank of North Fulton	Alpharetta	State Bank and Trust Company
22	24-Jul-09	Security Bank of Gwinnett County	Suwanee	State Bank and Trust Company
23	21-Aug-09	First Coweta Bank	Newnan	United Bank
24	21-Aug-09	ebank	Atlanta	Steams Bank, N.A.
25	25-Sep-09	Georgian Bank	Atlanta	First Citizens Bank and Trust Co
26	23-Oct-09	American United Bank	Lawrenceville	Ameris Bank
27	6-Nov-09	United Security Bank	Sparta	Ameris Bank
28	4-Dec-09	The Tattnall Bank	Reidsville	Heritage Bank of the South
29	4-Dec-09	First Security National Bank	Norcross	State Bank and Trust Company
30	4-Dec-09	The Buckhead Community Bank	Atlanta	State Bank and Trust Company
31	18-Dec-09	RockBridge Commercial Bank	Atlanta	No Acquirer
32	29-Jan-10	Community Bank and Trust	Comelia	SCBT National Association
33	29-Jan-10	First National Bank of Georgia	Carrollton	Community & Southern Bank
34	19-Mar-10	Bank of Hiawassee	Hiawassee	Citizens South Bank
35	19-Mar-10	Appalachian Community Bank	Ellijay	Community & Southern Bank
36	19-Mar-10	Century Security Bank	Duluth	Bank of Upson
37	26-Mar-10	Unity National Bank	Cartersville	Bank of the Ozarks
38	26-Mar-10	McIntosh Commercial Bank	Carrollton	CharterBank
39	14-May-10	Satilla Community Bank	Saint Marys	Ameris Bank
40	25-Jun-10	First National Bank	Savannah	The Savannah Bank, N.A.

	Close Date	Bank Name	City	Acquiring Institution
41	23-Jul-10	Crescent Bank and Trust Company	Jasper	Renasant Bank
42	30-Jul-10	Northwest Bank & Trust	Acworth	State Bank and Trust Company
43	17-Sep-10	The Peoples Bank	Winder	Community & Southern Bank
44	17-Sep-10	First Commerce Community Bank	Douglasville	Community & Southern Bank
45	17-Sep-10	Bank of Ellijay	Ellijay	Community & Southern Bank
46	22-Oct-10	The First National Bank of Barnesville	Barnesville	United Bank
47	22-Oct-10	The Gordon Bank	Gordon	Morris Bank
48	12-Nov-10	Darby Bank & Trust Co.	Vidalia	Ameris Bank
49	12-Nov-10	Tifton Banking Company	Tifton	Ameris Bank
50	17-Dec-10	United Americas Bank, N.A.	Atlanta	State Bank and Trust Company
51	17-Dec-10	Appalachian Community Bank, FSB	McCaysville	Peoples Bank of East Tennessee
52	17-Dec-10	Chestatee State Bank	Dawsonville	Bank of the Ozarks
53	14-Jan-11	Oglethorpe Bank	Brunswick	Bank of the Ozarks
54	21-Jan-11	Enterprise Banking Company	McDonough	No Acquirer
55	4-Feb-11	North Georgia Bank	Watkinsville	BankSouth
56	4-Feb-11	American Trust Bank	Roswell	Renasant Bank
57	18-Feb-11	Citizens Bank of Effingham	Springfield	Heritage Bank of the South
58	18-Feb-11	Habersham Bank	Clarkesville	SCBT National Association
59	15-Apr-11	New Horizons Bank	East Ellijay	Citizens South Bank
60	15-Apr-11	Bartow County Bank	Cartersville	Hamilton State Bank
61	29-Apr-11	The Park Avenue Bank	Valdosta	Bank of the Ozarks
62	29-Apr-11	First Choice Community Bank	Dallas	Bank of the Ozarks
63	20-May-11	First Georgia Banking Company	Franklin	CertusBank, National Association
64	20-May-11	Atlantic Southern Bank	Macon	CertusBank, National Association
65	17-Jun-11	McIntosh State Bank	Jackson	Hamilton State Bank
66	24-Jun-11	Mountain Heritage Bank	Clayton	First American Bank and Trust Co
67	15-Jul-11	High Trust Bank	Stockbridge	Ameris Bank
68	15-Jul-11	One Georgia Bank	Atlanta	Ameris Bank
69	19-Aug-11	First Southern National Bank	Statesboro	Heritage Bank of the South
70	2-Sep-11	CreekSide Bank	Woodstock	Georgia Commerce Bank
71	2-Sep-11	Patriot Bank of Georgia	Cumming	Georgia Commerce Bank
72	14-Oct-11	Piedmont Community Bank	Gray	State Bank and Trust Company
73	21-Oct-11	Community Capital Bank	Jonesboro	State Bank and Trust Company
74	21-Oct-11	Decatur First Bank	Decatur	Fidelity Bank
75	10-Nov-11	Community Bank of Rockmart	Rockmart	Century Bank of Georgia
76	20-Jan-12	The First State Bank	Stockbridge	Hamilton State Bank
77	24-Feb-12	Central Bank of Georgia	Ellaville	Ameris Bank
78	2-Mar-12	Global Commerce Bank	Doraville	Metro City Bank
79	23-Mar-12	Covenant Bank & Trust	Rock Spring	Stearns Bank, N.A.
80	15-Jun-12	Security Exchange Bank	Marietta	Fidelity Bank
81	6-Jul-12	Montgomery Bank & Trust	Ailey	Ameris Bank
82	20-Jul-12	First Cherokee State Bank	Woodstock	Community & Southern Bank
83	20-Jul-12	Georgia Trust Bank	Buford	Community & Southern Bank
84	27-Jul-12	Jasper Banking Company	Jasper	Stearns Bank N.A.
85	16-Nov-12	Hometown Community Bank	Braselton	CertusBank, National Association

Enablers of the Apocalypse and the Perils of Contemporary Banking: Pigs, Rats and Capital Requirements

"Every businessman knows that there are moments on which hang the destiny of years."

Mimi Moges

Friday, April 15, 2005
Atlanta banks vulnerable to home slump
Atlanta Business Chronicle - by Jill Lerner, Staff Writer

Georgia community banks are among the most vulnerable in the nation to a downturn in the housing market because of an unprecedented reliance on construction-related lending.

According to new figures from the **Federal Deposit Insurance Corp.**, construction and development lending at Georgia community banks jumped 45 percent last year, to $9.6 billion in 2004 from $6.64 billion in 2003.

The surge in so-called "C&D" lending, most of which came from metro Atlanta banks, means the Atlanta banking market is the second-most exposed to C&D lending as a percentage of total capital in the nation, behind only the Fort Walton Beach, Fla., area, according to the FDIC.

The housing market has experienced a long boom, fueled in part by ultra-low interest rates. If it were to decline sharply, builders could be unable to repay those loans, causing losses at many banks.

Although Atlanta leads the state in such lending exposure, Athens, Macon and Savannah also ranked among the top 10 markets nationally in terms of C&D lending exposure, meaning Georgia markets account for four out of the top 10 list.

"C&D and commercial real estate loans traditionally represent relatively high-risk portfolios where losses can mount quickly in a downturn. High concentrations in these loans have historically been associated with a higher frequency of failure among FDIC-insured institutions," said Richard Brown, chief economist for the FDIC.

That said, he added, "It needs to be recognized that not only is the banking industry in strong financial shape at present, but it is generally recognized that C&D and CRE loan underwriting and risk selection in this cycle have been more conservative than during the 1980s-early '90s real estate cycle."

Observers also point out construction lending long has been higher in Georgia than the rest of the country, and the region's banking industry has withstood previous housing slumps relatively successfully. Furthermore, the region's population growth continues to outpace the nation's, and Atlanta's economy is on the upswing.

Since 1993, when Atlanta was ranked 16th among metros nationwide for median C&D exposure, it has been in the top five for such lending concentration in the country.

However, Georgia community banks' current level of exposure is the greatest ever and far greater than it was during the recession of the early 1990s. In 1991, Georgia banks' C&D lending as a percentage of total assets was 3.2 percent; it is 13.7 percent today. (Emphasis RDK)

Nationally, the average is 5.5 percent of total assets.

And, at the same time that C&D lending has surged 45 percent, loan loss reserves – the money banks use as "cushion" against charged-off loans – grew only 12.4 percent, according to the FDIC.

My experience of the past several years has taught me that the failure of a business—any business—is an intensely *personal* affair. To the people who invested in it, managed it, were employed by it, sold, served and patronized it, their interactions were anything *but* "just business." The losses suffered on so many different levels are uniquely (and painfully) personal. Business is comprised *entirely* of personal interactions, from the mailman who makes a daily delivery, to the CEO who oversees his employees, his vendors...and his mother-in-law's investment in the company.

Riding On *Annus Terribilus*

Take a moment and visualize yourself on a thrill ride: you're rising slowly but imminently toward the top of a roller coaster. Your hands are clamped firmly around a cold metal bar (or are flailing in the air!) as the car is pulled deliciously skyward. The view is exhilarating—and it just keeps getting better. The world looks amazing from up here! Go ahead and summon up that feeling of dramatic anticipation—and the inevitable twist in your stomach. You're going higher, there's nothing you can do about it, so draw a breath, brace yourself and enjoy the ride...

OK, now that you're up there...pause at the summit and imagine just one more thing: imagine that within the past hour you've eaten three chili cheese dogs, two baskets of potato patch fries (extra cheese) and a cotton candy ball the size of a tumbleweed. Mom's been chiding all afternoon that you're eating too much junk food and that you're going to get sick to your stomach. You don't care. It feels good, and you're having fun. Now, as your cart approaches the summit of that coaster, your face begins to flush, your hands feel clammy, and that woozy feeling starts to take over. It's all downhill from here...

After several years of remarkably strong business conditions in the Atlanta regional economy, carts began flying off the rails in the latter half of 2007. Two charts below, courtesy of John Hunt at Smart Numbers, illustrate the dramatic falloff in Atlanta residential real estate that began during *annus terribilus*, the awful ride that was the year 2008.

First is a graph of Atlanta's metro county residential development permits between December 1996 and August 2012. The chart attests to a development trend that registered in the multithousands of units per month *for ten years*. Suddenly in 2007, new permits fell 90 percent from levels reached during the heights of 2005. Those chili dogs sure tasted good at the time!

Chart 29

Permit Trend 12/1996- 8/2012 Atlanta

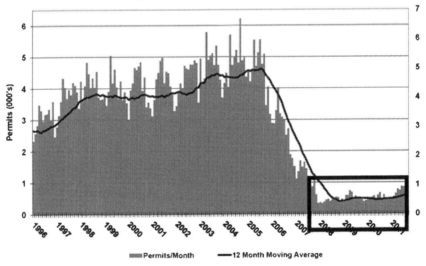

The national chart (courtesy of Bloomberg) is equally as dramatic. From a high of 2.27 million annualized housing starts in January 2006, the bottom was reached in April 2009 at 478,000. In February 2013 the graph registered at 917,000. The 20-year average is 1.38 million.

Chart 30

Annualized Housing Starts: 1993 – Feb 2013

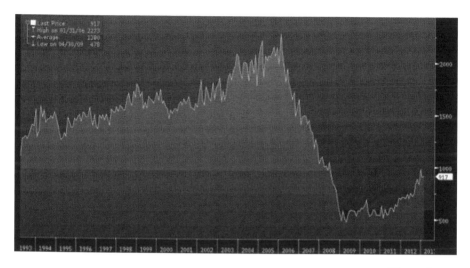

Bloomberg

The second Smart Numbers chart shows the corresponding amount of listed residential real estate in terms of years' supply of inventory. This is the data from which overhang and absorption rates are calculated. Notice that permits actually peaked in mid-2004 and just hung there through 2005. I personally hate it when roller coasters do that—but it's great for the economy! As the chart shows, inventory in 2006 began to balloon as demand went into free fall just as all those permits were coming on to the market as residential housing. Note that 2012 inventory levels ultimately returned to lows not seen since 2000. During those wonderful years leading up to 2007, real estate agents and developers could just about sell anything to anybody. *Those* were the days of irrational exuberance! The market in 2013 is just now returning to the long term trend. Those other lines point out the moment in January 2012 when inventory fell to levels not seen since January 2000. That graph tells quite a story!

Chart 31

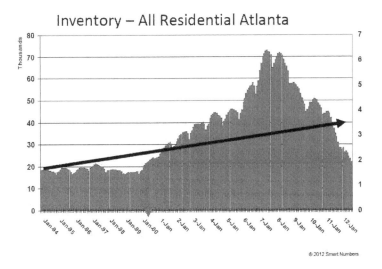

To be clear, the community banking industry participated only to a small degree in the business of mortgage lending—that is, providing 30-year financing for residential homes. While many institutions staffed mortgage origination departments, those loans were sold off into the enormous securitization industry that had kicked into high gear by the early 2000s. The vast majority of community bank real estate exposure came through the funding of property developers and the massive residential and commercial projects that were cultivated at the outskirts of the burgeoning Atlanta region. The key mechanisms that powered this growth enabled both leverage and funding to fuel a broad spectrum of housing demand.

The Four Enablers of the Apocalypse

Population growth and economic development provided the backdrop for a strong banking sector in the run-up to the economic crises across Georgia and the US as a whole. *Inside* the industry, there were four factors that fueled the growth of community banking through the Golden Age of Banking. To understand these elements is to understand how a state like Georgia could spawn 149 new community bank charters over ten remarkable years.

Trust Preferred Securities

A trust preferred security (TRuPs) is a bond issued by a bank holding company or insurance firm that financial institutions use to fund loan growth, acquisitions, or both. Between 2000 and 2007, the TRuPs market saw nearly $50 billion of issuance. Most of these securities were pooled into instruments similar to mortgage-backed securities on the premise of diversifying exposures across a range of issuing companies. Ninety percent of these issues were bank or bank-dominant. Most of this debt was also *bought* by financial institutions—like the banks themselves, who saw TRuPs as a way to hold a diversified earning asset with an attractive yield. The industry largely bought up its own debt: a bond originated by one bank served as an investment for another in a veritable kaleidoscope of security originations. Fascinating, huh? Kinda like what the Fed has been doing in earnest with its balance sheet since 2010.

Chart 32

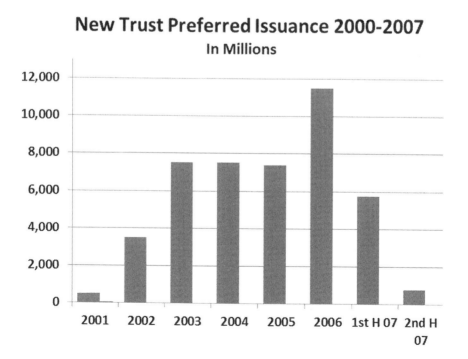

New Trust Preferred Issuance 2000-2007
In Millions

The trust preferred market was materially disrupted (read: shot dead) by the subprime mortgage meltdown in 2007. Funding sources largely disappeared, and the market entirely dried up by the end of that year. With the onset of failures and regulatory actions beginning in 2008, many issuers were forced to defer interest payments and the market value of these securities collapsed to pennies on the dollar. Billions of these securities remain on bank balance sheets today. The issued debt (the liability side) is still (of course) valued at the amount issued. TRuPs securities purchased, though (the asset side) are currently priced anywhere between 5 percent and 60 percent of issuing price. Resulting writedowns and impairment charges have been an enormous drain on bank capital levels. Silverton Bank, for example, was a big originator and distributor of trust preferred securities and bank holding company loans. While not widely recognized, this implosion has been one of the larger causes of capital deterioration, and has precipitated the failure of numerous community banks.

As of May 2013, literally hundreds of bank holding companies remain in interest deferral on their TRuPs. Deferrals began in the latter half of 2008. Indentures typically provide for 20 quarters, or 60 months of deferment. As such, the permissible 60 month deferral period will begin expiring for bank holding companies throughout 2013. It's going to be "interesting" to see which have the cash to pay out the accumulated deferred interest...and which will be facing insolvency. In the eyes of the Federal Reserve— which regulates bank holding companies, this is among their greatest concerns in the coming years.

Interest Reserves

Probably the most abused and controversial lending scheme employed in the heyday of development lending involved the practice of interest reserves. An interest reserve is a designated portion of a borrower's line of credit that is drawn on to make interest or principal payments on the borrower's asset-based loan. Say a bank puts in place a $10 million facility to fund a development of residential homes. Among the covenants of the facility might be that the borrower can draw down only $9 million for construction and build-out. The balance of the credit facility will be *managed by the banker* and used to pay interest that accumulates on the loan until the developer can finish and sell off developed lots and residences. Months—sometimes years—could go by without the developer ever writing a check to pay principal or interest! Instead, the debt could be serviced by the bank drawing on the remaining portion of the loan facility...in order to pay itself! And you thought only the US Treasury could come up with such schemes! A loan could remain current for months (or years!) regardless of the borrower's ability to pay—*or even after the developer has gone out of business!* In their lawsuit against the directors of Integrity Bank, the FDIC alleged that officers "replenished interest reserves, which allowed the bank to pay interest with more borrowed funds." This ploy enabled banks like Integrity to delay recognition of impaired loans...until those credit lines were maxed out or their auditors cried foul, revealing borrowers who had long since headed for the exits.

Brokered Deposits and Wholesale Funding

A bank generates revenue by taking in deposits and making loans. When loan demand outstrips available deposits, banks can borrow funds from institutional sources. So-called brokered deposits evolved from massive balances held in institutional brokerage accounts, which fund managers sought to invest to generate additional returns on their portfolios. These funds make their way into banks in the form of institutional CDs and money market deposits. The rate that a bank pays for a brokered CD depends on a quality rating: the better the rating, the lower the borrowing cost. Because these deposits tend to be transacted in larger blocks—usually $250,000 to $1 million—a deterioration of a bank's quality score could jeopardize renewal and put a strain on the bank's ability to pay out these large deposits at maturity. Some of the most aggressive lenders in Georgia during the boom period drew more than a third of their funding from such non-core sources in lieu of a historically more stable base of checking, savings, and consumer CDs. Once the regulatory agencies began to criticize institutional funding levels, banks backed off considerably and now rarely draw more than 10 percent of funding from brokered sources. Wholesale funding, though, encompasses a wider class of non-core borrowings, such as advances from the Federal Home Loan banks, institutional "money market" funds, deposits from other banking institutions and so-called jumbo CDs of more than $100,000.

Loan Participations

As discussed earlier, a bank is limited in the size of the largest loan it can put on its books—generally 25 percent of capital for a state-chartered institution and 15 percent for a national charter. Most banks prudently have in-house limits that are considerably less than the maximum. In order for a bank to take advantage of larger deals—or for rural banks to acquire loans from higher-growth markets—bankers can syndicate or share larger credits among several participating institutions. An originating, or "lead" bank underwrites and structures the deal, participating banks analyze the credit to their internal requirements, and the loan is then shared and funded on a pro-rata basis, with the lead bank administering and forwarding payments and documentation accordingly. This all works well and good when the borrower is healthy, the lead bank is healthy, and the participating banks are liquid and healthy, too. But what happens if the lead bank develops problems and becomes preoccupied with internal and regulatory challenges? Even worse, what happens if the lead bank or one of the participants fails and the loan is assumed by another banking organization? In short, the position of the remaining bank participants, *as well as the borrower*, becomes perilous, precarious and just a god-awful mess. For reasons that we'll cover later, a loan acquired under a so-called loss share agreement with the FDIC can incent the acquiring bank to become adversarial with both the borrower and the other banks in the syndicate.

Participation agreements were often standardized documents used on a one-size-fits-all basis. Negotiated modifications were frequently drafted by internal staff and open to interpretation. Such arrangements rarely hold up well if one of the banks gets in trouble.

Participation documents drafted through 2007 rarely anticipated events of default such as the sale of collateral or the priority of payment distributions. The formal agreements that parsed out the events of default, referred to as intercreditor agreements, were rarely completed among the banks sharing a credit, which meant that lenders were left to hash out such conditions only after the loan went bad. As you might imagine, such meetings are contentious affairs.

Loan participations present a unique challenge because *only the lead bank has an actual relationship with the borrower.* If you think about it, buying into a loan participation isn't nearly as sound as buying into a bond deal or an investment security. Loan participants other than the lead bank, after all, *hold no promise to pay from the borrower.* The only party obligated to pay the participating lenders is the lead bank in the syndicated deal. Think about what that means when a participating bank wants to exit a deal...and the lead has no desire (or ability!) to replace that participant in the pool. Consider, even worse, if the lead bank should fail...

Participation agreements tend to give a great deal of flexibility to the lead bank. Some provide no voting rights for the other participating banks at all. Participating institutions could (can) often be left out of key decisions or be forced to sue to assert their rights. Remember, times were *good.* Defaults were unheard of, and many of those deals were hotly competitive.

Clearly, too many Georgia loan participations were based more on relationships between bankers than they were on a fully vetted understanding *of* and relationship *with* the borrower. In cases documented all too frequently in FDIC post-mortem reports (published by the Office of the Inspector General), participating banks were purported to have relied entirely on the underwriting of the lead bank rather than on their own internal credit analysis. Current or updated credit information was hard to come by in the best of times, depending almost entirely on the diligence and attention of the lead bank to both gather and distribute this information.

For bankers who may argue that I'm broad-brushing these four instruments as weapons of mass financial destruction, let me clarify that all four mechanisms are fundamental to the trade of community banking—and when used in moderation, each is a viable contributor to the growth and prosperity of the business. But history shows that each of them can also be characterized as volatile accelerants. Just like gasoline.

Friday, July 6, 2007
Banks' sale of loans may spread ills
Atlanta Business Chronicle – by Joe Rauch, Staff writer

Problem loans such as those that have emerged recently at several Georgia community banks could trickle down to community banks throughout Georgia because of an obscure lending practice largely shielded from public view.

Alpharetta's Integrity Bancshares Inc. said June 29 it is adding $21 million to its loan loss reserves and restructuring a series of past due loans as it continues to work out $83 million in problem loans. Other loan problems have emerged recently at **United Community Banks Inc.** and **GB&T Bancshares Inc.** The reason some bankers are worried the problems could become more widespread is the practice known as "loan participations." They say this is the biggest issue facing community banks as the housing market slows and loan defaults rise.

A hallmark of community banking, loan participations are portions of loans, made by one bank, which are then sold to other banks. Several banks then hold pieces of the same loan made to a borrower. The buyers of those loan portions can be as close as the same city as the original lender, and as far away as the other side of the state or country.

The benefit of loan participations is they allow banks in areas with poor loan demand to find business in higher-growth areas. Banks in Savannah or Athens, for example, could tap into loans made in Atlanta, Macon or Valdosta. They also enable banks whose customers have large loan needs to get the resources of several banks to get deals done.

The state is a hotbed for loan participations. Banks such as Macon-based **Security Bank Corp.** run divisions that specialize in selling portions of loans to other banks statewide.

Other lenders such as Atlanta-based The Bankers Bank and Milledgeville-based **Empire Financial Services Inc.** work as middlemen for loan participations, matching loan sellers with loan buyers. But the practice comes with risk.

Bankers said because many of the deals involve property or projects outside a local market, extra due diligence and care has to be taken when evaluating where to buy a loan participation in an area where a bank might have little or no lending experience.

Although some banks avoid the practice, some of the newest community banks are increasingly relying on loan participations to grow in a market crowded with competitors and fewer quality customers, according to local bankers.

But data on banks' loan participations are not released publicly. Instead, the information is compiled by banks and shared solely with state and federal regulators during regular oversight examinations. Participations aren't publicly disclosed because they should be evaluated and held to the same standards of any other loan on a bank's balance sheets, said Rob Braswell, Georgia Department of Banking and Finance commissioner.

Banks don't usually disclose a loan participation unless the loan goes bad, with the borrower missing payments or defaulting on the loan.

Locally, a slowing real estate market is spurring demand, said one prominent correspondent lender who declined to be named because he works with banks across the state on loan participations.

Banks who can't repeat the returns of recent years on their own, he said, will look to loan participations as one way to continue growing. But in their desire to continue growing, they could outstrip their ability to evaluate what might be bad loans.

The issue isn't just on bankers' minds.

"We encourage proper underwriting, just as the originating bank does," said Braswell.

State regulations require each bank in a loan participation to document and evaluate the loan as if it were any other potential customer.

But last fall, state bank examiners found several new Georgia banks relying on the underwriting work of the original bank on loan participations.

"The Department has always stressed the need for participating banks to do their own underwriting" and not rely on banks' selling the loan participations, an October announcement said. The Bankers Bank cautions buyers to do their own due diligence on potential loan participations.

Meanwhile, Integrity Bancshares says no portion of the $83 million in problem loans was sold to other banks.

And CEO Steve Skow said despite the problem loans, demand for loan participations remains strong. "Forty-plus banks are looking to buy our participations," Skow said. "Business continues as normal."

He declined to discuss specifics on how many of Integrity's loans are participated out to other local banks, but said the loan participations average between $2 million and $10 million in size. **Integrity Bank** has never had a loan participation default, he said.

Why Banks ~~Fail~~ Close

In the words of the Comptroller of the Currency:

"Liquidity is a financial institution's capacity to meet its cash and collateral obligations at a reasonable cost. Maintaining an adequate level of liquidity depends on the institution's ability to meet both expected and unexpected cash flows and collateral needs without adversely affecting either daily operations or the financial condition of the institution."

Interagency Policy Statement on Funding and Liquidity Risk Management, March 2010

In other words, if you don't have the cash available to meet the obligations and the withdrawals of your customers, you're not liquid. Liquidity shortfalls are the cause of those nasty bank runs we've read about, and from John Mauldin's synopsis in an earlier chapter. Banks used to fail because they ran out of money and literally went broke. But since the establishment of the FDIC in the 1930s, banks rarely fail like that anymore (unless Senator Chuck Shumer gets involved like he did with IndyMac). The FDIC is a federally owned and operated insurance company that ensures that depositors will get paid in quick and timely fashion (remember, banking is above all else a confidence business). With the exception of the savings & loan debacle of the 1980s, modern-day banks are now "closed" rather than left to suffer the unseemly drama of "failure" with the associated queues of anxious customers lined up in front of teller windows.

In a brilliant and widely circulated open letter to bankers in November 2010, Kilpatrick, Townsend attorney Richard Cheatham took issue with the characterization of contemporary bank "failures" and proceeded to build a case for why it was wrong, illegal, and immoral for regulators to be closing Georgia institutions on the basis of what Cheatham characterizes as a legislative flaw. Here is Cheatham's opening paragraph:

Since 2006, forty-eight Georgia banks have been closed by the bank regulators. Only a handful of those banks failed. The banks that failed were primarily relatively new banks with very limited true core deposits formed principally to benefit from what turned out to be a real estate bubble largely created by Wall Street funding. The rest, the vast majority of the Georgia banks, closed by the regulators were closed because the regulators determined that their tangible leverage capital levels had fallen below 2 percent, a statutorily mandated minimum capital level.

Cheatham then shakes a noble fist:

Many of these failures have resulted in irreparable damage to the communities formerly served by these banks and often to their employees, not to mention ruinous financial losses to the shareholders whose sole financial asset in many cases was their bank stock. These community and personal tragedies could and should have been avoided. If current trends continue, many more Georgia banks will be closed by the regulators in the coming months.

Building on the analogy that "generals are always fighting the last war," Mr. Cheatham goes on to explain why:

The S&L as a business model was destroyed by interest rate deregulation in the late 1970s and early 1980s. Previously, S&Ls borrowed short by taking deposits and lent long by extending home mortgages. That model only works in a market with regulated interest rates. Rather than letting S&Ls fail when the inevitable rate mismatch took hold, Congress and the regulators rewrote the rules to permit the S&Ls to expand their operations to include enterprise with different risks. Also, S&L regulators kept institutions open long after they were hopelessly insolvent. None of these thumbs in the dyke held, and the inevitable had to be faced and paid for. Congress, declaring never again and attempting to shift most of the blame to the regulators, amended the banking laws to require regulators to close financial institutions as soon as their leverage capital ratios fell below 2 percent. There is no way to say it tactfully; that was a stupid response to a unique crisis primarily created by Congress.

Banks do not fail because their tangible capital ratios fall below some bright line number. Banks are liquidity businesses. They can continue to operate with no capital as long as they can continue to generate cash necessary to meet their customer's needs. If this 2 percent closure rule had been in place in the 1970s, all the banks in Atlanta and most throughout Georgia would have been closed. Hindsight tells us that would have made no sense and would have impaired Georgia's economic development for decades."

While I love this letter and thoroughly recommend that you find it in your browser, I include only one last broadside of wisdom from Cheatham:

The 2 percent rule is ill conceived because it elevates to gospel an unreliable, estimated number developed as an approximation useful in identifying trends.

Mr. Cheatham explains that banks necessarily make *estimates* and *forecasts* regarding the fair value of their balance sheets, and that in dynamic markets, those estimates are bound to change across a reasonable range. It's quite a letter and goes on for several pages with a considerable argument that bankers should defend their shareholders, their employees and their customers from the legislated ratios that have brought hundreds of banking institutions to ruin.

And supported by the wisdom of a legal superstar like Dick Cheatham, I chime in here with what I feel is one of my most important conclusions from this writing project:

a tragic, spectacular truth about the carnage of community bank failures over the past five years is that *many of them absolutely, positively did not have to be closed*. Indeed, the senseless inflexibility around an arbitrary metric like 2 percent tier-one capital has cost investors, bankers, borrowers, and depositors dearly. For every institution that piled on more risk than could ever be justified to shareholders (like the boneheads at Integrity Bank), there are three or four other closed institutions that did their level best to follow the rules. While many could have managed sufficient liquidity to serve depositors through stormy seas (forced metaphor), capital and businesses were destroyed because of the two percent rule.

Here is a contention that I believe encompasses a majority of closed institutions since the 2008 collapse: *Genuine community banking franchises would have ponied up any and all necessary capital to keep their businesses liquid had their directors not feared the intransigence of narrowly-focused banking regulators.* While the counterargument is that the FDIC feared even larger losses had the 2 percent trigger not been absolute, I find that to be a self-fulfilling contention. No one wants to invest with a gun to his head, or with the fear that Uncle Sam might swoop in and declare a bank insolvent "because I say so." Stories abound of banks being forced to charge down loans that management had demonstrated were performing and ultimately collectible (bankers refer to these dictates as "RAP vs. GAAP": Regulatory Accounting Policy vs. Generally Accepted Accounting Principles). As of December 2012, there are survivor banks in Georgia holding millions of "special classified loan assets" on their balance sheets that, while performing and paying as agreed, are characterized as nonperforming loans with significant impairment charges taken against them...because of a regulatory dictate. The ultimate revenge for these hobbled institutions will come on the day when they can write those assets back up and record substantial gains as those loans are repaid in full. Those will be the lucky ones. They're still in business...unlike the bank that we'll read about in the next chapter.

In the end, there were plenty of reasons for community bank failures across Georgia: overdevelopment, overheated competition for business, big bonuses, fast money, and the head-rush thrill of succeeding in a fast-paced business. And let's be clear: bank regulators are not uniformly the colorless, black-hatted bad guys, and community bankers aren't uniformly the Pollyannas of the financial service industry. They're all *people*: some more capable than others, some better managers than others, some more desperate than others.

The following article, reprinted with permission from SNL, is a testimony to the frustration experienced by many a bank director. Charles Loudermilk served as chairman of the Buckhead Community Bank, which failed in December 2009. Though Loudermilk is known for having resources beyond that of the typical community bank chairman, his points are wholly representative of closed community banks. I include the entire article here because it's chock full of excellent points.

December 4, 2012

Failed-bank chairman lashes out at FDIC for sullying reputation with D&O Suit
By Tim Zawacki for SNL Financial

Defendants in FDIC professional liability complaints have been generally reticent to publicly discuss the litigation pending against them. Not so with R. Charles Loudermilk Sr.

The FDIC named Loudermilk, a longtime Atlanta-area businessman and philanthropist known as "Mr. Buckhead," as a defendant in a Nov. 30 suit seeking at least $21.8 million for alleged negligence in the issuance and servicing of 13 "high-risk and speculative" acquisition, development and construction and commercial real estate loans issued in the mid-2000s by The Buckhead Community Bank. Loudermilk served as founder and chairman of the bank, which failed in December 2009.

"I've been in business all my life and this is the first time I've ever been personally sued," he told SNL. "The way I see it, the FDIC is trying to collect the $5 million in directors' and officers' insurance. The insurance company feels the same way I feel: We didn't do anything wrong. We have not made any brother-in-law loans or illegal loans of any kind whatsoever. I have a lot of money, so they put me in there as the poster child, I think."

The FDIC suit accused Loudermilk and certain of his former colleagues at The Buckhead Community Bank of permitting the institution to engage in "extreme" growth in CRE and ADC assets, both on an absolute basis and relative to the bank's total capital. Examiners had found the bank approved loans that exceeded acceptable loan-to-value ratios, failed to properly monitor outstanding loans, maintained lax underwriting practices and continued to issue speculative loans amid signs of weakening in real estate market trends.

Loudermilk, however, said the bank fell victim to circumstance, not, as the FDIC alleged, mismanagement.

"If we knew we were going to have the recession, we sure as hell wouldn't have made those loans," he said. "Maybe if we had a magic wand we would have known that we should not have grown that fast."

At the time the FDIC alleged The Buckhead Community Bank was growing too quickly — regulatory data as archived by SNL shows the bank's construction and land development loans spiked to $372.7 million in 2007 from less than $100 million just three years prior — Loudermilk said the Atlanta area was expanding rapidly.

"You didn't have to go out and get loans, they would come to you," he recalled. "We turned down a lot."

He also defended the bank's board, saying it included individuals with a background in real estate, as well as the underwriting practices that have been criticized by the FDIC.

"We were not going blind into these loans," he said. "We all felt they were good. I looked at all of the paperwork, and the No. 1 thing I would look at is the net worth of the borrower ... to make sure it was more than twice the value of the loan. For some reason, we were not able to go after those assets until they closed us down. It was a timing thing."

The FDIC's lawsuit accused bank officials, among other shortcomings during the underwriting process, of failing to collect sufficient information regarding the financial wherewithal of borrowers in loans and loan participations entered by The Buckhead Community Bank, and then relying on stale data when agreeing to extend or renew certain of the loans and participations.

As the bank's losses mounted amid the economic downturn that was particularly swift in the Atlanta metropolitan area, Loudermilk recalled two meetings with the FDIC in which he predicted the agency's deposit insurance fund would lose up to $250 million if the bank were to be closed. The Buckhead Community Bank had $191.2 million in noncurrent assets and other real estate owned on its balance sheet as of Sept. 30, 2009, the last quarter-end prior to its failure. A June 2010 material loss review pegged the estimated loss, as of the end of 2009, at $240 million.

"They should have let us work it out," he said. "We would have lost money of course, but we had the ability to work those loans out. Each one of these [development] projects could've been sold for something. ... They closed us down before we were able to go out and liquidate these assets."

At the same time, Loudermilk said, he and his fellow directors — most of whom he characterized as "basically rich" — were reluctant to agree to regulators' requests that they infuse more equity into the bank prior to its closure.

"Friendship means more to me than money, and I'm not going go out and ask my friends to put more money into this bank and have [regulators] shut it down in six months or a year," he said. "That's what they did to a number of small banks," he alleged.

Loudermilk said regulators turned down his offer to infuse $50 million in additional capital into the bank on the condition they refrain from seizing it for a period of two years.

While Loudermilk said he could not imagine a jury would find him and his former colleagues guilty of the FDIC's negligence claims — and he is not open to settling the matter — he said he is most concerned about the impact that news of the lawsuit could have on his reputation.

"Every bank in the world could be charged with the same things we're charged with: making loans that turned sour because of the recession," he argued. "I bet you we were cleanest of the banks that were shut down. ... We ran that bank to the best of our abilities."

If you're interested in reading more on this subject, check out the congressional testimony given by community bankers before the House Banking Committee in September 2011. Warning: if you have a conscience, this is going to make you angry. For the community bankers among us, remove sharp objects from the room before proceeding:

http://www.gpo.gov/fdsys/pkg/CHRG-111hhrg56240/pdf/ CHRG-111hhrg56240.pdf

Capital Requirements

As Dick Cheatham's article noted, banks since the early 1980s have been required to maintain statutory capital levels in order to avoid punitive action from the FDIC. Eight percent capital to average assets constitutes a "well capitalized" bank, 5 percent is deemed "adequately capitalized," and anything below 5 percent... is a problem. As of December 2012, the median US bank held 9.86% of tier-one capital on its balance sheet and 16.38% risk-based capital, which weights loan and investment assets by their potential for default (ratio source: BankIntelligence).

Should a bank slip below the 2% tier-one ratio for *one single day,* the institution is required to notify its primary regulator (who in all likelihood has been in close communication with the bank by this point, anyway). The primary regulator—along with the FDIC—then has ninety days to either allow the bank to source investors and restore a sufficient capital buffer, or locate an institution willing to acquire the "failing" bank. Here's a simplified example:

Of Pigs and Rats

Let's say we organize the Piggy National Bank, and it opens with $10 million of opening capital on the balance sheet. So long as we can attract $90 million in customer deposits after we open, our bank can build roughly a $100 million loan portfolio to generate income for our shareholders. To make our example really simple, let's say our entire loan portfolio is made up of ten loans secured by either consumer or commercial real estate. Our collateral is office parks and strip shopping centers, residential mortgages and apartment buildings. We're feeling nicely diversified!

Now let's introduce a recession (wouldn't you know...). Property values fall by 10 percent—which isn't unusual for even the mildest of recessions. What happens to our loan portfolio? Well, on average our collateral values have declined...and now three of our borrowers can't afford to make their payments. In short, some of the loans in our portfolio have become impaired. We need to make provision for that impairment, and on their next visit our examiners and auditors will expect (and assure!) that we have done so. We need to establish loss reserves for our three troubled borrowers and test the collateral values that support the troubled loans in our portfolio. Rats.

It turns out that one of our borrowers goes bankrupt, and his collateral is in really bad shape. We can only sell it for $5 million, and there are no other assets that we can recover from the borrower. That means we take a loss and write off $5 million... and so we only have $5 million of our starting capital left. We're worried about losses on our other loans—especially those two problem guys, so we charge ourselves another $1 million and use it to establish a reserve against potential future losses in our portfolio.

In meetings with the other two problem borrowers, it looks as though we may be able to restructure their loans and reduce their payments to something they can afford, but we need to order appraisals and probably lower the interest rates on their loans in order to make the restructures work. Rats again! And, uh oh: if we have to write down the value of those loans by even 10 percent, we've dug down to the ominous 2 percent minimum tier-one ratio ($5 million loss + $1 million charge to reserves + $1 million write-down each on our other two loans = $8 million vaporized out of our $10 million starting capital).

The Piggy National Bank board calls a special meeting at the trough and anxiously considers ways to prop up the value of its loan portfolio: take more collateral, reduce expenses and work with the borrowers in order to get our money back. That is the challenge that the Piggy National Bank faces *with only a 10 per-cent collateral reduction.* Between 2008 and 2011, property appraisals across all classes of real estate declined anywhere *from 20 percent to 70 percent in value.* That great sucking sound you heard as you drove by banks in those tumultuous years was capital blowing out of the windows.

From such downturns, a collateral-dependent bank is unlikely to recover without a fresh infusion of capital from its existing share-holders—or from new shareholders. Now speak up everybody: who wants to invest in a business where asset values are declin-ing...and we're not yet sure what our ultimate losses will be? How deep is the hole? How do you value the portfolio?

Hey, why are you all running for the exits!?

To understand this simple example is to appreciate the conun-drum of a banking industry in crisis: *If you can't value the asset, you can't execute a transaction—and so transactions cease to take place.* No reasonable person will invest in (or buy) something that they cannot value. When a builder, an owner-occupant, or a real estate investor (aka the borrower) informs us that he or she cannot fulfill the terms of a loan, our collateral is impaired. As bankers, unless we can accomplish some other means of repayment, subse-quent write-downs are drawn from either profits or capital.

The crux of the crisis in collateral-dependent lending is the requirement to equate *loan values* with *collateral values.* Banks are required to evaluate collateral and update appraisal values at least annually. An auditor generally won't sign off on year-end financials unless appraisals are both current and in line...and unless the numbers add up, the FDIC will fire up the barbeque pit for Piggy National Bank.

After The Bank ~~Fails~~: Banking Upside-down

So let's say then that the Piggy National Bank ~~fails~~ is closed. On that most unfortunate of Friday afternoons, Piggy held $100 million in assets. The FDIC steps in, and after negotiating a price, all of the Piggy Bank's deposits and loans are acquired by the Poultry County Bank at a cost to the FDIC of $40 million.

How this happens: an FDIC evaluation of the Piggy National Bank loan portfolio estimates that write-downs and borrower defaults will ultimately result in $40 million of credit losses, leaving $60 million of collectable loans. The FDIC cuts a check to the Poultry County Bank out of its insurance fund to cover the shortfall. Because the Poultry board is not willing to risk taking a loss on the acquired loan portfolio—even at a 40 percent discount—the FDIC provides those chickens with a loss-share agreement (LSA) that promises to reimburse Poultry County Bank for 90% of any losses incurred in excess of the $40 million.

In practice, FDIC loss protection agreements can exceed 90 percent of incremental losses—because coverage is based on the original loan amount (par) as opposed to the discounted value acquired by the Poultry County Bank.

An example: among the loans in the failed Piggy Bank portfolio is a defaulted $100,000 mortgage note to Farmer Bob that Poultry County Bank took over at a discounted value of $60,000—along with a 90% FDIC loss-share guarantee. After evaluating farmer Bob's loan and determining that Bob can't afford his loan payments, Poultry County Bank elects to foreclose on the property, and establishes a date to sell the farmstead at auction. Bob, who continues to farm on the property even though he's way behind on his loan payments, is distressed. When a notice is tacked to the farmhouse door instructing Bob to vacate, he pleads with the chicken bankers to restructure his loan into payments that he can afford. Unfortunately, there are two very upside-down reasons why the Poultry County Bank has no incentive to haggle with poor Farmer Bob.

The first reason is that Poultry County Bank has recently appraised Bob's farmstead, and believes it will easily bring $75,000 at auction. Because Poultry acquired the loan for only $60,000, auctioning the property will bring more than they paid for the mortgage note. What's more, *so far as the FDIC is concerned, the loan is still a $100,000 obligation*. Should Poultry follow the rules of their FDIC loss-share agreement and realize the $75,000 at auction, the FDIC will reimburse the bank for 90% of their $25,000 loss (the $100,000 original note less the $75,000 realized at auction), or $22,500. So the Poultry County Bank has a choice: work with Farmer Bob and *hope* to successfully restructure his loan...or sell the collateral and realize a handy $37,500 profit ($97,500 for the farm + the FDIC reimbursement less the $60,000 paid for the loan).

What do you think is going to happen?

Bob's got even more stacked against him. If the Poultry County Bank decided that it *wanted* to restructure the $100,000 loan, the farmstead collateral would only support 75% percent of the amount Bob actually owes (fair market value of the farm is $75,000). Poultry County Bank's underwriting guidelines require at least an 80% loan to value. He doesn't qualify!

Still further (as if there needs to be more), should the Poultry County Bank elect to restructure Bob's note, the loan will no longer be covered under the FDIC's loss-share agreement. Should Bob default again, the Poultry County Bank will have no FDIC insurance support and will have to contend with the loss. E-I-E-I-Owe.

Farmer Bob had better start packing.

Many hard-working borrowers have found themselves in circumstances similar to Farmer Bob due to the unintended consequences of FDIC loss-share agreements. For reasons they can't understand, their bankers are unwilling to accommodate on even the most minor of issues.

To be clear, banks that have acquired loan assets under FDIC loss share agreements have not suddenly turned dark-hearted or vindictive. These banks are simply taking actions in accordance with their best interests, and those interests are frequently at odds with agreements that were put in place by the bank that originated the loan.

That old adage is just too good not to repeat one last time: *"When it comes to breakfast, the chicken is involved (eggs), but the pig is committed (bacon)!!!."*

The Appraisal as a Weapon of Capital Destruction

In April 2012, I met Mike Turner of the Peach Appraisal Group at a Georgia Community Bankers' Association luncheon. Mike is an appraisal consultant who at the time was spending a lot of time in the courtroom, testifying as an expert witness about the appropriate use of professional appraisals. While Mike lamented that his testimony was at times bleeding capital away from Georgia's banks, he was committed to the transparency of his profession. We talked for a while about the environment that was setting bankers against bankers where appraisals were concerned.

There are several approaches that appraisers can take when evaluating a property. There are also timing parameters such as the "sale in the ordinary course" valuation, "quick sale" liquidation, or a "bulk sale" in which multiple properties are evaluated for disposal as a pool. Mike was busy through much of 2012 as an expert witness in cases where an FDIC loss-share bank had been ordering bulk-sale valuations. The appraisals in question were for a group of participated loans the bank had acquired in an FDIC loss-share acquisition. The other participating lenders were suing because they disagreed with the lead bank's approach to valuation. Under the terms of their participation agreement, the lead bank (the FDIC-covered bank) was contending that it had full authority to choose the valuation approach for the appraisals. Were the loss-share bank win the case, the other banks would be forced to write down their share of collateral to the predominant valuation as determined by the lead bank.

At the conclusion of our conversation, Mike scribbled some numbers on a scrap of paper as an example.

"Here is a deal that I am involved with," he said. "Bank 'A', the lead bank (with FDIC loss-share coverage), has ordered a bulk-sale appraisal that it intends to use in order to sell out of a busted residential development. The two other banks ('B' and 'C') have also ordered their own appraisals." Now recall that the collateral value has to support the amount of a troubled loan, or else the lender is required to write down and charge off the difference between the loan and the depreciated collateral market value.

"The outcome in this case will determine whether the borrower can be rehabilitated or foreclosed upon." Mike drew a circle around Bank A, handed me the paper and pointed to the circle with the tip of his pen. "That's the loss-share bank" he said. "It's the one in lead position and it holds 60 percent of the deal. Banks B and C each hold 20 percent."

The appraisal results submitted by each bank are listed under the percentage that they hold:

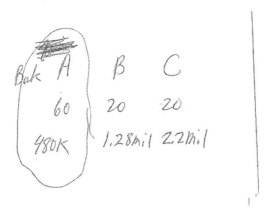

If lead bank 'A' wields a participation agreement that trumps the appraisals of 'B' and 'C', then the two smaller participants would be forced to write down their loans in accordance with the bank 'A' valuation. Brutal, huh?

The amount of loan assets covered under FDIC loss-sharing contracts is staggering. As of December 2012, US banks reported holding $68.5 billion of loans and leases covered by FDIC loss-share guarantees. This compares to $88 billion at December 2011 (FDIC call report data).

Side Articles: The Failure of Alpha Bank & Trust

September 19, 2009
Risky Loans Fuel Bank's Fast Fall
Russell Grantham, The Atlanta Journal Constitution

When federal regulators rolled into the parking lot of Alpha Bank & Trust last October to seize the bank, it became one of the quickest bank failures in the nation in recent years, losing almost half its assets after only 29 months in business, by regulators' estimates.

Loan stacking, or financing several separate subdivisions or other projects controlled by one developer, became common in Georgia, Florida, California and other booming regions as banks made loans to fast-growing real estate developers and home builders, said Jerry Blanchard, an Atlanta banking lawyer with Bryan Cave Powell Goldstein.

Georgia banking law has long barred institutions from lending more than 25 percent of their capital — or funds available to absorb losses — to any single borrower.

But most developers incorporate each project as a separate company. Many banks reasoned that each project was a separate borrower, even though they may all be owned by one individual.

"It was very common because most of these developers didn't have just one subdivision. They might be working a dozen different subdivisions," said Blanchard.

But in a deep recession, a developer can default on most or all of those loans, said Blanchard.

By the end of its first year in business, Alpha Bank had far outstripped its five-year growth plan, with $278 million in assets at mid-2007 and 75 percent of its loan portfolio invested in the real estate construction and development business. The bank later grew to $383 million in assets.

By mid-2007, the bank already had lent five times its capital to the boom-and-bust real estate development industry, despite warnings in 2006 by the FDIC and other regulators that a 300 percent concentration was considered excessively risky.

Action 'too late'

Alpha Bank bent several rules along the way, according to auditors. The bank ignored a state regulation by making loans to nine individual customers that each exceeded 25 percent of its capital.

A search of property deeds by the Atlanta Journal- Constitution showed that Alpha Bank's loans to only six of those customers totaled at least $58 million. That was more than double its capital, which continued to dwindle because of the bank's losses.

From the Office of the Inspector General's report on the failure of Alpha Bank and Trust (FDIC, May 2009):

Interest Reserves: Alpha did not have appropriate controls related to the use and tracking of interest reserves. Alpha's loan policy stated that the bank should not capitalize accrued interest when renewing or rewriting an existing loan unless the repayment of the capitalized interest is tied to an identifiable source of repayment in the near term. The policy also stated that any device that avoids the recognition of loan delinquency is prohibited. However, Alpha did not follow this policy and used interest reserves to mask the deterioration of loans. Based on a schedule of loans with interest reserves that Alpha prepared in January 2008, the OIG determined that Alpha used about $11.1 million in interest reserves to fund loans. Of that amount, $4.4 million (about 40 percent) was associated with loans that were adversely classified, as noted in the April 2008 ROE, because borrower payments were past due, and collateral values were insufficient. Additionally, the schedule showed two instances where the amount of used interest reserve exceeded the total amount of interest reserve set aside for the loan. We consider inadequate controls over the use and tracking of interest reserves to be a significant concern, which we will address in our summary reports covering multiple bank failures.

Chapter 10

The Downslide of Creekside

A man can fail many times, but he isn't a failure until he begins to blame somebody else.

John Burroughs

I commented in Chapter 3 (Caveat Emptor) that no organizing group in their right minds would have set about opening a new bank in the early 2000s had they known what the coming years would bring. The story of Creekside Bank in this regard stands as a testimony that even the most capable of business leaders was not equipped to negotiate the steep decline in asset prices that shook the economy from the precipice of 2006. This chapter relates the brief story (both figuratively and literally) of a Cherokee County, Georgia bank that suffered the same fate as many of its brethren, now collectively known as the infamous de novo banking class of 2006. The story fits entirely into one chapter: it doesn't take nearly as long to close a bank as it does to open one.

Friday, February 13, 2009

Bank crisis heading for historic level

Atlanta Business Chronicle - by Joe Rauch Staff writer

Atlanta banks' loan problems, which a year ago began to rival the peak of the late 1980s Savings and Loan Crisis, dramatically worsened in the fourth quarter of 2008.

On average, 12 percent of Atlanta banks' loan portfolios are in some form of delinquency. Statewide, the ratio is 8.69 percent for Georgia's 340 banks, according to data compiled by Atlanta-based investment bank **FIG Partners** LLP from fourth-quarter 2008 bank regulatory filings.

Both figures are far higher than the 4.41 percent problem loan rate reported by Atlanta-area banks in 1991 at the height of the S&L Crisis. The data is setting a new standard for industry woes in the region, leading to what some are calling the worst bank market in the state's history.

"We're beginning to see that we can't compare this downturn to 1990 or 1980 anymore," said Chris Marinac, FIG Partners banking analyst. "We're now going to measure future crises by 2009. A new bar is being raised for the industry."

Bankers throughout the state reported the fourth quarter of 2008 as the worst they could remember in their careers, concluding a year where little went right for the industry.

The new data buttresses that. Borrowers, centered in the increasingly weak home-building and development businesses, continued to default on loans statewide. Banks failed at a rising rate throughout the fall and early winter, peaking in mid-November and early December, when three banks were seized in a four-week period.

In December, Walt Moeling, a Bryan Cave Powell Goldstein LLP banking attorney who has worked with area banks for 40 years, described the industry as in a "free fall."

National economic news also continued to worsen with accelerating job losses and continuing shocks to the financial system.

"This is the worst environment I've seen in 45 years in the business," said Gordon Teel, CEO of **Georgian Bank**.

Part of the reason for the lag in bank numbers tracking the national economy, Marinac said, was the continued refusal of the industry to recognize the depth of its lending woes.

"Banks have had a difficult time coming to terms with the reality of where they are," he said. "They're doing now what they should have done two quarters ago."

Locally, 25 Georgia banks reported that their loan problems more than doubled between the end of third-quarter 2008 on Sept. 30 and the end of the year. Some banks reported enormous spikes, like Camilla, Ga.-based Flint River National Bank's 1,545 percent increase in problem loans, the highest figure statewide.

During the quarter, average statewide net charge-offs, or loans written off as unrecoverable, doubled from 1 percent to 2 percent.

Bankers attributed that rapid spike to the economy's year-end nose-dive, along with local banks' heavy concentration in residential real estate construction loans.

"This is the quarter where many of our builders just threw up their hands and gave up," said Marvin Cosgray, **Buckhead Community Bank**'s CEO. Cosgray's bank reported problem loans doubling during the quarter, with nearly one-fifth of the bank's $724 million in loans now in some stage of delinquency.

Teel's bank, one of Atlanta's largest community banks with $2 billion in total assets and a large residential construction loan portfolio, reported loan problems are well below local averages.

Roughly 7.2 percent of the bank's total loans are problems. But despite problem loans spiking 101.7 percent during the fourth quarter, he said the bank is continuing to work with borrowers, rather than foreclosing on projects aggressively.

"We'll try to fit the jigsaw puzzle pieces together to make it work," Teel said. "We are not in a liquidation mode."

Forty-three banks in the state have loans problems that now exceed capital, according to an industry metric known as the "Texas Ratio." Created during the S&L Crisis to measure how banks and thrifts in that downturn could absorb loan losses, the metric has become a clear gauge of which institutions are flooded by bad loans.

McDonough-based **FirstBank Financial Services** reported the highest Texas ratio in the state at 390 percent, or problem loans nearly four times as large as the bank's available capital to absorb losses.

That institution was seized by state and federal regulators on Feb. 6. And the potential cumulative losses continue to rise at a number of state banks. One-fourth of the state's banks, or 92, are reporting more than 10 percent of their portfolios are problem loans.

Norcross-based **First Security National Bank** leads the state, reporting 48 percent of its loans are problems. It also has the third-highest Texas ratio in the state.

Dan Baker, First Security National's CEO, said the bank's loan problems are due to its aggressive credit management. Baker said he expects the bank's problems to stabilize this spring.

Despite the industry's fourth quarter decline, Marinac said he believes the industry has further to go. "This is the tip of the iceberg for these losses and the recognition of problem loans."

A Victim of Impeccably Bad Timing

I have never met a more qualified community bank president than Larry D. Peterson. A (fellow) Penn State grad, Larry spent his formative years in Grove City, Pennsylvania, completed a degree in State College, PA and went on to distinguish himself in positions of progressive responsibility at Key Bank of Columbus, Ohio. In 1997, Larry was recruited to move south and take the reins as president at Fidelity Bank in Atlanta. His mission at Fidelity was to right the ship from some fairly serious credit problems and to repair a god-awful relationship with the bank's regulators. Repair the bank he did, and Larry ultimately departed from Fidelity in 2003 having accomplished a full rehabilitation. Though entertaining thoughts of retirement, Larry was open to opportunities to run another banking enterprise. It wasn't long before one found him.

In early 2005, Peterson was contacted by a group organizing a banking charter in northwest Atlanta. The bank was planning to serve the growing populations of south Cherokee, Cobb, and northwest Fulton counties. The organizers were part of a network of businessmen who planned to build out a Cherokee banking company in conjunction with several other charters, eventually forming a string of locally operated banks in a cooperative franchise across northwest Georgia.

The board included established community leaders like Dr. Johnny Hunt of Woodstock First Baptist Church, former Georgia state representative Garland Pinholster, and George Shropshire, a construction company executive who would serve as the bank's first chairman of the board. Shropshire was also a director for the Bank of Ellijay, another of the network's string of bank start-ups. All of the directors had strong community ties and were actively involved in the organization process. It was an ideal community bank board. After considering, Peterson accepted the position as president and chief executive officer of what would become Creekside Bank of Woodstock, Georgia.

Chart 33

$15 MILLION RAISED
TAKE STOCK IN YOUR COMMUNITY
Locations planned for Cherokee and Cobb Counties
Additional $3 Million Authorized
CREEKSIDE BANK
IN ORGANIZATION
770-544-2130
BOARD OF DIRECTORS
Larry Peterson
President and CEO, CreekSide Bank, I.O.
George Shropshire
William Archer, III
Retired Executive Vice President, Georgia Power Co.
Paul Beckham
Chairman, Hope-Beckham, Inc.
Gregory Bowen
Owner
Mike Evans
Owner
Dr. Johnny Hunt
Senior Pastor, First Baptist Church of Woodstock
Larry Nelson
Professional Golfer and Owner, Larry Nelson Enterprizes, Inc.
Dr. John Peacock
Dentist, Woodstock, GA
Dr. Garland Pinholster
Former State Representative, Georgia General Assembly
Kenneth White
Manager, White Capital Group, LLC
Orlando Wilson
Owner, Northside Agency, LLC
CREEKSIDE BANK, I.O. OFFERS TO THE PUBLIC
1,800,000
~~1,500,000~~ SHARES (300,000 ADDITIONAL SHARES)
OF STOCK AT $10.00 PER SHARE
Creekside Bank I.O. is pleased to announce the receipt of $15 million in subscriptions and commitments. The stock offering has been such an overwhelming success that the Organizing Directors have decided to raise up to an additional $3 million in capital.
Call now for more information - 770-544-2130
These securities will be offered through an offering circular and may not be sold nor may offers to buy be accepted prior to the time an offering circular is delivered to prospective investors. No person has been authorized to give any information or make representations other than those to be contained in the offering circular and, if given or made, any such information or representations may not be relied upon as having been authorized. This advertisement shall not constitute an offer to sell or the solicitation of an offer to buy these securities, nor shall there be any sale of these securities until the offering circular is delivered to and reviewed by prospective investors. Offers may be made only by an offering circular. The securities are neither insured nor approved by the FDIC. Any indication of interest in response to thisadvertisement will involve no obligation or commitment of any kind.

Creekside's 2005 capital raise was a textbook example of community bank outreach. The bank took out half-page ads in local papers like the *Marietta Daily Journal* to solicit funds directly from the community. After quickly exceeding its initial $15 million goal, Creekside closed out its offering early in 2006 at $18 million with a solid base of local shareholders. The organizers themselves, pleased by the prospects for their success, put up considerable equity of their own to fund the start-up. Creekside received its charter and opened for business on July 24, 2006.

Participations

While Peterson and the Creekside board were as intrigued as any other bank by the lure of real estate development lending and its quick, fat margins, the bank's business plan reflected Peterson's commercial lending background and called for a diversified lending approach across consumer and commercial lending, wealth management and treasury services.

Building a commercial lending staff would take time, however, and experienced commercial lenders (in comparison to real estate, or "dirt," lenders) were hard to come by in construction-focused Atlanta. In order to accommodate a diligent lender search while at the same time advancing toward profitability, the Creekside board felt pressure to take on some exposure to the real estate markets in order to kick-start earnings for its shareholders. At the end of 2006, the bank elected to fund a series of real estate development deals.

Because Creekside didn't have a long-term real estate focus (and had no plans to build a staff of real estate lenders), it made sense to buy into loan participations from other institutions rather than to staff up and originate its own deals. Real estate development was clicking along at a fast pace in late 2006, and banks were routinely booking fees upwards of 5 percent annually on A&D transactions in addition to the robust margins that those deals provided. The plan seemed to offer a compelling interim path to profitability. Creekside originated and participated out a couple of big residential real estate projects and bought into numerous others. The bank grew its portfolio in earnest through 2007 with deals scheduled to be completed and paid out by the end of 2008. Proceeds from these projects were expected to fund a more diversified commercial portfolio by the first half of 2009. Or so that was the plan.

By December 2007, Creekside's loan assets amounted to $72 million. Just shy of $52 million was real estate secured…and just over $30 million was composed of construction and development deals.

In December 2008, the bank's construction & development portfolio amounted to $31.8 million. The market was dead…and every single one of those 2007 C&D deals was still on the balance sheet. None had successfully rolled out of the portfolio. And every single deal was showing signs of impairment.

While the strategy seemed fool-proof at the time, the underpinnings of the real estate markets were coming unglued throughout the very months that Creekside was building its portfolio. Because the information hasn't been made public, I am not at liberty to relay the amount of the bank's loan portfolio that was specifically composed of participations. But almost without warning, the real estate development markets hit a wall in the fall of 2007. Creekside's timing could not have been worse.

From an $18 million capital raise in 2006, Creekside opened with $16.7 million of capital on its balance sheet and a sported an opening tier-one capital ratio of 80.45 percent. By the end of 2008, total equity capital had declined to $14.2 million, core equity had deteriorated to 12.9 percent, and the bank began laying off staff. Non-accrual loans in December 2009 amounted 12.8 percent of the portfolio. By December 2010, the ratio had risen to 24.6 percent, or $16.7 million out of a $68 million loan portfolio. By the end of 2010, equity had dwindled to $2.9 million, and core equity was a mere 2.69 percent of assets.

Creekside Bank Historic Performance Ratios (in thousands)

	Dec-06	Dec-07	Dec-08	Dec-09	Dec-10	Jun-11
Average TA	20,735	79,718	108,130	114,338	106,563	104,572
Total Equity Capital	16,682	16,458	14,118	8,298	2,870	651
Charge-offs	-	-	60	3,026	2,832	700
Net Income	(1,035)	(772)	(3,100)	(5,980)	(5,519)	(2,271)
Tier 1 Leverage Capital	80.45%	20.63%	12.90%	7.26%	2.69%	0.57%
Total Risk-Based Capital	173.40%	23.98%	16.77%	10.08%	4.86%	1.56%

Source: FDIC

Creekside acquiesed to a consent order from the FDIC in January 2010. A consent order is an authoritative measure taken by the FDIC to require corrective actions when a bank's capital position weakens or when practices are discovered that trigger some sort of disciplinary response (more than half of all Georgia banks were under some sort of regulatory action by year-end 2010). In Creekside's case, the FDIC order mandated that the bank re-establish and maintain well-capitalized ratios. The Creekside board formed a capital committee, hired T. Stephen Johnson (quoted several times in the ABC articles throughout these chapters), and began extensive measures to identify potential investors. The loan portfolio continued to deteriorate. This was now a crisis. A full-blown, asset-based financial crisis.

Friday, June 12, 2009

Money-hungry banks get the cold shoulder
Atlanta Business Chronicle – by Joe Rauch, Staff Writer

As Georgia banks look to raise millions in additional capital to survive the current financial downturn, they are running into unexpected resistance: their own shareholders.

Rather than finding directors and existing investors ready to open their checkbooks, bank execs are finding those shareholders to be some of their toughest critics.

"It is incredibly hard to sell stock right now for any institution, even amongst the insiders," said Byron Richardson, a consultant with **Bank**

Resources Inc. who has raised capital for new and existing banks for two decades.

Consultants, bankers and investors said dozens of smaller, local banks are pursuing private capital raises. The banks are initially courting existing shareholders, directors and management, rather than outside investors, because the market for new investment in banks has all but evaporated, consultants and bankers said.

***

They are looking to raise as little as a few million dollars, or the offerings can climb into the tens of millions.

Smaller, community banks' boards are (also) typically made up of local business owners and, in some cases, are dominated by people with ties to the real estate industry. Many of those investors and directors have had their personal wealth wiped out by the current economy.

Others are simply hoarding the cash, waiting for signs of economic recovery and signs their bank will be one of the survivors.

Meanwhile, the main question existing shareholders have about reinvesting continues to be the condition of banks' battered real estate loan portfolios.

"There's still a concern that unless you can stop the bleeding in the real estate portfolio, why should they invest?" said Lee Bradley, the locally based managing director of Dallas, Ga.-based **Commerce Street Capital** LLC's bank development group. Bradley raises capital for both new and existing banks.

"As an investor in several de novo banks [in Georgia and elsewhere], what I am seeing are attempts by the struggling banks to sell new shares to their existing shareholders at prices substantially above what they can get from private equity firms or others, and at prices that may not yet reflect the true condition of the banks' underlying assets," said one local investor and director in several Georgia banks via e-mail. He requested anonymity because of his position in the industry.

"More disturbing is that the directors of these banks are not fully subscribing to the rights offerings, which indicates they are not convinced the values have bottomed out," the director said.

Investors' hesitation puts the banks in a precarious position, consultants and bankers said.

Without a cash infusion, already weak banks become more likely to fail, wiping out the stock holdings of shareholders entirely when the institution is seized by the **Federal Deposit Insurance Corp.**

Bankers said several of the 11 banks that have failed in Georgia since August 2008 did so, in part, because they could not raise enough capital to satisfy regulators.

Bradley said existing shareholders who are investing "realize the bank is in a survival mode. They're not worried about diluting their investment anymore."

Searching For Capital Along The Boulevard Of Broken Dreams

Larry first approached me about working with him at Creekside in October 2010. In a devastating turn of events, several of his key executives had resigned in succession: George Shropshire was required to step down as chairman when the Bank of Ellijay failed in September 2010 (an executive who causes the FDIC to suffer a loss has historically been disqualified from service at other chartered institutions). Both the CFO and the bank's senior lending officer gave notice of their resignations the very next week. Ouch.

Larry and I met for several hours one beautiful October afternoon. We concluded that as a couple of Penn State grads with pragmatic Midwestern roots, we could hit it off and work quite well together.

My mission as a contract CFO (I was initially engaged through my company, BankForward Consulting, LLC) was to assist with the bank's recapitalization. A diligence review was already underway with an investor considering a capital injection. By January 2011, though, it was increasingly apparent that continued loan deterioration was making the required capital injection a moving target (read: the hole was getting bigger).

The "Texas ratio" became synonymous with problem banks in the course of the 2008 crises. The metric—named after the Texas savings and loan debacle of the 1980s—measures total problem loan assets to a bank's equity capital and loss reserves—its cushion to absorb losses. A figure approaching 100 percent means that problem loans are overwhelming a bank's capital base. Creekside's Texas ratio in December 2011 stood at 471 percent.

Plenty of opportunistic investors began circling troubled banks in 2008, looking for compelling deals. Because most didn't understand that banks can't afford to jettison foreclosed property at fire-sale prices, transactions were rare.

Creekside reached out to several capital funds in pursuit of an investor. Two funds seemed genuinely interested. The problem with the mission, though, was that the bank's loan portfolio had been deteriorating at a perilous rate throughout 2010. After Larry hired longtime banker Chuck Barnes in November to assist with managing the portfolio, it was nearly January 2011 before we had our hands around the size of Creekside's challenge.

While it may seem obvious in hindsight, one of the shortcomings of the community bank model during the boom years was that the borrower's relationship manager and *lender* was often the same person. Commercial real estate lending officers with an established base of developer relationships were veritable rock stars of the industry in the early 2000's, often commanding six-figure signing bonuses and lucrative production payouts. The most productive were recruited from start-up to start-up...and their payouts got bigger as they went along. In the downturn, however, loyalties become conflicted. Lender/relationship managers naturally sought to protect their portfolio of borrower relationships rather than bite the hand that had fed them. The banks, however, needed to triage deteriorating loans and get out ahead of struggling projects. While the appropriate crisis management move would have been to get those troubled relationships away from the lenders and into the hands of a no-nonsense, "junkyard dog" workout manager, it was difficult to pry relationships away from the relationship manager who controlled them. In most cases, after all, there *wasn't* a workout-specialist on board at the bank. The workout specialist-in-chief was usually the bank president... which created enormous management pressures at troubled institutions. By 2010, lenders with workout experience were in high demand. Real estate lenders were not. It was a hard, hard time for real estate lenders.

Recall my earlier contention that community banks are *highly regulated small businesses.* In an environment where management is consumed with fighting fires, there is no time to focus on building or even maintaining the enterprise of the business. As a result, *good* relationships go wanting for attention, and the overall business is left to cast about on troubled waters while management is consumed with the urgency of with troubled loans. It is a very tough spiral to exit.

For the first six months of 2011, I worked on what I came to call the "Bank*Forward* Plan" to fund capital investment into a select group of Atlanta community banks—including Creekside. The model offered what I believe was a compelling investment opportunity for outsized returns...at least on paper! I contacted everyone I knew with experience in property investment, portfolio acquisition, and bank mergers and acquisitions. I met with 14 prospects in all. I summarized my experience in a blog post that I published on my website in July 2011:

Condensed from *Salvage Efforts in the Skittish Landscape of Community Banking*

Bank*Forward* Consulting, July 2011

Early this year I began to analyze metro Atlanta community banks with good market demographics, a strong deposit base, and nonperforming assets (NPAs) that have been written down to a level such that the bank's remaining capital and loan loss allowance could serve as a sufficient buffer against any "burn" of newly invested capital into the business. My investment premise is that **new capital can be injected into qualified bank targets at a stock price amounting to a small fraction of book value, enabling an investor to gain majority control of an operating bank at a nominal cost.** Cost efficiencies in combination with a focused business plan could yield compelling returns over a three- to five-year time horizon. The filters I employed surfaced several de novo institutions and a few "seasoned" but impaired banks, each holding between $100MM and $225MM in assets.

Armed with my analytics, I reached out to institutional investors that I know...but the general response was that my project was "too small" to warrant consideration: the effort necessary to underwrite a $10-$20MM equity deal to "start the ball rolling" was just not worth the risk/return when much larger projects were available with larger-scale results. The smaller funds that I knew had already been burned by bank investments and the larger guys couldn't be bothered. Sheesh.

On the other side of the table, I found out that it's just as hard to convince a bank director to dilute his ownership by selling shares for pennies on the dollar—until the moment of truth arrives and there is just not enough time to get a deal done before the bank fails. From a human nature standpoint, I guess I can understand that one, too. Unfortunately, we are finding in this environment that *He Who Hesitates Is Lost.*

After a recent July 2011 meeting that I hosted, an intrigued portfolio manager contacted Renova Partners for summary evaluation of First Citizens Bank of Dawsonville, GA (one of my "viable candidate" banks). Now, I had previously scrubbed First Citizen's balance sheet and was confident that the bank was worth somewhere between $1 million and -$4 million. Renova's estimate was an astonishing -$15 million. Read: they wanted to be *paid* $15 million in order to assume 100 % ownership of the bank. Needless to say, the portfolio manager was unimpressed with the opportunity. At least he offered to pay for my lunch.

I puzzled over Renova's valuation, and decided after several more attempts to abandon project Bank*Forward* with this notation:

Institutional investors are applying excessive discounts when valuing open banks—especially those with any measurable level of asset challenges. Large institutional investors are just not scaled to give these institutions serious consideration. The underwriting size is below their interest level, and bigger discounts are available for the assets alone—without the headache of actually owning a regulated business. Lastly, the lucrative gains available for failed bank acquisitions are effectively accomplished with a "post-bankruptcy" cleansing that is unavailable with an open bank acquisition. The fact is that there is no "warranty" period when acquiring an open bank. You can't take it back to the FDIC if the results aren't what you expected! Unless an open bank in search of capital is willing to swallow extreme dilution, the likelihood of attracting capital is small indeed. That doesn't feel very good—but it has enabled me to appreciate the ruthless efficiency of an FDIC-controlled marketplace.

In the first quarter of 2011, First Citizens of Dawsonville had tier-one capital amounting to $4.1MM (3.43 %) and a loan loss allowance of $1.6MM. The bank at the time held $9MM of Real Estate Owned (foreclosed property) and was confident that it had stabilized its remaining troubled loans. Total assets amounted to $120 million. As of March 31, 2013, the bank has posted a modest $87 thousand profit for the first quarter, tier one capital amounted to $2.72 million (2.94%), the loan loss allowance stands at $1.3 million and REO stands $11.4 million. Total assets have been condensed to $92.6 million. While First Citizens looks like it's hanging on by a thread, the bank is making progress. The Georgia real estate markets are in recovery at the outset of 2013, and odds are now in First Citizens' favor.

My point: In conjunction with a capital injection—First Citizens could have written down its ORE from $10MM to $5MM in 2010. If foreclosed property was written down below market price, selling it ultimately for, say, $7MM would have yielded a $2MM recovery gain to the acquirer. These gains would have been independent of accretive returns accomplished by acquiring a controlling interest in the bank at a fraction of book value. Charles Buckner, CEO of First Citizens, is a capable community bank survivor. Mr. Buckner and his board have managed to steer their bank through the past five years without *any* injection of capital. While a capital injection or buy-out is likely in First Citizens' future, I wager that closure is not an option the board will permit with the Georgia markets now in recovery. Sometimes survival is the best revenge. I'm betting that the First Citizens board will ultimately prevail.

This Way Out...No Souvenirs

This chart, courtesy of McKenna, Long & Aldridge, captures the enormity of the capital losses suffered by Georgia banks through worst of the crisis. Between 2008 and 2011, 47 percent of Georgia's bank capital evaporated in real estate write-downs! $14.3 billion of shareholder investment and retained earnings were destroyed.

Chart 34

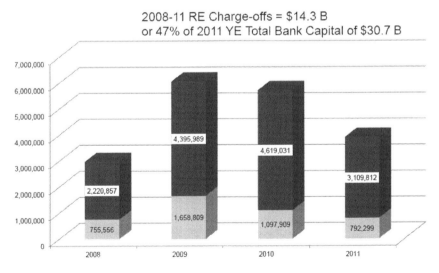

2008-11 RE Charge-offs = $14.3 B
or 47% of 2011 YE Total Bank Capital of $30.7 B

McKenna, Long & Aldridge, LLP

Documenting the Inevitable

Chuck Barnes set about evaluating Creekside's loan portfolio in early December, and I in turn, began fitting his conclusions into the bank's loan loss calculations. At the January 2011 board meeting, we took a deep breath and recommended a fourth quarter charge-down of a little over $1 million to recognize losses. As a result, Creekside reported full-year 2010 charge-offs of $2.8 million and a full year loss of $5.5 million. Discussions with the bank's potential investors ceased within a few weeks of filing our reports with the FDIC in late January. The state banking department visited for several days the following month to get a better handle on Creekside's tenuous position.

Like most of Georgia's bankers, I had never been in a role like this one before. Garland Pinholster, Creekside's new board chairman, made only two requests of Peterson and me through the course of Creekside's travails: first was to continuing the search for capital. Second was to preserve as many employee jobs as possible in the event of failure.

In spite of its tough run, Creekside Bank benefitted enormously from a group of branch employees who had stuck together almost from the time the bank opened in 2006. Creekside operated from two locations (Woodstock and Acworth, GA) and had built up an enviable franchise in both communities, largely as a result of good service and rapport from the branch management staff (branch managers, tellers, and customer service reps). The bank's internal controls, procedures and annual audits had always received high marks. The branch employee group was everything a small business employer could hope for: they were dependable, flexible, and experienced, and they all got along well together. Unfortunately, none of this could overcome the huge write-downs suffered in the loan portfolio.

The resolve of the lending staff, unfortunately, was another matter altogether. Because of their cultivated relationships with the bank's healthier borrowers, Creekside's lenders were recruited away and hit the exits in the spring of 2011. By June, Larry Peterson was the only remaining bank employee with lending experience (Barnes and his successor Scott Hudgins were both consultants). The fact that the lenders bolted is in no way intended as a criticism—people gotta eat and provide for their families. And, after all, these lenders weren't the ones responsible for the bank's portfolio of busted loan participations—that guy had left the previous year! In most cases, the remaining lenders had no relationship whatsoever with the participating borrowers. That made communication even more difficult. What I had heard to be the case at other troubled institutions was coming altogether true for Creekside: management had become consumed with the administration of problem credits. There was *no* time to proactively manage the business of banking. Clients looking for refinance opportunities, extensions, or expansions of their credit relationship found the bank unable to assist. The result was atrophy by way of the bank's better clients jumping ship—or being drawn away to stronger competitors. It was a ruthless downward spiral.

Friday, March 19, 2010

New wave of bank failures about to hit
Atlanta Business Chronicle – by J. Scott Trubey, Staff Writer

The calm appears to be ending before what could be a new storm of bank failures.

***

At least five struggling North Georgia banks are said to be up for bids through the **Federal Deposit Insurance Corp.**, and regulators are expected to sell the ailing lenders to rivals in bundles on March 19 and March 26, multiple banking sources have told Atlanta Business Chronicle.

The anticipated seizure of at least five banks through the end of the month is expected to bring new buyers into Georgia as stronger players see attractive opportunities to enter the state.

***

To be well-capitalized under federal regulatory standards, banks must have at least 10 percent total risk-based capital. Fifty-eight Georgia banks, including 32 in metro Atlanta, have fallen below that key regulatory measure. There were 42 banks below 10 percent total risk-based capital at the end of the third quarter.

***

Another measure of financial health, Texas ratios, are also climbing for many struggling banks.

Appalachian Community had a Texas ratio of 561 percent, the third-highest in the state, at the end of the fourth quarter.

The figure — named for the Texas savings and loans where it was used to gauge financial health during the Savings & Loan Crisis — compares total loan problems to a bank's total equity capital. A figure approaching 100 percent indicates problems are exceeding the bank's available capital, and outstripping its ability to absorb losses.

Among the other lenders with the highest Texas ratios are **McIntosh Commercial Bank of Carrollton** (885 percent) and Century Security Bank of Johns Creek (741 percent).

There is much speculation that some deals to come in Georgia might involve the bundling of a relatively desirable bank with another bank that is either in an undesirable location geographically or that has so little franchise value it is unlikely to be acquired alone in an FDIC-assisted transaction.

Some within the industry are privately saying there might not be bidders for some of Georgia's troubled banks because they have little true value — either because of loan portfolios littered with rotten development loans and a lack of real deposits, or because they are located in markets with poor growth prospects.

The failed-bank version of a two-for-one auction is known as a "linked bid." Using "linked bids" improves the regulator's efficiency at disposing of failed banks, sources say. Bundling lenders together to more quickly dispose of some struggling Georgia banks puts less pressure on the resources of regulators and eliminates multiple troubled banks at once.

Georgia has already seen the FDIC sell unrelated banks in this fashion. State Bank & Trust acquired metro Atlanta lenders The Buckhead Community Bank and **First Security National Bank** in December in a bundle.

Private equity-backed State Bank also acquired the six bank subsidiaries of the failed **Security Bank Corp. of Macon** last July.

"It brings new bidders to the table and makes it easier to resolve these things," said Brennan Ryan, an attorney with Nelson Mullins, Reilly & Scarborough.

***

Among the out-of-state banks said to be interested in building in Georgia are: **First Citizens Bank** & Trust Co. of South Carolina, the acquirer of the failed Georgian Bank; IBERIABANK of **Louisiana and BB&T Corp.**

Another interested suitor could be Community & Southern Bank, the private equity-backed acquirer of the failed **First National Bank of Georgia**. Community & Southern is headed by Pat Frawley, a former regulator and noted turnaround specialist who is estimated to have more than $150 million in additional capital in his war chest.

The Way of All Flesh...And Failed Bank Shareholders

To ensure that there was never a repeat of the crisis that saw *six thousand* banks fail during the Great Depression, Franklin Roosevelt signed a federal bank deposit insurance program into existence on January 1, 1934. Since then, every bank in the United States has paid a quarterly insurance premium to the Federal

Deposit Insurance Corporation to insure, within limits, the savings of individual depositors. The 465 banks that were closed between January 2008 and December 2012 (85 in Georgia) have depleted the fund—and insurance premiums have increased significantly for the less healthy banks. To reduce losses and speed up recoveries to the fund, the FDIC sells closed banks at auction whenever possible, and then transfers that institution's loans and deposits to the acquiring bank. This would ultimately become the path for Creekside Bank.

The FDIC demands strict compliance surrounding the confidentiality of bank closures. No information under any circumstances can be removed from bank premises. Directors and executive managers risk serious fines—and even jail time—by disclosing the particulars of an intended closure with customers or rank-and-file employees. This is for obvious reasons: the worst possible event for a bank (or its regulators) is to see clients lined up at the door out of concern for their deposits. Further, document copies removed from the bank could compromise customers or the FDIC's subsequent efforts to pursue the insiders (all of the material for this work, by the way, was constructed from outside resources and from my own personal recollections). Early on in the Georgia crisis, employees were often shocked and completely taken by surprise when the "hit squad" of regulatory turnover specialists arrived at closing time on a carefully rehearsed Friday afternoon. By late 2011, though, scheduled closures were among the worst-kept surprises in the industry. Failures that were leading news stories in 2008 and 2009 were hard-pressed to make the front section of the local paper by the fall of 2011. In some ways, this was a good thing: it meant that the public was largely confident that a trustworthy transition would take place and that deposits would be available without a hiccup. In practice, this has always the case. Tragic, yes—but also effective.

While I had to tread carefully when talking with employees about the bank's weakened position, in reality the staff knew where things were headed. Most of them were understandably frustrated that as loyal team members they were kept in the dark on the specifics. To a great degree, that just couldn't be helped. Short of an angel investor coming to the rescue, the range of outcomes was limited—and all of the options were dramatic:

1. Creekside would be acquired by a bank with local operations, and its customer base would be absorbed into a competing franchise. Most of Creekside's staff would be let go.

2. Creekside would have no bidders, and the bank's assets would be liquidated by the FDIC. All of Creekside's staff would be let go.

3. Creekside would be acquired by a bank with no local operations but looking to expand into their markets and at least some of the local staff would be retained.

All of us, of course, were rooting for option three.

The best way to accomplish this, I encouraged (over and over), was for Creekside's employees to stay focused, smother their customers with good service, and maintain the high quality of their internal work in order to demonstrate expertise to incoming suitors. As part of my staff evaluations (I was de facto head of HR), I requested that employees update their job descriptions and provide work experience details for their employee HR files. Beyond that, I stressed that employees should go the extra mile to assist in any way possible during the upcoming diligence sessions. These may seem like obvious recommendations, but employees understandably become desperate and depressed when the outlook is bleak. We all needed an optimistic distraction! I often felt like "cheerleader in chief" for a group of employees and directors who were organizationally transitioning through the seven stages of death. There were not suitors anymore. The bank's ratios were terminal. In effect, we were awaiting regulatory euthanasia.

While Creekside had little to offer employees in the way of long-term job security, keeping them on board until closure would be incredibly important for success of the transition process. File accumulation, the on-site diligence reviews, the regulatory turnover process and data conversion required experience and familiarity with the books and records of this intensely process-driven business. Without experienced personnel who are intimately familiar with the books and records of the company, it would be a challenge for any regulatory team to piece together a smooth transition to the acquiring bank. Such a shortfall would reflect poorly on the executives and directors of the bank. Even more, keeping the team together through transition would position them for interviews at the acquiring bank...or at least a severance package! As you can surely imagine, the job environment for bank employees in 2011 was even more dire than it is today. The reality of it was that the branch staff had little to risk by staying on for the duration...prospects elsewhere were hardly better! The bank's tellers, service reps and branch managers play a crucial role in determining the ultimate outcome of the bank—both for the FDIC and for the acquiring institution.

Where was Larry Peterson throughout this process? To his considerable credit, Larry spent countless hours documenting Creekside's responses to every regulatory request, every compliance concern and every examination from the time the bank first went under a compliance order in 2010. There were quarterly progress reports, capital plan updates, consent order compliance—all of which required time, organization and documentation in meticulous detail. Peterson's work ethic was impressive. Larry also had the able assistance of attorneys like Jim McAlpin, Walt Moeling, and Ken Achenbach from the Bryan Cave law firm and Angela Holguin, who expertly consulted on the bank's documentation process. In fact, I recall helping Larry finalize the bank's final capital plan update to regional FDIC director Tom Dujenski in mid-July—nearly a month into the regulatory marketing process that formally began on June 8, 2011.

There were no "fat cats" fending for themselves at Creekside Bank. No self-serving gamesmanship or greed the likes of which we've all heard about in the news. The Creekside Bank directors and officers were diligent, hardworking, and honorable people, all doing their best in the midst of a terrible industry crisis. While their own hard-earned investments in the bank suffered along with those of other shareholders, they dutifully followed banking regulations and the direction of regulatory supervisors. These were professionals *acting* like professionals in the "other 99% of American banking.

Labor Day Redux

Creekside fell below the 2 percent "critically undercapitalized" trigger in early June 2011. On June 8, the board was called to a special meeting with the FDIC and the Georgia Department of Banking and Finance. The meeting was stiff, somber, and instructional. The heavy curtains and fabric wall coverings of the Creekside boardroom took on the feel of an upholstered funeral parlor. After reading from a prepared statement, Frank Grey, an assistant regional director for the FDIC, outlined the purpose of the somewhat hastily arranged meeting. Mr. Grey was *requesting* board approval of a resolution that *granted* the FDIC authority to identify prospective bidders for the bank. While it took a moment for this positioning to sink in, the Creekside directors soon came to realize that this was not going to be orchestrated as a ham-handed government seizure...but rather as an authorized handover by the unanimous *consent* of the Creekside board. Kevin Hagler, Georgia's assistant banking supervisor, put on his best face to encourage the group in a continued search for capital. (By all accounts, Hagler has been a solid supporter of Georgia's community banks. These meetings must have been painful for Kevin). As I watched the resolution make its way around the table for each director's signature, it was apparent that everyone was getting the message. This was *their* bank. The responsibility to determine its fate was *theirs*. The authorization for FDIC assistance to market the bank would be *theirs*. This led to more than a little (understandable) squirming in the seats. So *this* is what "ultimate responsibility" meant in all of those board-approved bank policies! Creekside's directors were signing a resolution that *endorsed* the FDIC's *request* to market the bank. In the most respectful tones, Hagler explained that neither the Georgia State Department of Banking nor the FDIC had the legal right to force the bank to sell. The statutes, rather, mandate that the FDIC "resolve" an institution within sixty days of tripping the 2 percent capital trigger by either overseeing a capital injection that reestablished safety and soundness, or by means of auction/closure of the bank within a defined time frame. Signing the resolution was solely to enable the FDIC and the DBF to market Creekside to potential bidders. Should the board *object* to the bank being marketed (and you might imagine that certain objections were raised...), Hagler explained that the FDIC would then be forced to sue the directors in order to "prove" that the bank was illiquid. In such an event, the FDIC would be asking a court to authorize seizure by means of a verdict. The resolution, he explained, avoided such unpleasantries. The plush curtains intensified the silence. The entire meeting took less than an hour. Within days, the FDIC had an advance manager on-site to assist with the coordination of documents that would enable a bidder to assess the bank's condition. By July, we were on alert for diligence teams that were scheduled to come by and kick the tires.

At the time of the June 2011 FDIC resolution, Creekside Bank employed seventeen managers and branch staff at two locations. Staff was at a bare minimum. Were we to lose a *single* branch employee, Creekside would have been forced to shutter its Acworth location on account of having less than the required staffing. We knew that having to do so would be an embarrassment—and would broadcast the fragility of the charter to our customers and to the public. In response, our two branch managers structured "all hands on deck" schedules. Employees from Woodstock commuted periodically to the Acworth location to serve as "a warm body in a chair" over sick days and lunch hours, etc. It was an effort of genuine teamwork.

We were notified in July that the first of five banks that would be arriving to kick the tires in a limited diligence review. Because Creekside had never instituted a document scanning process, loan files had to be served up on a two-tiered rolling cart that was loaded from a secure document room. After having been thumbed through over the years, those were some seriously stapled, paper-clipped, dog-eared, and shuffled files! Scott Hudgins and the branch staff proved themselves to be patient, diligent, and attentive over the course of the serial on-site visits. Over five separate visits, banks descended for a whirlwind diligence review, ordering up loan jackets and detail history by the stack. On each occasion, Scott and his team filed through the "stacks," for loan jackets and returned with organized document sets. Five times, employees stayed late to reorganize, replace, and re-load the file room for the next diligence team. *Remember: unless you can value the asset, there is no way to reach a transaction price.* The employee group was committed to a fair and full assessment of value.

Despite our best efforts, Creekside was unable to negotiate a capital infusion. The final Creekside board meeting took place on August 16, 2011, at which time the board was asked to sign another resolution affirming that it "would not oppose" the FDIC taking possession of the bank and its property. I read the resolution several times; it was a moment in history that I would rather have been watching from a greater distance.

The FDIC is not staffed to operate or close down banks with regularity—especially the regularity witnessed in the course of a banking crisis. As discussed in the last chapter, the agency instead solicits healthy institutions to bid on the assets and liabilities of a distressed charter. In most cases, the FDIC subsidizes the buyer by selling the loans at a discount and then insuring against losses in the portfolio. While specifics vary by institution, examiners estimate what they believe ultimate loan losses will be, and then reimburse the acquiring institution for losses above an established threshold.

Less than two weeks after the August 16 board meeting, Peterson was notified that Creekside's closing would take place on Friday, September 2, 2011. The employees would be expected to work through the weekend at a pay rate of time and a half in order to assist the FDIC acquisition team with the turnover. Monday was the Labor Day holiday. Some of the staff would be expected to work the holiday in order to coordinate final arrangements with the acquiring bank.

On Thursday, September 1st, several of us met in the Creekside boardroom after closing time. It was a surreal moment. The bank was about to be shuttered...but we felt as though we'd just won a victory. All seventeen employees were still at the bank, and *everyone* was planning to work through the weekend. There were no tears—only heavy sighs of relief! We were all going to hang together through the closing. Kim Kunkel, our operations manager—who had previously worked through the close of Bank of Ellijay, joined me for a shot of bourbon before we set the alarms Thursday evening. More than any of us, Kim knew that it was going to be a *long* weekend.

In its six years of its operation, Creekside Bank had not managed a single profitable year. Eighteen million dollars of shareholder capital had been rendered worthless as result of the failure. Exactly four years earlier, I'd been working like gangbusters to get Touchmark's prospectuses mailed ahead of the Labor Day holiday. Now I was administering palliative care to a bank that was about to be euthanized as Georgia bank failure #70. Another coaster car was about to take a jarring leap from the rails...

The Circus Comes To Town

When Creekside's doors closed at 5:00 p.m. on Friday September 2nd 2011, the parking lot was already filling with a variety of vehicles that represented an advance wave of more than fifty special-purpose FDIC employees. They would descend on the Creekside branches to administer closure and conversion. The DRR (Department of Resolution and Recovery) would coordinate with a precision gained from the numerous failures worked prior to this one, and as they gathered, many hailed each other and renewed old ties in recalling previous "jobs" they'd worked across Georgia and across the country. It was a cacophony of personalities and equipment that set up shop across the lobby of the bank, not at all unlike the chaotic organization of a circus.

"Keep in mind what they're going through," a takeover manager is recorded to have counseled ahead of a previous closure. "We're going to outnumber them, and it's almost going to be like a herd of locusts descending on the place where they work." Indeed: we ultimately counted a total of fifty-seven staffers working across our two branches, arrayed amongst our loyal band of seventeen employee holdouts!

When the FDIC supervisors arrived, we were all ushered into the Creekside boardroom. A woman with big hair and an over-sized "FDIC" badge read (another) scripted explanation pertaining to the bank's closure. After that, a kinder and gentler looking man moved to the front and explained that we would all be "very important" over the next several days as the FDIC worked to transition the bank to its new owners. Dinner would be brought in—and we were sternly cautioned to stay on for the evening unless only the most exceptional of circumstances required that we go. Most of us should expect to be working a full day on the Monday holiday as well. And did anyone have any questions?

This was September 2011. We were Georgia bank failure #70. We'd been preparing for this moment for weeks. While there was surely a level of anxiety across the room, the only real question that I remember from our group was "What we're having for dinner?"

The meeting ended and I walked back toward to my office. There was a yellow band of tape stretched across my doorway that read "SECURE AREA." Two staffers were inside, shuffling through papers and pulling files from my desk drawers. I leaned in, smiling, and asked them not to touch my family photos or the cactus that I kept on my desk for companionship. They both shot me quizzical looks and nodded in unison. Neither one smiled or said a word. I pivoted and made my way to the lobby in search of dinner. I was serious about the cactus.

I wrote the following note to myself on Saturday evening, September 3rd: "The FDIC is surely not an employer of choice. The crowd in our lobby looks more like a misfit jamboree than a troop of career bank regulators. " The thought wasn't intended to be snide, but rather an acknowledgment that most of the specialists on site at Creekside Bank had joined the FDIC only after their previous employers...had failed. Failed banks, after all, were an obvious repository from which to draw competent, experienced staffers. Though the positions required extensive travel and odd hours, the FDIC was hiring furiously at the onset of the crisis to staff up for what it expected would be a wave of sequential failures across the country. As I negotiated through Friday evening and then returned on Saturday morning (the line outside my office was at times three and four specialists deep), I had opportunity to meet with nearly every one on the transition team, who in turn were fairly open about their stories: Superior Bank, American Marine, Charter Bank, and Horizon were alma maters that I recalled among the specialists. While each had a unique story, they also came equipped with a question or task—or had come to secure a particular document thought to have resided in my files. As I repeatedly turned over information and files (the cactus and photos were ultimately safe), I developed a strange sense of appreciation for the buzz of humanity that formed the steady comings and goings from my office. What would they be doing once this cycle came to an end? It was then that I realized why most of us would be working on Labor Day. For the FDIC staffers, the hours would represent double time pay—because Monday was a holiday! Even though Creekside was a small bank, and so the turnover should have been fairly straightforward, bankers are smart and know how to pace their work when they're paid by the hour!

Georgia Commerce Bank of Marietta was the winning bidder in the auction for the closure of Creekside Bank. GCB had acquired Creekside as part of a linked bid with Patriot Bank in Cumming, Georgia, which was closed over the same September weekend. Both were relatively small community banks—Patriot held about $150 million in assets at closure.

Distinction in Failure

While the basics of an FDIC conversion can be conducted in a single night, Creekside didn't have Saturday hours, so a more complete turnover was possible over the extended holiday weekend. While several customers noticed the crowded parking lot and knocked at the glass doors throughout the weekend, none showed any signs of panic or spoke derisively about the bank in any way. Where earlier failures were known to draw calls of "good riddance" for the management and shareholders, Creekside saw nothing of such derision. While a few customers were unsettled because they didn't fully understand the process, they were accepting once assured that their funds would be available when the bank was next open for business. And, if necessary, the ATM in the drive-through was open to handle their withdrawals...

Creekside Bank cost the FDIC insurance fund an estimated $27.3 million on account of its busted development loans. *In spite of this loss, Creekside Bank* (along with Patriot Bank) *was the first Georgia bank closure since the start of the 2008 crisis in which the winning bank at auction chose to acquire all* (both) *physical branches, retain all of the employees, and absorb the entire franchise into its operations.* From the standpoint of its employees, Creekside was a distinguished failure.

Chart 35

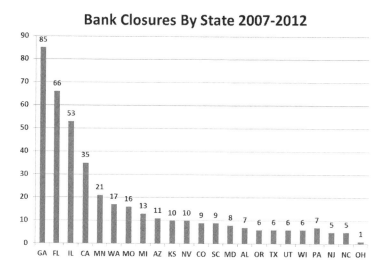

Bank Closures By State 2007-2012

Chart 36

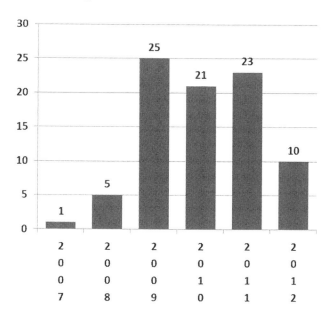

Georgia Bank Closures 2007-2012

Source: FDIC

Friday, September 4, 2009

Golden age of new banks likely over

Atlanta Business Chronicle – J. Scott Trubey, Staff Writer

The era of selling new banks for a quick profit might be over.

A decreased appetite by investors for new banks and new regulation will help ensure the de novo banks of tomorrow look a lot different than the startups of yesterday, industry experts say.

"For a while, just like doing construction loans funded by brokered deposits was a can't-lose deal, building banks to grow and then sell was a can't-lose investment," said James Stevens, banking attorney with **Kilpatrick & Stockton** LLP.

New bank charters have been all but frozen as equity capital has dried up. Some insiders say the government has put a quasi-moratorium on startups because regulators already have enough on their plates.

But when the industry rights itself over the next few years, expect the new breed of de novo banks to look much different than their forbearers, said Walt Moeling, banking attorney with **Bryan Cave LLP**.

"It's going to have to be a tighter ship, with slower growth," Moeling said. "We won't see the same level of new banks for the foreseeable future."

For many years, investors poured money into Georgia startups, attracted by hefty returns that could come from selling a new bank fueled by a booming population and a burgeoning real estate market.

From 2000 to 2007, 123 banks were chartered in Georgia.

"Those days are gone. We're not going to charter community banks like we used to," said Tony Plath, banking professor at the **University of North Carolina at Charlotte**. Georgia, he said, will likely charter fewer than 30 banks over the next decade.

From 1985 to 2006, billions of dollars in equity capital poured into banks. Returns were high, sometimes 3-to-1 for banks sold within a few years, Plath said.

Of the 23 banks that have failed in Georgia since August 2008, 16 failed within the first decade of operation.

Fifteen new charter applications were made in Georgia in 2008 and 10 were granted, according to **Federal Deposit Insurance Corp.** data, but the market has largely dried up as the financial crisis has deepened.

On Aug. 28, the FDIC issued new rules extending the period in which new banks are examined under greater scrutiny. The rules were not unexpected, and in some ways mirror an evolving regulatory climate in the current financial crisis that has claimed 84 banks nationwide in 2009, with scores more under regulatory orders to improve their balance sheets.

Newly insured banks, the FDIC said, "pose an elevated risk to the **FDIC Deposit Insurance Fund**. Depository institutions insured less than seven years are over-represented on the list of institutions that failed during 2008 and 2009, with many of those failures occurring during the fourth through seventh years of operation."

Federal regulators said many failed de novo banks made changes to business plans "that have led to increased risk and financial problems where accompanying controls and risk management practices were inadequate."

Other problems observed have been rapid growth leveraged on brokered deposits and high concentrations in real estate.

***

Historically a lack of funding, i.e. core deposits, kept early growth from being too great, Moeling said, but as wholesale funding came about, banks could grow a lot faster in early years.

Georgia was prime territory. **Alpha Bank** & Trust opened in 2006, smashing growth records, and then failed in 2008.

Alpha, like nearly all 23 Georgia banks that have failed from August 2008 to August 2009, was a new bank over-weighted in a hot real estate market that cooled at an unprecedented rate. The bank also relied on costly brokered deposits, which left the bank without a solid source of funding when losses started pouring in.

Investors won't be able to realize the same rate of return because de novo banks won't make a quick buck off real estate lending, Plath said.

Real estate values that were once inflated have imploded, and regulators won't let over-concentration happen again, Plath said.

The charters of tomorrow will be long-term plays for banks designed to fill a geographic or retail niche, Moeling said.

There is precedent, Moeling said. Georgia chartered about 100 banks in the five-year period from 1988 to 1992, but following the banking crisis of the early 1990s, the number of startups fizzled to about two dozen from 1993 to 1997.

"The real control over new banks is the flow of capital," he said.

At his first meeting with the bank's employees on the Saturday afternoon of takeover weekend, Georgia Commerce CEO Mark Tipton stressed his appreciation for the fine work of beleaguered Creekside employees and assured them that they could all find a home in the GCB franchise. *Every employee who elected to stay on kept his or her job.* To this day, I count the retention of those seventeen jobs among the highest accomplishments of my banking career. I stayed on to head up the bank's accounting conversion team...and rolled off the payroll on December 31, 2011.

Larry Peterson and I keep in touch. We have both moved on to new adventures.

And there you have it. In the five years between 2007 and 2011, I both opened a bank and closed a bank.

It was the most fun I never want to have again.

List 3

Time Line: Banking Crisis and Business Launch of Touchmark National Bank

"There are decades where nothing happens; and there are weeks where decades happen."
—Vladimir Lenin

The banking crisis that began in 2007 has transformed the world's financial landscape. Institutions of enormous size and influence failed or were bailed out with unprecedented intervention from governments and central banks. "Toxic mortgages" on bank balance sheets dramatically slowed interbank lending, resulting in a global liquidity crisis. After an initial stock market upswing, equity markets swooned as global economies entered the Great Recession of 2008. The stagnation of Western economies revealed weaknesses in underpinnings of the European Union, now advancing toward default by individual members and perhaps eventual dissolution. During it all, Touchmark National Bank of Norcross, Georgia organized and opened for business.

2007	
Feb 7: HSBC announces losses linked to US subprime mortgages.	**Feb 13:** Short and Koncerak attend a de novo banking conference hosted by Banker's Bank (Silverton Bank) at the Ritz Carlton Hotel in Atlanta.
	April 26: The group selects Touchstone National Bank and Touchstone Bancshares, Inc. as names for the bank and holding company.

May 17: Federal Reserve Chairman Ben Bernanke says growing number of mortgage defaults will not seriously harm the US economy.	**May 20:** Short and Koncerak submit 105 pounds of application paperwork to the Office of the Comptroller of the Currency to establish a bank in Norcross, Georgia. Shortly thereafter, the group moves into temporary offices at Davinci Court in Norcross.
June: Two Bear Stearns-run hedge funds with large holdings of subprime mortgages incur large losses and are forced to dump assets. The trouble spreads to major Wall Street firms such as Merrill Lynch, JPMorgan Chase, Citigroup, and Goldman Sachs, which had loaned the firm money.	**June**: Applications for a bank-holding company and SEC registrations are developed and submitted. A prospectus is developed to solicit investment in the enterprise. The closing date for the offering is set at October 31, 2007.
August: French bank BNP Paribas freezes withdrawals in three investment funds.	**August**: The group receives approval from the OCC to establish a national bank charter. The twenty-two organizers gather addresses and refine contact info.
Sept: UK bank Northern Rock admits financial difficulties, approaches The Bank of England for assistance. Share prices fall as customers queue up to withdraw their money.	**Sept 3**: Touchstone Bancshares, Inc. mails roughly 2,300 prospectuses to potential investors over the Labor Day weekend holiday.
Oct 1: Swiss bank UBS announces losses liked to US subprime mortgages.	**Sept 28**: Short reports that the organizers have raised $12,914,500 toward $31,250,000 required to break escrow and open the bank.
Oct 5: Merrill Lynch reports losses of $5.5 billion.	**Oct 12:** The group receives preliminary conditional approval from the FDIC for deposit insurance.

Oct 15: Cititgroup announces $6.5 billion third-quarter losses. Citigroup, Bank of America, and JPMorgan Chase announce plans for an $80 billion Master Liquidity Enhancement conduit to purchase highly rated assets from existing special-purpose vehicles.	**Oct 19:** Short reports that escrow funds amount to $18,424,500. The impact of global headlines slows incoming receipts, and the group considers extending the offering.
Oct 31: The FOMC votes to reduce fed funds target by twenty-five bps to 4.50 percent. Fed votes to reduce prime rate by twenty-five bps to 5.00 percent. Merrill Lynch announces losses to be over $8 billion.	**Oct 31:** Escrow funds reach $21,361,480. Touchstone extends offering period to December 15, 2007.
Nov: Financial market pressures intensify, reflected in diminished liquidity in interbank funding markets.	**Nov 20:** Short relays that escrow funds amount to $26,008,480. The group hires Commerce Street Capital to assist with soliciting funds through the necessary minimum to break escrow. Prospectus is updated, and the offering is extended through March 31, 2008.
Dec 11: FOMC votes to reduce fed funds target by twenty-five bps to 4.25 percent. Fed votes to reduce prime rate twenty-five bps to 4.75 percent.	**Dec 13:** Short and Koncerak still pressing for close by year-end but anticipate extension into January. Escrow fund amounts to $27,021,500.
Dec 12: Fed announces creation of a term auction facility (TAF), in which term funds will be auctioned to depository institutions against a wide variety of collateral. FOMC authorizes temporary reciprocal currency arrangements with European Central Bank and the Swiss National Bank. Fed commits up to $20 billion and $4 billion to the ECB and SNB, respectively.	**Dec 21:** Short announces that group will not reach minimum in 2007. Letter mailed to subscribers on December 22 updating status, additional subscriber events planned for January. Escrow fund amounts to $28,438,500.

Dec 21: Citigroup, JPMorgan Chase, and Bank of America abandon plans for the Master Liquidity Enhancement Conduit, stating that the fund "not needed at this time."	**Dec 28:** Escrow fund reaches $29,074,750.

2008

Jan 15: Citigroup reports $18.1 billion 4th Q loss.	
Jan 17: Merrill Lynch reports $11.5 billion 4th Q loss. Washington Mutual posts losses.	**Jan 17:** Group has no limits on percent ownership. Drs. JJ and Meena Shah invest additional funds, which bring group within $500K of minimum.
Jan 18: Fitch downgrades Ambac Financial Group's strength rating to AA, Credit Watch Negative. S&P places Ambac's AAA rating on Credit Watch Negative.	**Jan 18:** Short announces that escrow fund will reach $31,250,000 minimum on Tuesday, January 22. Bank anticipates opening for business on January 28.
Jan 30: FOMC votes to reduce fed funds target rate fifty bps to 3.0 percent. Fed votes to reduce prime rate fifty bps to 3.5 percent.	**Jan 28**: Touchmark National Bank opens for business and establishes its first customer accounts.
March 16: Bear Stearns, 5th largest investment bank, collapses and is acquired by JP Morgan.	
April 1: German Deutsche Bank credit losses of $3.9 billion in first quarter.	**March 30:** TMAK offering closes with $34,500,000 and 560 shareholders.
May 12: HSBC writes off $3.2 billion in the first quarter linked to exposure to the US subprime market.	**May 21**: TMAK holds first annual meeting of shareholders and hosts its grand opening gala at the Atlanta Athletic Club.
June 5: Federal Reserve approves Bank of America to acquire Countrywide Financial Corporation.	

July 11: OTS closes IndyMac Bank, F.S.B.	
Sept 7: Fannie Mae and Freddie Mac effectively nationalized by the US Treasury, placed into conservatorship.	**August 29**: Integrity Bank fails, Alpharetta, GA
Sept 14: Lehman Brothers files for bankruptcy. Stock markets plummet.	
Sept 15: Bank of America announces intent to purchase Merrill Lynch for $50 billion.	
Sept 25: WaMu sold to JP Morgan.	
October 10: "Black Friday"- Dow crashes nearly seven hundred points before regaining lost ground.	
Oct 11: Fed endorses Wachovia takeover by Wells Fargo.	
Oct 24: PNC buys Nat City	**Oct 24**: Alpha Bank & Trust fails, Alpharetta, GA
Nov 26: Fed approves Bank of America to acquire Merrill Lynch.	**Nov 28:** Community Bank fails, Loganville, GA
Dec 19: Treasury authorizes up to $13.4 billion in loans to General Motors and $4.0 billion for Chrysler from TARP.	

Chapter 11

What Happens Now?

Go as far as you can see; when you get there, you'll be able to see farther.

J.P. Morgan

Karl R. Nelson, CEO
KPN Consulting

Those who have been around the banking industry for some time know that this latest crisis pales in comparison to the last one. As an industry, we have faced some difficult moments, but none quite so bad (at least in modern times!) as the decade of the 1980's. Most of us who lived through the *last* crisis would prefer to write the whole ten-year period off – unfortunately, not so easy to do.

This current "crisis" (or what remains of it) began in late 2007 and, continues in varied forms through the writing of this book. During the period from January 2007 through the end of 2012, we experienced 468 US bank failures. Now, that is a lot of banks to lose, but it pales in comparison to what happened during the 1980's. The decade started off slowly with 22 failures in 1980, followed by another 40 failures in 1981. But, then it was "Katy-Bar-the Door" for the remainder of the decade! From an average of 100 failures per year between 1982 and 1984, the situation became quite serious as the decade wore on. Between 1985 and 1992 an astonishing 2,484 institutions were closed by the FDIC (yes indeed – 310/year!). In 1989, the single worst year of the decade, a remarkable 534 banks were taken down by the FDIC. In retrospect, one wonders how this got done over only fifty two weekends in the year!

Why is this important? Because projecting our future is a function of understanding our past, and I can assure you that a little reflection will be well worth the effort.

As it happened, the cleansing of the 1980's was followed by the very best banking environment ever. In fact, just looking at the bank failure rate from the 1990's on, we note that the FDIC seemed to be significantly under-utilized in terms of managing failed banks – only 120 *in total* were closed between the end of 1992 and the end of 2006. Put another way, the failure rate fell from 310 banks per year...to nine. Even more interesting was the fact that there were *no* failures in either 2005 or 2006 – an event that had never occurred in the history of the FDIC. Industry profitability was also something that had not been seen before: industry net income in 2006 amounted to a record $145 billion. Industry return on assets in 2006 exceeded one percent! Extraordinary times for all of us and, I think, a reminder of what we can achieve when we have good underwriting and a decent economy.

Crisis environments offer an aspect that we in this business need to consider – the competitive environment for banks. At the end of 1990, there were 15,158 banks and thrifts in the United States. By the end of 2006, that number had been reduced to 8,680. As of this writing, we have 7,083 – think about that. *More than half of the competition has disappeared in the past 22 years!* When you add in the fact that many of the "shadow" banking players have also been hit by this economic crisis, it becomes apparent that the survivors of our industry should have a much easier time in the future based strictly on the competitive environment. And with a Gross Domestic Product (GDP) exceeding $15 trillion, it seems obvious that our industry is operating on a playing field with the scale to do very well in what is looking more and more like a slowly improving economic situation.

Planning, Products and People

What will it take to succeed? In my mind it will require the right *planning*, the right *products* and the right *people*. To say that it won't be "business as usual" is clearly an understatement. Equally clear, at least to me, is the fact that more will be required from our management teams and our Boards of Directors. The days of a nice dinner (with lots of wine) followed by a leisurely Board meeting are over! We must, as management, prepare our Boards for a much better understanding of the business than ever before. It is not that our Boards are lacking in intelligence – much to the contrary. Our boards have generally been built around individuals who have achieved financial success and have a demonstrated ability to help us grow. So, it is not a question of their not understanding – it has been our *inability to present them with a clear business plan that they can act on* that that has caused many of our board members to seem detached and ineffective. We must do a better job of providing training and of creating information in a language that our boards understand and in a format that they can act on. We need to give them something to sell! If we want our boards to be part of our future success, we must make certain they understand and appreciate what we do and how we do it. To say that the successful banks of the future will be high quality "teams" is apparent to anyone who understands how difficult it is to make a buck, particularly in today's highly regulated environment. That "team" will be comprised of Management, Staff, and Boards all following the same plan. And, it will require that all team members have "a dog in the fight". Operating by "the seat of my pants" is simply not going to do it in the future. Success will require a sound strategic plan and execution of that plan. Performance management will, in my view, separate future winners from losers.

Some of our most important banking products are our delivery channels. Only time will tell if the predominant distribution channel of our industry – namely the branch system - will flourish.

Many industry veterans believe that a significant share of banking clients will continue to prefer doing business "face-to-face", in the confines of a branch location, for years to come. If I were making a bet, however, it would be on offering as many channels as our customer's desire. Consider, for example, how long the ATM distribution channel was in the making: it was quite a challenge in the early years to get customers to simply try the machine. In the early days of ATM's, many banks actually stationed employees in locations where the first ATM's were located. Their *job* was get people to use the machine! Now, it seems odd today to think that a simple ATM would have presented such a challenge. After all, online banking has become a "must have" for every bank and customer acceptance was much faster than that for the ATM. One can only imagine that the next step, mobile banking – will be accepted much faster than either ATMs or online banking. Profit-Stars, one of the largest banking technology providers, estimates that by 2017, 70% of adults will own a smart phone. If that's true, then bankers need to be introducing their mobile banking platforms right now! This kind of technology will not only change our business model, it will also create a much less expensive distribution system and eventually result in real cost savings to our industry.

Another issue facing our industry has to do with the kind of people we employ. While we have all learned to operate more like "retailers", the change has been a struggle for many. In this day and age, the "customer experience" is with a critical element of every transaction. The experience *must* be a good one. Keeping our staff reminded that the customer is not an annoyance, but is instead *the reason we exist*, can sometimes be lost in a crowded, fidgety teller line—but this we must do! Every customer transaction must be one they will remember as pleasant, efficient, and something to be repeated. Regardless of whether it's a telephone contact or a teller line – good retailers want every experience to be a positive one. Bankers that take this to heart will execute a strategy that rewards such behavior and will, I think, be winners in the new world of banking. This kind of change will be difficult for some and will require significant training in the future. While banking is by nature a service model, it is surprising how inconsistent the service experience can be from transaction to transaction to transaction. We need incentive programs that create necessary behaviors and reward employees who make our customers want to return to whichever delivery channel they prefer.

Finally, we will have to have products that make sense and make money for our institutions. Too often, we charge for services that our clients think should be "free". Figuring out what our clients value—and are willing to pay for, will separate the winners from the losers. We are already seeing mobile services that create marketing rewards for depositors. When coupled with a checking account, such a vehicle provides easy justification for a monthly fee. Rebranding overdraft products so that they are appreciated as a *convenience* rather than as a penalty is another way to earn fees in a way the *depositor* feels is justified. We need to figure out what *each* of our customers *wants* and is *willing* to pay for. This will require marketing, product diversification, and some very specific demographic targeting. Technology will make it all happen. Spending and focus in this area will be necessary for those who intend to succeed.

Planning (strategy), Products (distribution channels) and People (service with a smile) – this is where we see the battle for market share developing now. For these reasons, our opportunity is as good as it has ever been! If done right, the sequel to this story could well be titled "The Most Fun I Could Ever Want to Have!" Taking advantage of this moment is, we think, the key to the next cycle of banking. We hope that all of you in the banking industry will succeed, and we wish you all the best.

Karl Nelson can be reached at kpnconsulting.net.

Epilogue: What's an Investor to Do?

We have met the enemy, and he is us.

Pogo

The trials you encounter will introduce you to your strengths

Epictetus

So, if you're among the tens of thousands who purchased community bank stock in the past fifteen years, or if you are among the millions who either work at or serve the community bank industry in some way, you've read all the way to this point for one of several reasons: it could be that you've been on this roller coaster ride yourself...and you've found this to be a copasetic story. It could be that you found my storytelling and rapier wit to be so compelling that you just couldn't put this book down (Thanks, mom!). Or it could be that you own bank stock that is worth a miserable fraction of what you paid for it—and you're exasperated in looking for clues as to whether or not you're ever going to get your money back. I include these last paragraphs for shareholders and directors.

I wrote in an early chapter that community banks at the beginning of 2013 might best be described as an industry of highly regulated, beat up small businesses. Certainly there are some banks that have remained profitable through the past several years. Many more have had their values and prospects pulled down by industry averages. But as Karl Nelson relayed in the previous pages, the next phase of this story will distinguish the remaining winners...from the remaining losers.

Karl does a lot of speaking and educating, and our paths have crossed often in recent years. Among his contentions for the community bank industry is this prediction:

Roughly a third of community banks have been so damaged by the 2007 downturn that working back to pre-crisis valuations will be impossible in any reasonable time frame. Between the capital lost to bad loans and residual foreclosures and non-accruals, the damage will oblige them to find a buyer while they still have a reasonable chance of providing value to shareholders through the strength of an acquiring institution.

Another third may prosper, but will only do so by strategically acquiring or being acquired by a rival in order to reach a sustainable size. They either don't have the capital or the expertise to succeed on their own. They need to do something...it's probably a merger...and they're probably not going to be the winners. These banks need to find "dance partners" and the music has only just begun to play.

The last third has the most exciting opportunity ahead of them: they already have the talent (or the ability to acquire it), they are operating in good markets and can succeed by gaining market share and asset size through branch or whole bank acquisition. They have either worked down poorly performing loans in their portfolios or never really got themselves in trouble to begin with. These banks need to recognize who they are and not squander the opportunity ahead of them. In many cases, capital will be better deployed for acquisitions as compared to the funding of individual loans.

I think Karl is right. I believe that all bank boards have some essential questions to ask themselves. And the answers need to be delivered to their shareholders.

As you know from these pages, I own stock in a community bank. I paid $10 per share in November 2007. As of July 2013, the stock is trading at $4.25. If you're like me, I know your pain. I want my bank to succeed, and I surely want the leadership team to know what questions to answer—and then address.

Three Essential Questions

I want my bank to be a wildly successful investment. I want it to take every advantage of the opportunities that Karl and others see ahead for the industry. Before any bank, can become success-ful however, their boards need to address three essential ques-tions for the stakeholders of their enterprise: their shareholders, employees and vendors.

1. **Are we buyers or are we sellers?** In which "third" does the bank find itself, and why? It is common for a bank executive to exclaim "we can grow organically" or "we don't need to sell or acquire anything in order to gener-ate good returns". That sounds good, but it doesn't answer the question. *Every* bank board should have a stock price in mind that represents a compelling exit opportunity for shareholders—and the board should be prepared to eval-uate offers that *will* come their way. Every bank board member should be able to explain how their management teams are advancing (or recouping) shareholder value. If swapping stock with a higher-performing bank would provide a better opportunity for earnings growth, then the board should identify plausible candidates. Every commu-nity bank board should have an exit strategy, and be pre-pared to put an acquisition price on their company. Banks not capable of acquiring other institutions should know at what price their own stock would provide a fair return—or a better opportunity, for shareholders. *In my experience, few bank executives can do this, and fewer want to.*

Candidly, here's the biggest problem that I see in this regard: many small banks are not being run to generate shareholder returns—instead they're being run to generate income streams for their management teams. The salaries and bonus plans that most management teams receive *far outweigh* any return that can be generated on their stock. So guess what? Such management teams are more focused on preserving their existing jobs than they are on maximizing shareholder value. After all, if the number of banks is only shrinking...then which of two presidents will get the job in a merger situation? Which CFO? Which Chief Credit Officer? Management teams are hired by a board of directors to run the daily affairs of the company. The awkward and uncomfortable truth of this situation is that all too often, the agenda of the board and the agenda of the management team are at odds: one seeks to grow, the other seeks primarily to *preserve*.

2. **What is the plan for maximizing shareholder value?** The highest responsibility for a board of bank directors is to *maximize shareholder return in a safe and sound environment*. Unless the board can describe what "success" looks like and can articulate steps they're taking to become successful, how will they recognize success when they get there? Is success "just keeping the doors open"? Really? If your board can't lay out a plan that makes sense and seems achievable...you've got a problem. As a shareholder, the questions are simple ones: what are you doing to get my money back? If you can't do it, then who can we merge with or sell to improve our chances? These are fundamental board issues.

3. **How does the board "champion" the bank in its community?**
   Every organization needs champions. If the board of directors isn't "championing" the institution, then who will? How is the board advancing the bank's interests across the communities that it serves? What are the products and services that everyone in the community should *want* to be using? What is the board doing to foster introductions and bring business to the bank?

If you are a shareholder, *you* elect the board of directors. The reality is that community bank stocks are thinly traded issues. Often times, there is no market for the stock when a shareholder wants to sell. The only alternative is to ask questions...and demand good (better) answers.

These paragraphs won't make me popular at bank director conferences...but they are exactly the questions that bank *investors* should be asking their companies.

A Note Regarding the Adjudication of Closed (Failed) Bank Directors

Since director lawsuits began in earnest in 2010, the allegations have had a familiar refrain:

...an unsustainable growth strategy concentrated on lending for allegedly high-risk and speculative real estate ventures, which resulted in substantial losses when the real estate market collapsed and the bank failed. In these and other lawsuits, the FDIC has asserted claims for (i) breach of fiduciary duty, (ii) ordinary negligence under state law, and (iii) gross negligence under the federal Financial Institutions Reform Recovery and Enforcement Act of 1989 ("FIRREA").

Jones Day, 2012

Cases like *FDIC v. Steven Skow, et al.,* (Mr. Skow was CEO of Integrity Bank) have established that the bar is set fairly high when it comes to the personally liability of directors in the event of a bank failure. The *Skow* case determined that even "ordinary negligence" and breach of fiduciary duty as result of ordinary negligence won't result in legal judgment. Nothing short of fraud, bad faith or abuse of discretion—claims of *gross negligence,* seems to be making it through the courts. This seems reasonable. Unfortunately, as the headlines have shown us, fraud has played a part in several bank failures. In these cases, though, it's frequently been *lenders* rather than directors who have violated the law. It is sad, in any case, that the losses have been so great. From the research I have done, the FDIC seems to have been both diligent and responsible in initiating director suits. The primary goal is recovery to the FDIC insurance fund. The bureau responsible for troubled bank administration is, after all, called the Department of Resolutions *and Recovery* (DRR). Prosecutions thus far have shown that it is primarily those *criminally* liable who have been convicted. Those who merely demonstrated some lesser degree of negligence (my word: bonehead), have avoided personal liability. It's certainly been an anxious time for ex-directors, as the FDIC has three years post-failure in which to file such a claim. If you're in that mix, may time pass you quickly by!

One Final Thought: Consolidation in Metro Markets Has Merit

Here's one last slide to drive home the case for coordinated mergers and asset growth in my adopted city: the chart comes by way of Lee Burrows at Bank Street Partners. Among the 99 banks operating across metro Atlanta in March 2013, fewer than half have the capital to originate even a $5 million loan. Most of the community banks are fighting for the same business customers, because they don't have the capital to move into more rarified markets. Consolidation will provide the best opportunity to generate shareholder value...until the next round of de novos are ready to launch!

Chart 37

Competition Case Study - Atlanta

- ▶ Community banks compete ferociously for the market share left over by the money centers and super-regionals
- ▶ Most banks can compete to make a $1 million loan, but relatively few can make a loan greater than $5 million to a single borrower
- ▶ Of the 99 banks operating in the Atlanta MSA, only 41 can make a loan to one borrow greater than $5 million and only 26 can make a loan greater than $30 million*
- ▶ Loan competition becomes less intense as banks move up the asset scale

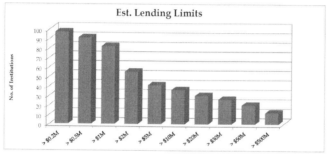

Est. Lending Limits

* Loan-to-one borrower limits estimated at 10% of Tier 1 Capital
Source: SNL Financial

B · S · P

Community banks in rural markets will have more time to react than those in the metro markets. The competition is fierce in metro geographies—both for customers and for good employees. For example, if you're a struggling bank and you lose either a good customer or a good employee...how can you replace them? The challenge gets tougher with each occurrence. Recall my epiphany # 4: one of the greatest privileges in life is to have *choices*. Excellent customers and excellent employees will move to maximize their opportunity. Don't let excellence pass you by!

Indeed, the past few years have constituted *The Most Fun I Never Want To Have Again*, and I am hopeful that my next years will absolutely be a thrill a minute. That will only happen, though, if I can be candid, optimistic and effective in my work. Perhaps Karl is right, and there will be a sequel to this book. I'd be delighted to write it someday if like this one, the story is worth retelling. Perhaps I can title it *I Thought I Was Done The Last Time!*

335